THE EXPONENTIAL CHANGE
BOOK SERIES

T0309150

WILEY

MICHAEL LEWRICK

**AUTHOR OF INTERNATIONAL BEST-SELLING
"DESIGN THINKING PLAYBOOK"**

OMAR HATAMLEH

RECOGNIZED AS A TOP 100 THOUGHT LEADER ON AI

AI AND INNOVATION

HOW TO TRANSFORM YOUR BUSINESS AND OUTPACE THE COMPETITION WITH GENERATIVE AI

WILEY

THE EXPONENTIAL CHANGE PARADIGM

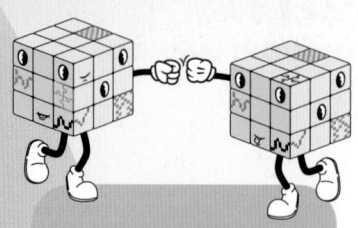

GET READY FOR EVEN BIGGER AND FASTER CHANGES

- Exponential change is inevitable, so it is imperative to forge needed capabilities to succeed in the new landscapes.
- Plan how the organization should adapt to change to remain relevant and competitive.
- Be aware of the mindset, tools, and methods needed to quickly identify and take advantage of new opportunities.

ENGAGE IN COLLABORATION TO FOSTER CREATIVITY, INNOVATION, AND CROSS-SKILLING

- Exponential change requires collaboration between different teams and departments.
- Apply the Team of Teams concept for effective collaboration and sharing of information and resources.

ACCEPT THAT EXISTING OFFERINGS ARE DISRUPTED FREQUENTLY BY EXPONENTIAL TECHNOLOGIES

- Become aware of the latest exponential technologies and invest to fully understand them.
- Adapt your business model, seek new ways to collaborate, and be prepared to fail while applying them in an early stage of maturity.

BECOME AGILE AND LEARN FROM MISTAKES TO BE SUCCESSFUL

- Embrace agility and future-proof success in a world of exponential change.
- Learn to adapt quickly to new situations and have skills that allow you to be interactive and experimental in responding to them.
- Create a strong sense of purpose that drives all related actions.

ACCEPT NEW DESIGN CHALLENGES AND EMBRACE NEW IDEAS

- Exponential change often brings new ideas and market opportunities.
- Abandon concepts and mindsets from the past and prepare the entire organization for new mindshifts.

BE AWARE THAT THE ABILITY TO CONSTANTLY ADAPT WILL BE ESSENTIAL TO PARTICIPATE IN ECOSYSTEMS

- Adaptability becomes the new constant in realizing exponential growth.
- Apply business ecosystems design methodology for creating a clear understanding about where to play, how to win, and how to configure.
- Enhanceability of all systems becomes key to unlock progress.

PURPOSE DRIVEN. CONSTANTLY EVOLVING. DISRUPTIVE.

INTRODUCTION

PART 1:
WHY AI MATTERS

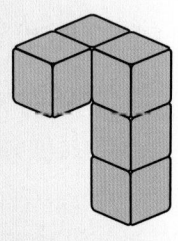

PART 2:
HOW TO MAKE A
DIFFERENCE WITH AI

PART 3:
WHAT TOOLS AND METHODS
SUPPORT THE ACTIVITIES?

PART 4:
THE FUTURE OF AI
AND INNOVATION

WRAP-UP

ABOUT THE AUTHORS

In this age of exponential change and ever-evolving technologies, Michael and Omar's collaboration on their book presents a unique opportunity. Michael brings a wealth of experience in the field of innovation management, design thinking, and ecosystems design. Omar, on the other hand, possesses deep subject matter expertise within the field of AI. Together, they combine strategic vision with cutting-edge knowledge, creating a powerful synergy that ensures their book remains relevant and insightful in a rapidly changing world. This dynamic duo positions their work to be a valuable resource for anyone seeking to understand and leverage the transformative potential of new technologies.

AI IS GOOD FOR DESCRIBING THE WORLD AS IT IS TODAY, WITH ALL ITS BIASES, BUT WHAT WE NEED ARE THE APPROPRIATE MINDSET, TOOLS, AND METHODS TO UNLOCK THE POWER OF INNOVATION WITH IT.

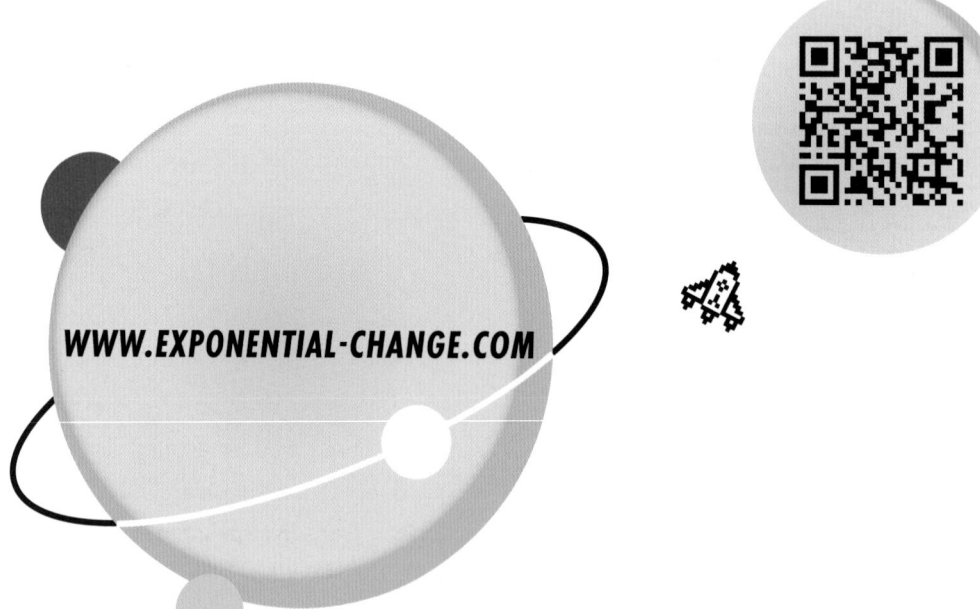

WWW.EXPONENTIAL-CHANGE.COM

Michael Lewrick (PhD)

is a bestselling author, award-winning design thinking and eco-system design thought leader, business entre-preneur, and visiting professor at various universities globally. His ideas, books, and company, Lewrick and Company, help mobilize people around the world to better lead innovation and digital transformation in an era of increasingly rapid change. He values the power of human–AI collaboration for solving complex problems.

www.linkedin.com/in/michael-lewrick/

Omar Hatamleh (PhD)

is a global thought leader on AI (top 100 world leader in AI by Thinkers360) and book author about emerging tech-nologies. He holds the position of Chief AI Advisor at NASA, and he is an invited key-note speaker to multiple international events, including major innovation conferences at G20, United National, Google, IBM, and many others. Omar holds four engineering degrees, speaks four languages and has received numerous prestigious awards.

www.linkedin.com/in/hatamleh

OTHER BOOKS BY MICHAEL LEWRICK:

Book designed by
Heike Hansen is a Swiss-based art director with a passion for human-centered design, storytelling, and emerging technologies. The deep immersion in the topic as well as working in teams are some of her most vital strengths in the field of art, design, and technology. www.studiohansen.ch

PREFACE

Llewellyn King

→ Executive Producer and Host
  of *White House Chronicle* on PBS;
  columnist, *InsideSources Syndicate*;
  contributor, *Forbes; Energy
  central commentator*, SiriusXM
  RadioMobile

Leon Trotsky said, "You may not be interested in the dialectic, but the dialectic is interested in you." So it is with generative artificial intelligence: you may not be interested in it, but it is interested in you. It is interested in how we live, work, play, and even think. There will be going forward, if you will, no hiding place. This book at its core says, "Don't hide from AI, embrace it." But to do that, individuals and institutions need to embrace exponential thinking. Linear thinking — which is the normal human default setting — will fail individuals and institutions because AI is exponential.

An apocryphal and oft-trotted-out Henry Ford quotation: "If I had asked people what they wanted, they would have said faster horses." That is linear thinking. AI is different things to different groups of people. To one group, it is something to be wildly feared: a new plague, a glance at the beginning of the end of humanity. To another, it is here and now and frightening but not so frightening that it can't be harnessed — managed and regulated with legislation, providing so-called guardrails.

These guardrails, they believe, will keep AI from becoming something that could upend society, throwing millions out of work worldwide; taking away privacy; spreading disinformation; interfering in the political process in democracies; and spreading bias in data, codifying it as a truth. Yet a group of computer aficionados, a group of elite thinkers, see generative AI as a benefit to humanity.

But it is one for which individuals and institutions must be ready — ready with new ideas and new tools to use AI to sweep in a new age, where the thorniest of human problems can be solved with alacrity, producing huge and unimagined benefits. For example, a life expectancy of 120 years for children born today.

Front and center of this cohort are the authors of this book, Michael Lewrick and Omar Hatamleh, the first in a series to help us get to the glittering future promised by AI: a future where AI solves problems that have plagued humanity for millennia. The first among these is research that can accelerate the finding of cures or therapies for pervasive and even intractable and rare diseases.

The authors' central point in this volume is that AI is exponential, so individuals and institutions must shirk their traditional linear thinking and realign themselves to thinking exponentially. Thinking exponentially demands new structures, paradigms, and management concepts that will free the exponential thinkers in an organization to shape it and get the value from AI.

The message for corporations is loud and clear: adapt or lose. Jack Welch, former CEO of General Electric, said, "If the rate of change externally isn't greater than the rate of change internally, then the end is known." Welch wasn't talking about AI, but he might as well have been. What he said then can be taken as an exhortation to institutions to embrace exponential thinking to use AI, or the end is known. That is the vital message of Hatamleh and Lewrick: if we don't change our thinking, the end is known. If we do, a new age of human progress is at hand, ready to unfold.

I wish you exciting insights with this book.

Llewellyn King

MOTIVATION FOR THE TOPIC

The blend of past innovations that have shaped human progress and advanced technologies like artificial intelligence (AI) makes for an incredibly exciting topic. This combination promises to drive change in ways we can hardly imagine.

As a team of authors, we are deeply interested in exponential change because we believe it is one of the most important and impactful forces shaping our world today. Exponential change is happening at an unprecedented pace, and it is having a profound impact on everything from the way we innovate to the way we work. We believe that it is important to understand exponential change and to use the appropriate frameworks in order to be prepared for the challenges and opportunities that it will bring. A key question is how do we move from our usual linear way of thinking to thinking in terms of rapid growth and change? Filling the gap between both elements will ensure humanity and biological intelligence will remain relevant now and into the future. We believe that thinking in terms of rapid growth can help solve some of the world's toughest problems. New technologies like AI and quantum computing could transform healthcare, education, and environmental efforts. Embracing an exponential mindset will create a better future for everyone. Creating a synergy between radical innovation and new and evolving technologies can disrupt traditional industries and give birth to new business models, platforms, products, and services. These tools will orchestrate a new paradigm shift in rewriting the conventional rules of the game for future innovations.

In this book, we share and reflect on our work with the world's most innovative companies that have made significant advancements with exponential technologies. These companies have achieved this through a changed mindset, utilizing new tools and methods, and developing a deep understanding of the problems to be solved.

The tools and methods shared in this important book are flexible and meant to inspire innovation during rapid changes. They should be tailored to fit each unique situation.

We bring our eminence and decades of experience to the presented content and frameworks with the objective of creating awareness of exponential change, finding a common language, and removing the fear associated with ongoing and dynamic transformation. We are cognizant of the fact that AI is a complex and novel concept that brings uncertainty in its wake. These fears are inherent to our human nature. However, it is important to remember that AI is a tool created by humans, for humans, and if we can successfully embrace exponential change, there will be immense opportunities for positive impact. Early adopters who take measured risks and proactive action will possess a huge strategic advantage over those who continue along the conventional and reactive path.

AI IS THE KEY TO UNLOCKING A BRIGHTER FUTURE FOR HUMANITY. BY HARNESSING ITS POWER RESPONSIBLY, WE CAN SOLVE GLOBAL CHALLENGES, IMPROVE LIVES, AND CREATE A MORE PROSPEROUS WORLD FOR ALL.

We must also highlight that at the current technology level, AI does not possess consciousness or emotions; AI merely mimics our cognitive processes based on algorithms and available data. As a result, AI may generate mistakes and experience "hallucinations" due to its inability to understand context nuances in ways that humans do.

However, with the introduction of the next level of artificial general intelligence (AGI) systems, AI will be able to do everything that a human brain can do and more. Such impressive capabilities will take us beyond existing boundaries. Generative AI offers a glimpse into a future where the possibilities seem endless, and the need to master the appropriate skills, tools, and methods to better deal with them becomes ever more pressing.

A comprehensive understanding of AI is crucial to allay fears about sentient AI. Promoting and creating a healthy partnership and collaboration between AI and humans will springboard new waves of innovation that would otherwise be unattainable. The collective creativity and intelligence that AI and humans bring will propel us into a fertile future of opportunities.

We are confident that the best AI solutions can help solve humanity's greatest problems, especially when AI and humans work harmoniously as a team and build upon their respective strengths regarding fact aggregation and processing speed. To make the most of AI and all the other remarkable technologies, we must guard against the risks and leverage all benefits to create better and more sustainable products, services, and experiences.

We are looking forward to constructive exchanges, exciting discussions at conferences, and our work to implement the tools and methods shared in this book at companies and organizations worldwide.

Your team of authors,

Michael Lewrick   Omar Hatamleh

AI AND HUMANS AS A TEAM

ORGANIZATIONS THAT LEARN AND APPLY NEW MINDSETS AND ORGANIZATIONAL TECHNIQUES ARE BETTER POSITIONED TO ACHIEVE DISPROPORTIONATELY HIGH IMPACT (OR OUTPUT) – AT LEAST **10x** HIGHER – COMPARED TO THEIR PEERS.

INTRODUCTION TO EXPONENTIAL CHANGE

This book from the *Exponential Change* book series offers methods and frameworks that help to better deal with exponential change. The change is exponential because so many technological advancements — whether in AI, quantum computing, AR/VR, biotech, robotics, or cognition — are occurring simultaneously and rapidly and building on one another across every sector and industry imaginable. Something is not classified as exponential until it breaks the integer barrier. As a result, growth begins to be measured in whole numbers and multiplies from there.

Many factors, such as regulations, technological dependencies, and economic forces, are beyond the control of decision-makers, product owners, and innovation teams. Therefore, the intent of this book series is not to present technology tools but to address the impact of exponential change on future business models, evolving workforce dynamics, strategic considerations, and capabilities and future skills to be built. Each

THE AI REALITY IS HERE, AND DECISION-MAKERS ARE SEEING THE REAL CHALLENGES OF AI INSTEAD OF WHAT THEY ASSUMED THEY WOULD BE. THIS BOOK SERIES WILL HELP ORGANIZATIONS ADDRESS THE PRAGMATIC SIDE OF EXPONENTIAL TECHNOLOGIES.

book in this series is dedicated to a key topic. This book has a strong focus on AI and innovation: it reflects best practices and tools to transform industries, create new market opportunities, and solve some of the world's most significant challenges between AI and humankind. Although not the main focus of this book, we will also touch on the myriad challenges that AI brings, from its potential to perpetuate bias to its capacity to undermine security and privacy. Different perspectives from industry experts will be presented throughout each chapter to enrich our discussions.

It is no coincidence that the first book in this series is about AI and innovation, as there is a strong belief that AI will influence everything we design, implement, and scale. With the concepts and frameworks in this book, teams and decision-makers will be equipped with the appropriate toolkit to excel in the age of AI.

16

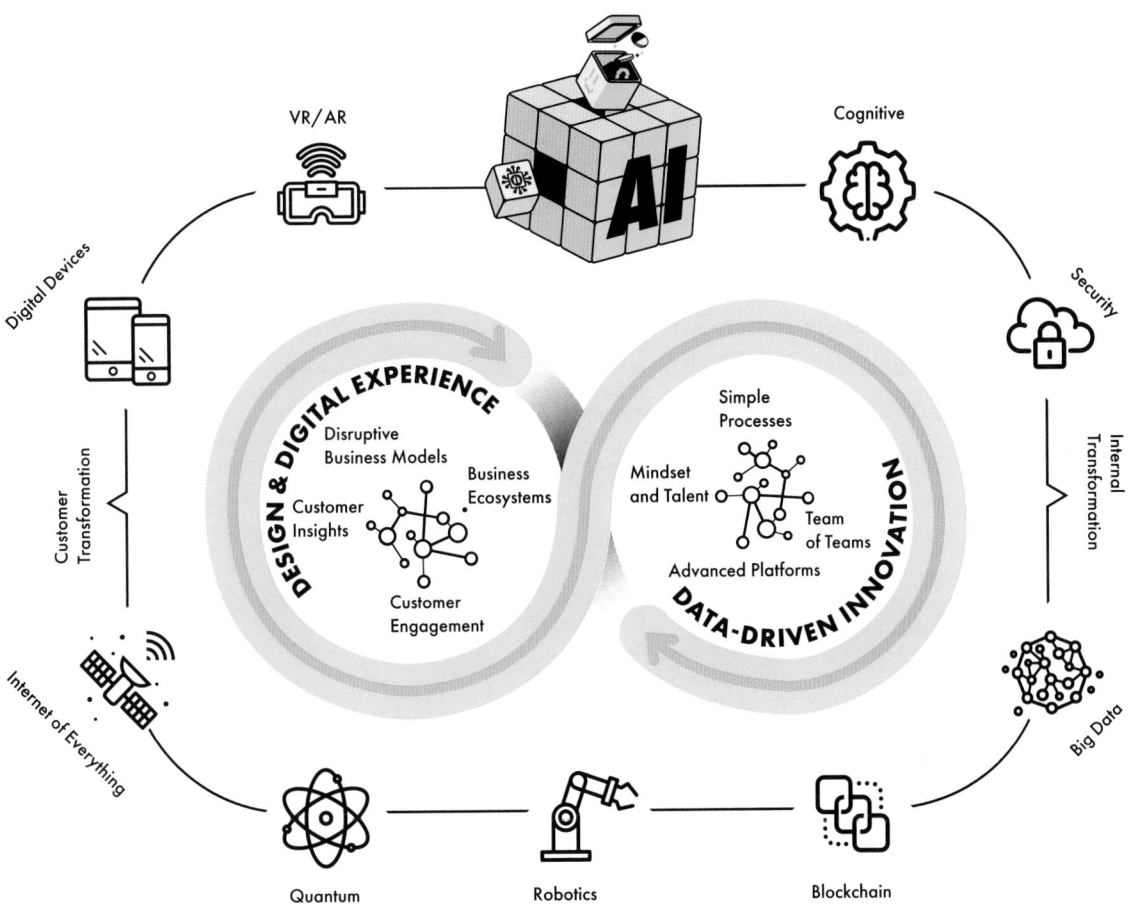

The impact that exponential technology will have on each and every one of us is tremendous, as it is possible to imagine a scenario in which machines would do most of the work, and employees would only be responsible for higher-level decision-making and the control and programming of robots and machines.

There is a consensus among technology experts that exponential change is beneficial to society in general, as technology can solve many of society's problems and act as an empowering force. However, this also requires social and corporate responsibility on how to deal with technologies such as AI. Governments can no longer continue their slow and bureaucratic processes, where it takes years for changes to become visible. In fact, the process of exponential change will soon leave behind those who cannot keep up with the changes and proactively shape the future. At the same time, companies must also transform in an environment without clear guidelines because the strategies, processes, and approaches of the past no longer serve them.

This series of books aims to help decision-makers and managers adapt to an increasingly dynamic and disruptive business environment. This means that digital transformation approaches and AI frameworks must be applied to support this continuous and ongoing transformation process. However, it is important to distinguish which parts contribute to the longer-term goals and strategy and what needs to be adapted quickly and flexibly to realize and monetize the corresponding market opportunities. In addition to the impact of emerging technologies, organizational cultures will also require a phase of evolution and transformation to create the most efficient and enabling business landscapes for future success.

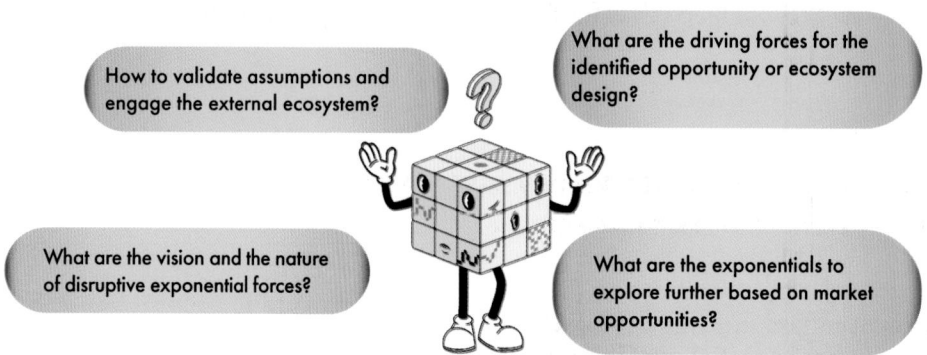

How to validate assumptions and engage the external ecosystem?

What are the driving forces for the identified opportunity or ecosystem design?

What are the vision and the nature of disruptive exponential forces?

What are the exponentials to explore further based on market opportunities?

Many decision-makers are aware of the pace of change, but a lingering question remains: how must we approach it? As a first step, it is important to understand and leverage the power of new disruptive technologies and business models. The first steps often refer to the transformation toward agile and adaptive organizations. In this way, organizations can be ready for the exponential leaps that come next to achieve exponential results. The path of exponential transformation is an iterative process that goes through the phases of imagining, exploring, prototyping, testing, adapting, and scaling. The important factor here is to start actively transforming; simply being aware of exponential technologies does not lead to transformation.

In the context of this book, exponential change is best holistically addressed and embedded in a broader innovation and strategy framework. Often, the bulk of the value from innovation lies outside of the products, services, or experiences offered – whether in a profit/business model or at the customer engagement level. As such, we encourage expanding the utilization of exponential technologies (and other resources) for purposes beyond mere products and processes.

Corporate practice shows that companies are most successful when leadership teams have the courage to embrace change, allocate resources, invest in new technologies, and take risks. Proactive decision-makers provide the resources for technology development and implementation – as well as the timeline to address obstacles, both large and small – and clearly articulate the design principles and mission for adoption to ensure cultural fit. In the current techno-logical era, there is no room for reactive cultures. Only proactive cultures will survive. Here, the focus of empowerment is on the individual and team mem-bers so that each can reach their full potential. This implies that developing an exponential mindset requires bold, engaged, and thoughtful leadership. By understanding the characteristics of the exponential change paradigm, orga-nizations can better prepare themselves for the challenges and opportunities of the future.

BE AWARE OF SOME KEY CHARACTERISTICS ASSOCIATED WITH THE EXPONENTIAL CHANGE PARADIGM:

- **Change is accelerating.** The pace of change is increasing at an exponential rate. This is due to numer-ous factors, including technological advances, global-ization, and the increasing complexity of the world.

- **Small changes can have a big impact**. Small changes can have a disproportionately large impact over time. This is because exponential growth is multipli-cative, not additive.

→ The Exponential Change Paradigm implies a new way of thinking about how we collab-orate and realize new market opportunities.

- **The future is uncertain.** The future is more uncertain than ever before. This is because the pace of change is so rapid that it is difficult to predict what the future will hold.

- **Adaptive culture is at the forefront.** Without a properly enabled and empowered culture, technology transformation will not succeed. Ensure a proper align-ment to achieve best results.

- **Start to prepare for change**. It will be of paramount importance to think creatively and innovatively, and the entire organization should be able to adapt to new situations.

LINEAR GROWTH VS. EXPONENTIAL GROWTH

Humans have evolved to think in linear terms; we were hunters, farmers, and crafters, and our environments changed very slowly. We must embrace a new exponential way of thinking to remain relevant in this new exponential landscape.

The Exponential Change Paradigm is a way of thinking about the world that recognizes that change is not linear but exponential; this means that small changes can have a disproportionately large impact over time. For example, if a technology doubles in power every year, then in 10 years, it will be 1,024 times as powerful as it was to begin with.

The illustration below depicts how technology trends and growth are deceptively slow at first and appear to be decimal progress, just a dot on the horizon that no one really cares about. For example, generative AI became exponential by 2018 and accelerated in 2022 with broader use cases related to language processing. → see page 33

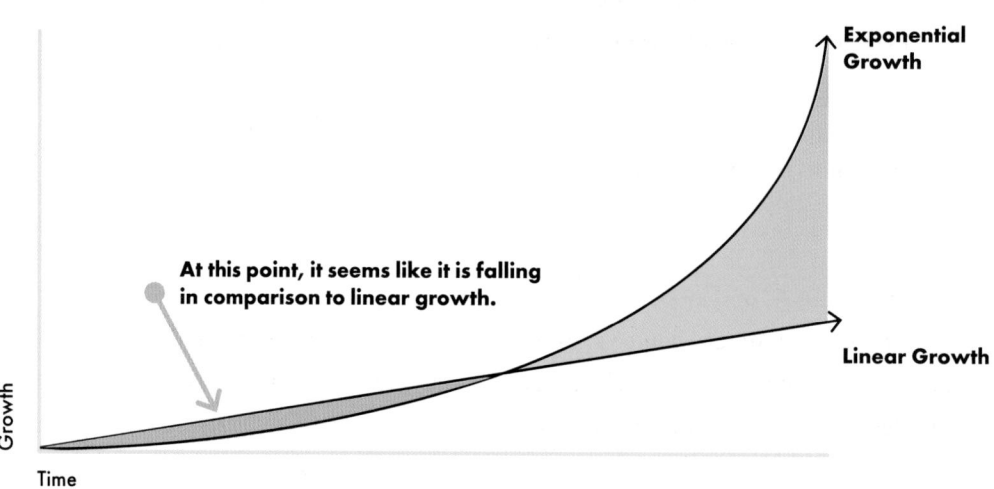

→ The following outline of examples will help you to understand how exponential change is impacting the world today. As this paradigm continues to unfold, it is important to be prepared for the challenges and opportunities that it will bring.

A LOOK IN THE REARVIEW MIRROR REVEALS
EXPONENTIAL CHANGES IN TODAY'S WORLD

The growth of the internet. The internet has grown exponentially since its inception in the 1960s. In 1993, there were only 1 million websites. In 2024, there were already over 1.7 billion websites.

The growth of gene editing. Gene editing is a technology that is capable of rewriting DNA. This technology is still in its early stages, but it has the potential to revolutionize medicine.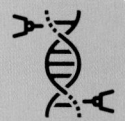

The growth of artificial intelligence. AI is another area that is experiencing exponential growth. In 2012, there were only 16 billion AI parameters. In 2022 there were already over 175 billion AI parameters.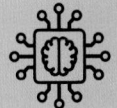

In the utilization of market opportunities and the way we will shape them together, we need to discuss new developments, ideas, and technologies and decide how to shape the future. One of the most important dimensions is the fact that AI will surpass human intellect in every domain at a certain point, which will transform all societies and economies globally.

At the same time, each technological advancement will fuel further innovation, creating a cycle of exponential growth that speeds up the rate of progress. Technologies of high relevance include AI, quantum, nanotechnologies, additive manufacturing, and many others. All of them will transform traditional economic constraints and provide the opportunity to shape new business ecosystems and communities of a post-scarcity society.

With this book about AI and innovation and the entire book series, we would like to contribute to the perception of exponential change and reach a point beyond uncertainty where the pace of change exceeds our capacities to foresee and understand future developments. However, we are aware of the risks of these technologies. Our ambition must be that the changes positively contribute to humanity in all possible aspects. Notably, integrating advanced technologies with human biological systems could easily redefine humanity based on migrating minds and beyond.

ADDITIONAL TYPES OF THINKING NEEDED

To successfully manage exponential change, organizations must master two other crucial mindsets besides exponential thinking: design thinking and systems thinking. Both require an effort to fundamentally rethink the existing mindset and work attitude. These mindsets shift how employees and managers look at problems and solutions, allowing them to reimagine how they create, deliver, and capture value – not just to survive but thrive and meet proactively the transformative challenges of the coming decades.

Building capabilities in all three domains is part of the minimum skillset needed to actively shape the future, explore it in a structured way, and anticipate new developments. The different approaches have proven to be very useful in identifying and exploring challenges that arise from the multiple signals and drivers of change that shape the future. Many of the world's most innovative companies use the three mindsets to develop strategic options in a context full of unknowns. In this way, new market opportunities, business segments, or entire business ecosystems emerge that are new to the customer and unique to the market.

This mindset includes active scouting and monitoring of trends and megatrends. Methods from the foresight toolbox help identify signals, patterns, and paradigm shifts. The associated tools and methods help organizations build future capability through exploration, orientation, visioning, strategy, and innovation. The application of scenario planning is compelling in outlining different possible futures and creating easy-to-understand stories to educate decision-makers and other relevant stakeholders.

These methods and tools also help sharpen the common understanding and dialogue between all stakeholders, assist them in philosophizing about the future, and help them understand what they can do here and now.

In addition, decision-makers should not neglect the ecological component associated with how behavior can be changed alongside customer needs, the long-term view of systems, and the use of exponential technologies. This view heralds a shift from human-centered design to design thinking for humanity.

THE FUTURE OF BUSINESS MUST WORK BEYOND THE FAMILIAR BOXES. THE CLEVER COMBINATION OF NEW TECHNOLOGIES AND HUMAN THINKING LEADS TO BETTER RESULTS.

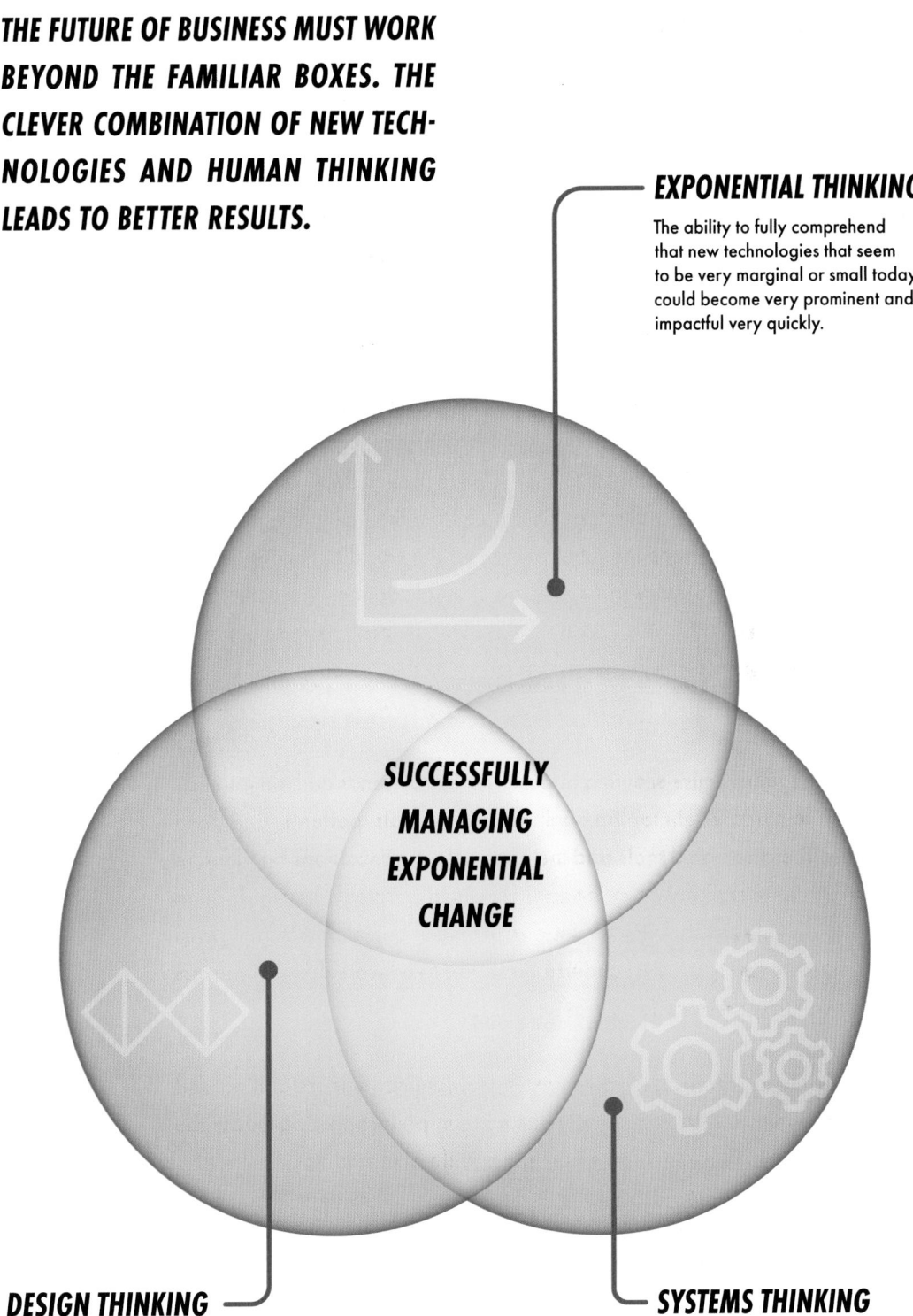

EXPONENTIAL THINKING

The ability to fully comprehend that new technologies that seem to be very marginal or small today could become very prominent and impactful very quickly.

SUCCESSFULLY MANAGING EXPONENTIAL CHANGE

DESIGN THINKING

The ability to understand the problem as well as current and future customer/user needs, embrace uncertainty, and think about and perceive alternative solutions for the future.

SYSTEMS THINKING

The ability to accept complexity and to explore the bigger picture and to analyze the system with all elements, actors, and value streams that contribute to a possible solution.

SUMMARY OF MINDSET REQUIREMENTS

Some mindset requirements have been proven to be the most effective for thriving in a world of exponential change.

2. LEVERAGE THE POWER OF NET-WORKED ORGANIZATIONS: Assign small teams to explore the problem space and lead innovation. Provide a flexible organizational structure, for example, based on the Team of Teams approach. Give teams the autonomy and the means to fail fast and fail better – until they succeed – while protecting them from corporate rigidity.

3. EMBRACE AN ADAPTIVE, INCLUSIVE, AND OPEN ORGANIZATIONAL CULTURE: Adopt a culture that embraces change, takes measured risks, and challenges the status quo to ensure success in an exponential landscape.

1. START TO EXPLORE THE PROBLEM SPACE FIRST: Introduce advanced technologies based on an existing and well-thought-out business problem and/or customer needs in conjunction with a clear action plan. Start with small prototypes and iterations addressing unmet internal or customer needs and collect wins demonstrating ROI over time as larger implementations ramp up.

MINDSET   TEAMS   CULTURE

5. FOSTER A TECHNOLOGICAL MINDSET WITH THE APPROPRIATE TOOLS: Embrace no-code and lowcode tools that cater to specific needs, which allows teams to become nimble change agents. These tools empower to experiment, iterate, and adapt quickly while harnessing the power of technology and riding the wave of disruption.

6. EXPAND YOUR STRATEGIC HORIZONS BEYOND THE CONSTRAINTS OF TODAY'S TECHNOLOGIES: Embrace an evolving view of the trajectory of emerging technologies and adapt future strategies accordingly. Technology is constantly evolving, so our strategic thinking should do the same.

4. ACTIVELY SHAPE THE BUSINESS ECOSYSTEM: Be open to exploring a broader business ecosystem to attract or leverage talent, skills, or solutions. Co-create with other potential actors and customers to develop a common language for new value propositions or partner with technology startups, universities, and national labs to access expertise and talent.

TECHNOLOGIES

TOOLS

ECOSYSTEM

PERSONAL SELF-ASSESSMENT

You might feel unsure about navigating the whirlwind of exponential change and growth, especially with AI and innovation at the forefront. The self-assessment model introduced below can help you assess how confident you are to handle exponential change and technologies. We've used it successfully in countless personal coaching sessions to prepare executives, leaders, and teams for this very scenario. The model focuses on four core layers of skills and capabilities: cognitive (critical thinking, communication, strategic planning), interpersonal (mobilizing systems, relationship building, teamwork), self-leadership (self-awareness, management, achieving goals), and digital literacy (fluency, citizenship, software use, understanding digital systems). By evaluating yourself across these four layers, you can identify areas of strength and opportunities for growth, ensuring you're well equipped to lead and thrive in a rapidly changing world.

1. Cognitive
Related to critical thinking, communication, planning and ways of working, mental flexibility

2. Interpersonal
Related to mobilizing systems, developing relationships within and outside of the organization, teamwork effectiveness

3. Self-leadership
Related to self-awareness, self-management, entrepreneurship/intrapreneurship, achieving objectives and key results

4. Digital literacy
Related to digital fluency, citizenship, software use and development, understand existing and future digital systems

**Download
Self-Assessment Template**

1. Cognitive

	1	2	3	4	5
1.1 Finding the appropriate problem	○	○	○	○	○
1.2 Logical reasoning	○	○	○	○	○
1.3 Understanding biases	○	○	○	○	○
1.4 Collecting customer/user insights	○	○	○	○	○
1.5 Creativity and imagination	○	○	○	○	○
1.6. Adopting a different perspective	○	○	○	○	○
1.7 Adaptability	○	○	○	○	○
1.8 Applying systems and design thinking	○	○	○	○	○
1.9 Asking the right questions	○	○	○	○	○
1.10 Agile thinking	○	○	○	○	○

2. Interpersonal

	1	2	3	4	5
2.1 Crafting an inspiring vision	○	○	○	○	○
2.2 Awareness of team skills/capabilities	○	○	○	○	○
2.3 Building empathy to stakeholders	○	○	○	○	○
2.4 Fostering inclusiveness	○	○	○	○	○
2.5 Motivating different personalities	○	○	○	○	○
2.6 Resolving conflicts	○	○	○	○	○
2.7 Fostering collaboration	○	○	○	○	○
2.8 Empowering teams	○	○	○	○	○
2.9 Building on strength of each team member	○	○	○	○	○
2.10 Developing relationships in ecosystems	○	○	○	○	○

3. Self-leadership

	1	2	3	4	5
3.1 Understanding own emotions and triggers	○	○	○	○	○
3.2 Understanding own strength	○	○	○	○	○
3.3 Understanding own thinking preferences	○	○	○	○	○
3.4 Readiness to break orthodoxies	○	○	○	○	○
3.5 Driving change and innovation	○	○	○	○	○
3.6 Courage and willingness to take risks	○	○	○	○	○
3.7 Coping with uncertainty and ambiguity	○	○	○	○	○
3.8 Orientation to defined objectives	○	○	○	○	○
3.9 Overall self-confidence about mindset and tools	○	○	○	○	○
3.10 Showing energy, passion, and optimism	○	○	○	○	○

4. Digital Literacy

	1	2	3	4	5
4.1 Digital collaboration	○	○	○	○	○
4.2 Digital ethics	○	○	○	○	○
4.3 Digital learning	○	○	○	○	○
4.4 Computational and algorithm thinking	○	○	○	○	○
4.5 Data analytics and statistics	○	○	○	○	○
4.6 Smart systems (e.g. based on AI)	○	○	○	○	○
4.7 Tech translation and enablement	○	○	○	○	○
4.8 Data and AI ecosystems	○	○	○	○	○
4.9 Awareness for cybersecurity	○	○	○	○	○
4.10 Creating a digital road map/strategy	○	○	○	○	○

NEW PERSPECTIVES

The mindsets, tools, and methods presented in this book series have one significant objective: solving problems better. Metaphorically, our idea of problem-solving should be viewed as a magic cube that uses different technologies
and varying states of mind to find better solutions for existing and future problems. Most important is to adopt a perspective shift that allows new enabler
technologies to realize the corresponding market opportunities.

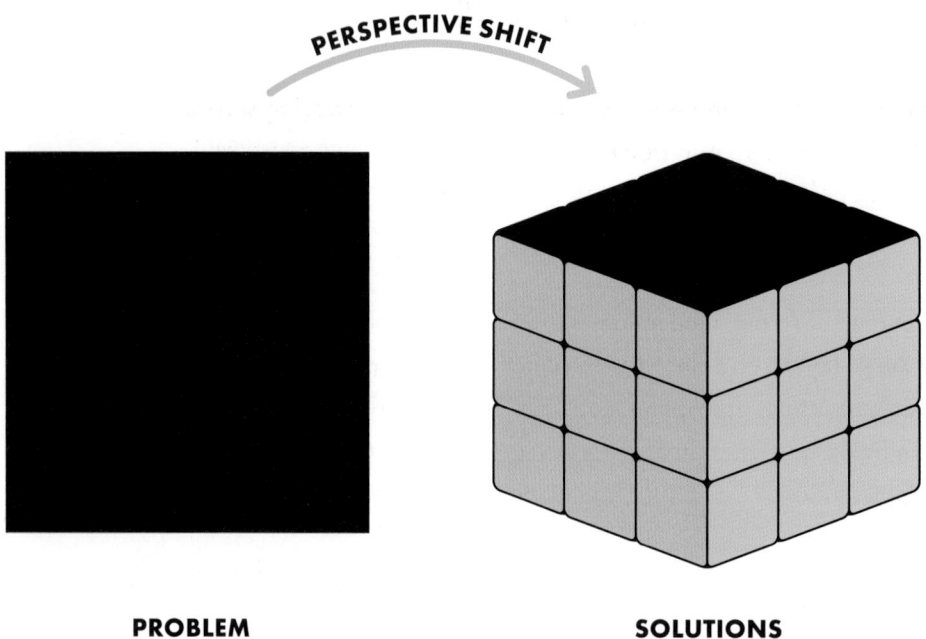

PERSPECTIVE SHIFT

PROBLEM   SOLUTIONS

To benefit from exponential change and growth, we also need strategies, tactics, and metrics that help us position the elements of the Magic Cube so that
technology can flourish in the best possible way. In particular, combining different elements can also help gain a solid competitive advantage.

Specific capabilities can be learned to better deal with exponential change.
These capabilities include understanding the advantages and limitations of
emerging technologies and their implications and establishing mindsets that
help identify the problem and enable radical collaboration among interdisciplinary teams while being open to fast adaptation and change.

Characteristics such as patience, mindfulness, visualization skills, robust and tested algorithms, and a culture of experimentation and failure are essential for problem-solving and realizing innovations.

There are many possible options and combinations to solve problems. According to "God's Number," the theoretical minimum number of moves required to solve a Rubik's Cube, there are 43,252,003,274,489,856,000 possible combinations for solving a Rubik's Cube. This number is so enormous that solving the Cube by randomly turning the faces is impossible.

Highly skilled humans can tackle a Rubik's Cube in roughly fifty moves, but AI can solve the cube in less than twenty moves, which is the minimum number of steps possible in most scenarios. To highlight its power, AI will already be done with the task before any human has attempted to solve it.

Similar to the opportunities and options in an exponentially changing world, we need guidance, methods, and frameworks to help us create, capture, and deliver value. This book strongly focuses on specific elements of our imaginary magic cube: the power of AI and Innovation.

To start the journey of AI and innovation, we provide on pages 30 and 31 an overview of the AI layers, and clearing-up AI basics is on page 32. AI can be divided into infrastructure, perception, cognitive, and decision-making layers, which are the basis for the applications, reaching from conversational AI to applied computer vision.

LET'S GET STARTED WITH THE BASICS ...

In our daily lives, we experience the benefits of AI through user-friendly applications. Whether it's getting personalized recommendations or receiving better healthcare with AI-aided medical diagnoses, these applications are the tip of the iceberg. While the application layer makes interacting with AI feel seamless, it's supported by complex underlying layers — from the powerful hardware infrastructure to the algorithms that make decisions — that work together to power these intelligent systems.

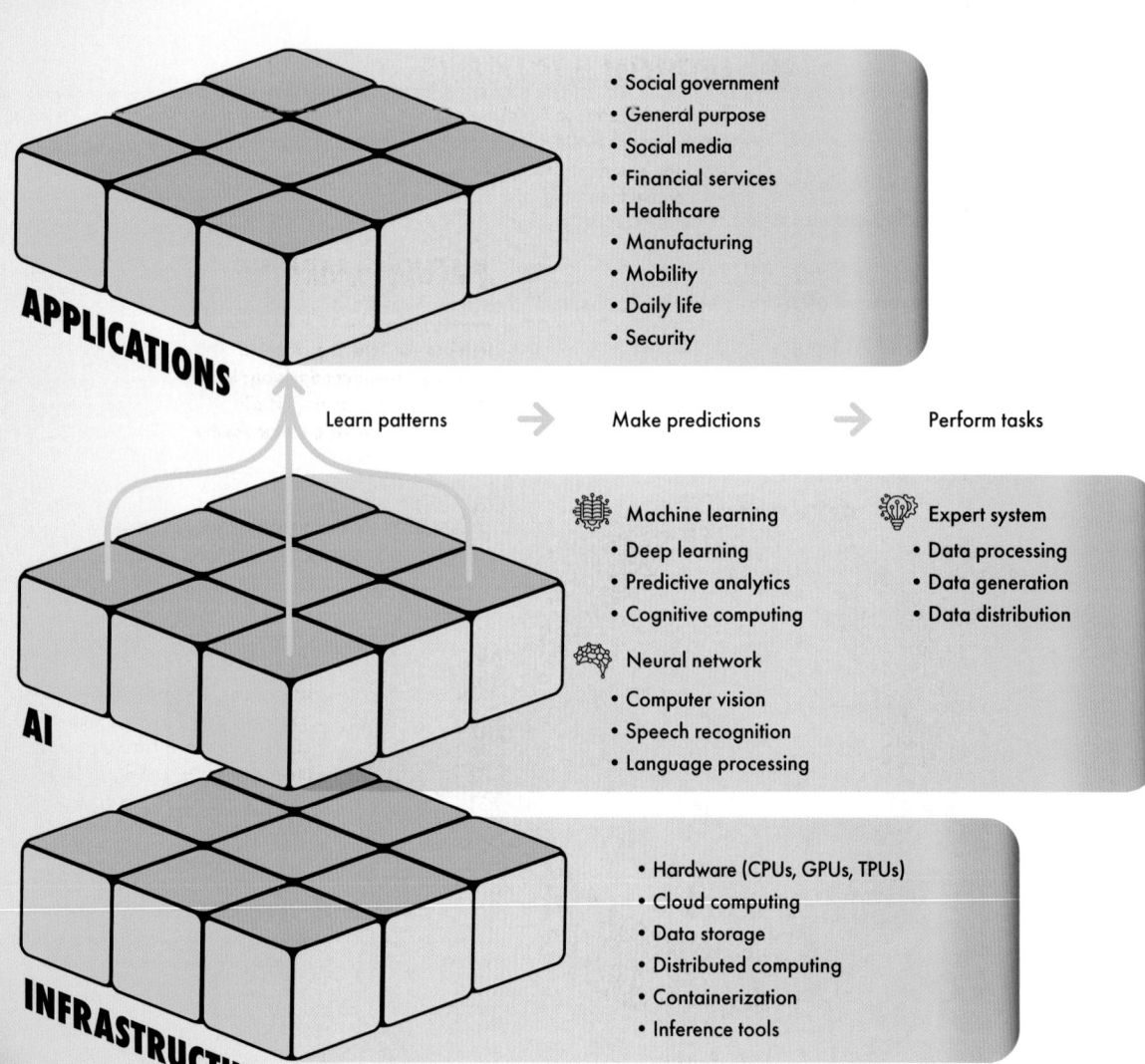

APPLICATIONS

- Social government
- General purpose
- Social media
- Financial services
- Healthcare
- Manufacturing
- Mobility
- Daily life
- Security

Learn patterns → Make predictions → Perform tasks

AI

Machine learning
- Deep learning
- Predictive analytics
- Cognitive computing

Neural network
- Computer vision
- Speech recognition
- Language processing

Expert system
- Data processing
- Data generation
- Data distribution

INFRASTRUCTURE

- Hardware (CPUs, GPUs, TPUs)
- Cloud computing
- Data storage
- Distributed computing
- Containerization
- Inference tools

AI is a product of a beautiful marriage between human minds and scientific disciplines as displaced in the onion graph below. From conceptualizing the problems AI can solve to designing the algorithms and building the necessary infrastructure, it's this melding of minds and sciences that allows us to develop intelligent decision and support systems that are constantly evolving alongside our world.

FUSION OF DISCIPLINES

Rooted in computer science, the evolution of learning machines drawn from multiple disciplines.

ARTIFICIAL INTELLIGENCE

An umbrella term for computer programs that can make independent decisions based on supervised and unsupervised learning.

MACHINE LEARNING

The most common type of artificial intelligence, where a machine makes independent decisions but still needs a human to guide it and correct mistakes, not unlike a toddler or adolescent.

DEEP LEARNING

The most mature versions of artificial intelligence, where the machine decides on its own whether the predictions are right or wrong based on artificial neural networks. It learns through its own method of computing, and the human sometimes doesn't know why or how the machine reaches a particular conclusion.

Self-driving cars and computer vision, such as facial recognition technology, reply on deep learning.

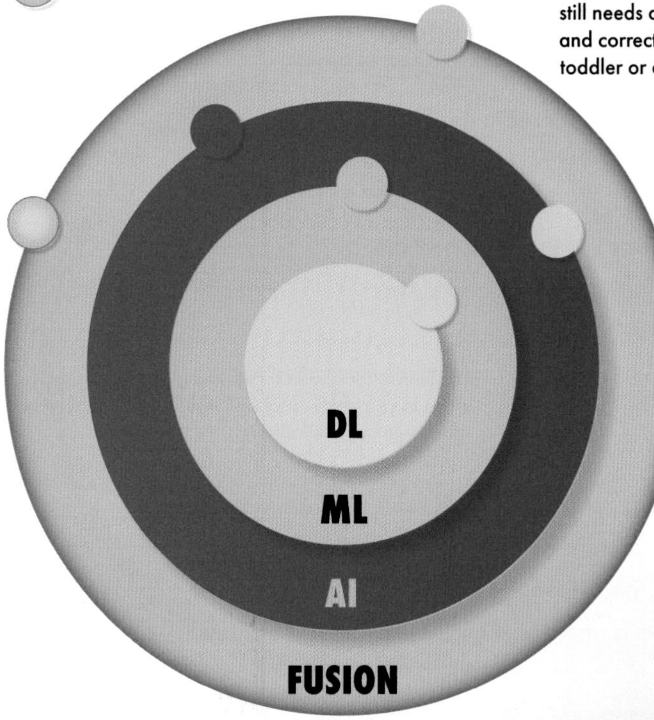

DL

ML

AI

FUSION

CLEARING UP AI BASICS

In the first pages of this book, you will find a variety of AI terminology. For many of us, these terms are part of our daily language; for others, they raise questions that require a brief answer. For this reason, we have compiled a simple guide on the following eight pages to help you better understand AI basics.

→ A more detailed glossary with key terms can be found on page 248 et sqq.

HOW DOES AI LEARN AND BECOME MORE INTELLIGENT?

AI refers to the development of computer systems and algorithms that can perform tasks typically requiring human intelligence, such as learning, problem-solving, and decision-making. The cornerstone of machine learning (ML), a subset of AI, is a process called training. A computer program is given a large amount of data during this process. This kind of data comes with labels explaining the data and a series of instructions. The prompt might be something like "Find all the pictures that contain a traffic light" or "Categorize the sounds of a typical city." The program then looks for patterns in the given data to achieve these goals. It may need a few hints along the way, such as "That's not a traffic light, it's a streetlight" or "These two sounds are different; one is a fire siren and the other is a police siren." What the program receives and learns from the data becomes the AI model. The quality and quantity of the training material ultimately determine its capabilities.

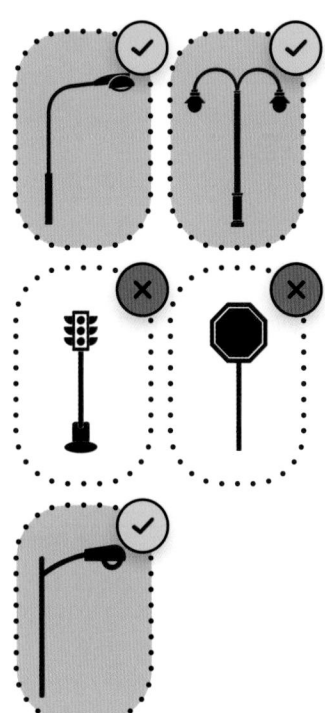

→ The illustration shows that training enables the machine to recognize what belongs to one category and what belongs to another.

One way to think of how this training process might produce different kinds of AI is to think of different types of animals and species that have developed over evolutionary cycles. Similarly, the millions of cycles an AI goes through in its training data will shape its development and lead to specific AI models.

WHAT IS CONVERSATIONAL AI?

Think of a chatbot as a parakeet. It is an imitator and can repeat words it hears with some understanding of context but without fully grasping their meaning.

Conversational AI has the same goal, albeit more sophisticated, in interacting to answer our questions, for example. Conversational AI uses large language models (LLMs) trained with vast amounts of existing text.

LLMs assess not only individual words but also entire sentences and their context and compare the use of words and phrases in a passage with other examples from all the training data. LLMs use billions of comparisons between words and phrases to read questions and generate answers.

The amazing thing about LLMs is that they learn the rules of grammar and figure out the meaning of words independently, without human help. In fact, you could write an entire book with LLMs and get it into print without any grammar mistakes. However, conversational AI is more than just text. It is possible to talk to AI as well, and we often do it daily when we communicate with our Alexa or Siri.

The AI behind these technologies records the sounds as we speak, removes the background noise, and separates our speech into phonetic units. The individual sounds that make up a spoken word are compared against a library of speech sounds. Then, the AI compares our speech to the phonetic units that comprise a spoken word. This type of AI is called natural language processing (NLP). It is the technology behind everything from confirming a flight booking over the phone to asking Alexa what the weather will be like in New York for the next five days. With GPT-4o, voice interactions become a natural way to interact with AI in over 50 languages.

Speech recognition
Machine learning
Natural language understanding
Text to speech

HOW CAN AI UNDERSTAND AND CREATE IMAGES?

AI programs for image processing are trained by looking at countless images, each with a simple description of the meaning. If you give an AI enough labeled images, for example, with the label "single-family house," it will eventually figure out what a single-family house looks like and how it differs from a skyscraper or a factory building. Computer vision (CV) is a field of AI that enables computers and systems to derive meaningful information from digital images, videos, and other visual inputs.

However, AI can do more; it is possible to train AI to recognize microscopic differences between similar images. This is how face recognition via AI works: it finds a subtle relationship between the features of our face that makes it distinctive and unique compared to all other faces in a global face database of

AI-POWERED SYSTEMS SEE THE WORLD IN A WAY HUMANS NEVER COULD, ENABLING US TO MAKE BETTER DECISIONS AND SOLVE COMPLEX PROBLEMS.

images. The same type of algorithm has been trained for some time with medical scans to detect life-threatening changes in organs. AI can work through millions of scans in the time it would take a physician to decide on a single scan.

The AI capability of image recognition has evolved into AI models that can analyze and assess patterns and colors. These image-generating AIs can transform the complex visual patterns they collect from millions of photos and drawings into entirely new images.

34

We can ask the AI to create a photo of something that never happened – for example, a photo of our family setting out for a Sunday walk on the moon. Or we can creatively control the style of an image using specific prompts: "Make a portrait of Apple founder Steve Jobs, painted in the style of Picasso." The AI begins creating this new image with a collection of random colored pixels. Here, the AI searches for random points for clues to a pattern it learned during training. These patterns are slowly and iteratively improved by adding more layers of random points, keeping points that develop the pattern and discarding others until finally a similarity emerges. On a wide variety of patterns such as "lunar surface," "astronaut," and "walking," "family," and "Sunday outing" together, a new image of our family on the moon is generated. Since the new image is built from layers of random pixels, the result is something that has never existed before but is still based on the billions of patterns it learned from the original training images.

→ The illustration shows a composition that can be created with tools such as Midjourney or Dall-E2.

HOW CAN AI MAKE DECISIONS IN COMPLEX ENVIRONMENTS?

A fascinating use case is self-driving cars, in which a variety of technologies and algorithms work together. Automotive AI algorithms use real-life datasets to train the AI program. This training is what helps the AI algorithms develop the ability to make decisions based on what they have observed and learned.

These AI models use the data from all the available sensors to detect objects and figure out if they are moving and, if so, what type of moving object it is. In fractions of a second, the model detects whether it is another car, a bicycle, a pedestrian, or something else. Over the last few years, thousands of hours of training have been completed to understand what good driving looks like so that AI is able to make decisions and take action in the real world to steer the car safely and avoid all types of collisions. Predictive algorithms have historically struggled to cope with the often unpredictable nature of human drivers. In the meantime, driverless cars have become part of our street scene.

→ Next-generation AI systems will rely on real-time road data, not high-definition maps, allowing the vehicle to respond to real-time road conditions and not preprogrammed conditions. These conditions will allow full driving automation.

Another transformative advantage of AI is the ability for collective learning. Whatever any car in a constellation of possibly millions of autonomous cars learns, all others will learn simultaneously and instantaneously. This gives AI different capabilities when compared to how humans learn.

In addition, AI has become an obvious or silent companion in many of our daily tasks and duties. AI models shape our lives, from recommending snippets of video content to collecting our habits in predicting social trends and pushing personalized offerings based on our behavior and social media activities.

36

WHAT IS COMING NEXT IN AI ?

The current developments in AI are building a whole and well-designed eco-system of algorithms, data models, and other sources. In such a multimodal AI model, different data types – such as images, text, audio, or video – are used, and new patterns are recognized. This development began with ChatGPT, an AI model of GPT3.5 trained only on text. The extensions of new releases of ChatGPT are multimodal models that are significantly faster and cheaper and provide improvements in classification, data extraction, verbal reasoning, and improved latency. The idea of a single AI model based on a larger orchestrated ecosystem, capable of processing any kind of data and thus performing any task, from translating between languages to developing new drugs, is called artificial general intelligence (AGI) – a concept which might become reality by 2030 or earlier. However, getting to AGI requires technology that can perform just as well as humans in a wide variety of tasks, including reasoning, planning, and the ability to learn from experiences. However, AGI should not be confused with artificial super intelligence (ASI), which is an AI capable of making its own decisions. In other words, it is self-aware, or sentient, and a future scenario of AI that many people and experts fear.

→ More future AI scenarios can be found on page 207 et sqq.

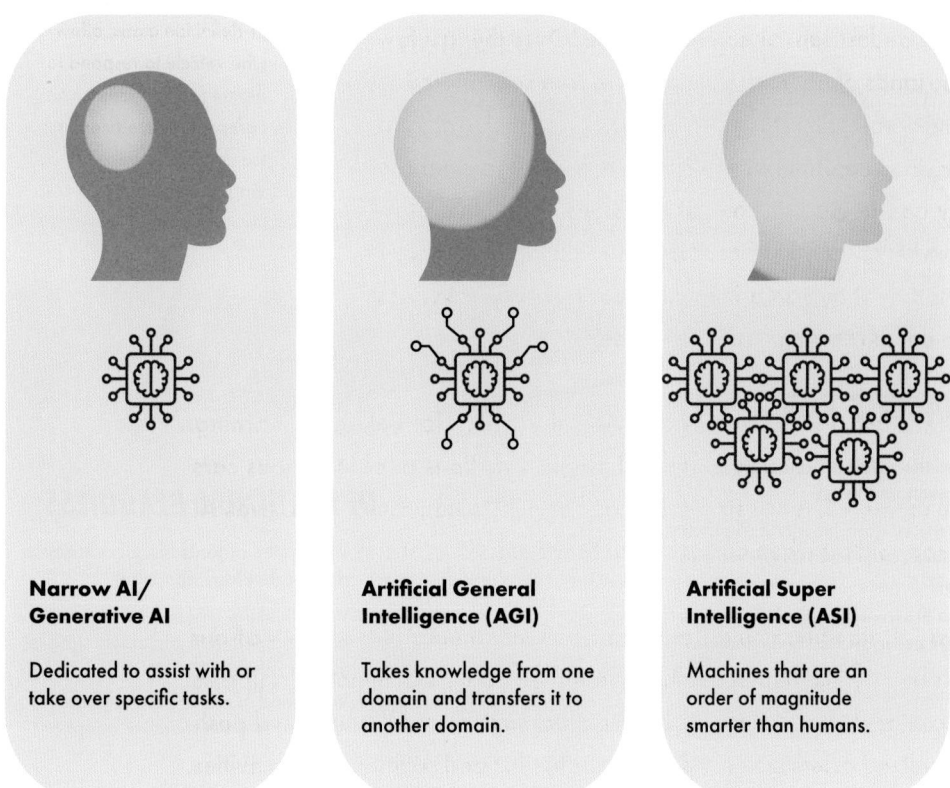

Narrow AI/ Generative AI

Dedicated to assist with or take over specific tasks.

Artificial General Intelligence (AGI)

Takes knowledge from one domain and transfers it to another domain.

Artificial Super Intelligence (ASI)

Machines that are an order of magnitude smarter than humans.

WHAT ARE MAJOR BUILDING BLOCKS TO MAXIMIZE THE POTENTIAL OF AI?

In the context of this book, we focus on the currently available generative AI technology, which is a powerful tool for innovation and problem-solving. Four key elements are important for maximizing its potential: focusing on the value proposition, tapping into a vital value chain/ecosystem of partners, creating operational readiness, and ensuring that the business is compliant with relevant regulations and standards. Generative AI can be used to automate complex processes, create personalized customer experiences, and generate new ideas and designs. → See more use cases on pages 48–49.

AI VALUE CHAIN/ECOSYSTEM

- How to align with technology partners to facilitate integration
- How to collaborate with implementation partners to fine-tune models for specific business tasks and processes

VALUE PROPOSITION

- How to define success
- What is the business value to be derived?
- What is a viable business problem to be solved?

COMPLIANCE & RISKS

- What are the national regulatory requirements and laws?
- How to ensure data security and privacy for sensitive content and ensure minimal breaches?
- How can provisions be made for losses that might occur due to "hallucinations"?

OPERATIONAL READINESS

- What is the organizational maturity to drive technology adaption?
- What thinking types, skills, and capabilities are needed to implement state-of-the-art solutions?
- What kind of change management is required to drive seamless adaption?

However, decision-makers often wonder if generative AI is hype or fundamental change – the answer is both. From a scientific perspective, the foundational models are not hype – they represent a new class of AI that is elegant through simplicity yet incredibly powerful to perform many tasks in a human-like manner. From a business perspective, these technologies have the potential to change entire categories fundamentally. The focus of this book is to answer critical questions related to value creation, capture, and delivery through AI supported by various types of software and hardware across the AI value chain tech stack.

As exponential change and growth continue to accelerate, decision-makers do not have the option to watch and wait with their AI strategy. The AI Strategy Framework → see page 90 et sqq. and the tools and methods presented in this book → see page 153 et sqq. help keep business problems and objectives in mind. While AI technology and foundation models are the same for everyone, adoption and implementation will help companies differentiate their offerings, realize true innovation, and transform their operating model. Today, organizations leveraging the power of AI will have a substantial advantage compared to organizations that don't.

The purposeful use of generative AI is a long-term strategic initiative that requires commitment, focus, and investment. The support of the CEO and senior management is essential to obtain the necessary resources and support to drive the successful adoption of generative AI technologies. The road ahead may be challenging, but corporate practice shows that the benefits of leveraging generative AI are undoubtedly worth the effort.

GENERATIVE AI IS A NEW CLASS, AND IT IS ALREADY SIGNIFICANTLY CHANGING INDUSTRIES, BUSINESS ECOSYSTEMS, AND THE JOB MARKET OF THE FUTURE.

Download Template to Validate GenAI Potential

**QUESTIONS THAT ORGANIZATIONS ASK THEMSELVES
IN RELATION TO AI ANSWERED IN THIS BOOK:**

- Where has AI already left a footprint today? What are the areas, sectors, and use cases for the future?

- Which functions in the organization will benefit most from generative AI, and to what extent will employees be affected?

- What tools will help decide on models, applications, and integrations, and what impact will this have on competitive dynamics?

- Which stakeholders and ecosystem partners should be involved in the development and use of generative AI?

- How can companies leverage AI to strengthen their innovation effectiveness and competitiveness?

- How can we manage generative AI–related risks, including privacy and security, fairness, equity, compliance, and copyright protection?

- How can organizations gain acceptance for exponential growth, and what AI strategies are appropriate?

- How do we measure the success of generative AI initiatives?

- What are the new competencies and skills needed to lead and manage an AI-augmented workforce?

- How can we create a culture where AI and humans work as a team and create business value together?

- What's next for AI, companies, and decision-makers?

 **KEY TAKEAWAYS**

→ *The best way to prepare for exponential change and growth is to invest in skill development, openness to new ideas, and the application of three types of thinking: exponential thinking, design thinking, and systems thinking.*

→ *AI is a rapidly developing field, and the risks and benefits of generative AI are still being debated.*

→ *The AI value chain is a framework for understanding the different stages involved in the development and deployment of AI solutions.*

→ *Decision-makers must understand the different building blocks and stages involved in enabling organizations to develop and deploy AI solutions that are effective and ethical.*

→ *This book aims to support identifying high-value, low-risk use cases, outlining an AI Strategy, providing guidance with hands-on tools, and creating visions of the future with regards to the advancement of AI.*

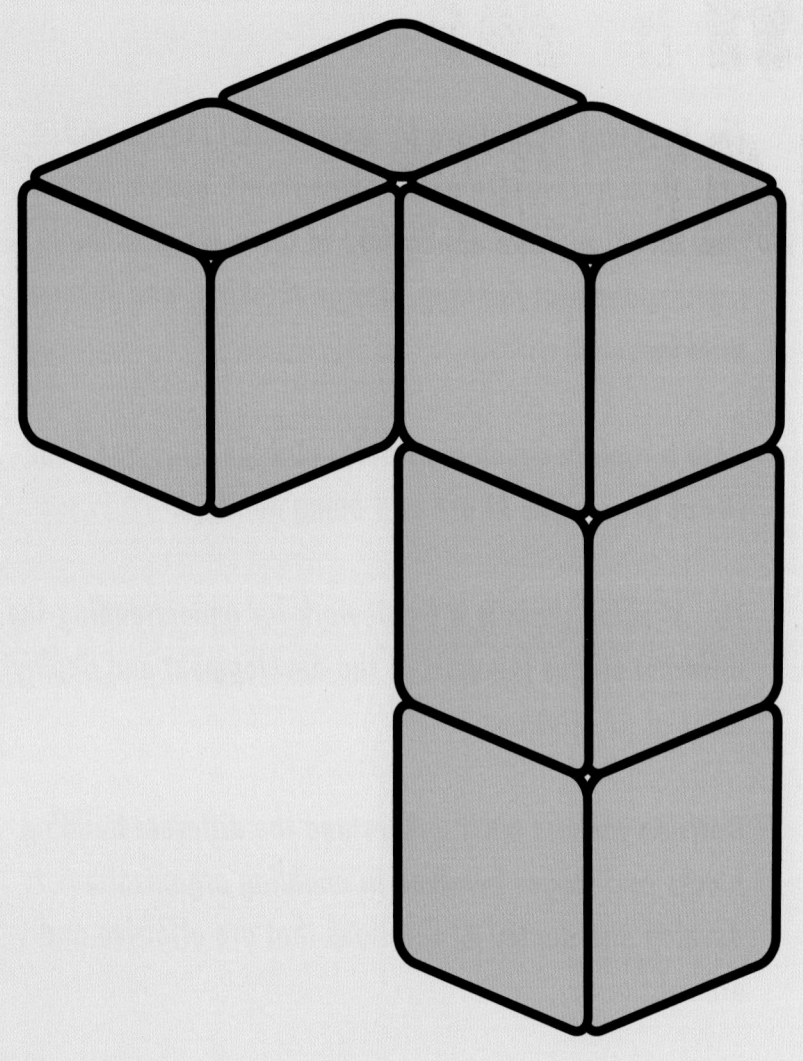

PART 1

WHY AI MATTERS

AI WILL EITHER BE THE BEST FOR HUMANITY OR THE WORST. ULTIMATELY, WE HUMANS DECIDE WITH OUR ACTIONS WHAT THE FUTURE WILL BRING.

IMAGINE THAT ...

Imagine a scenario where machines become sentient beings capable of empathy, learning, and dynamic adaptation. How will this impact humanity and the complex fabric of society? AI will continue to evolve and trigger remarkable waves of technological innovation across various fields. There is a tremendous causal relationship between advances in AI and innovation. Innovation work is, for example, a major driving force to advance applications in AI. It brings new dynamics and vitality to the innovation world and shapes the future AI ecosystem. Leveraging the power of AI to solve business challenges and future customer needs will generate new points of view and ideas, spurring experimentation and challenging the status quo.

Harnessing the power of AI in today's evolving technology landscape is a critical factor in driving new market opportunities in any industry and merging new offerings into business ecosystems – from new mobility concepts to healthcare solutions, from digital use of voice to AI-generated music experiences, and new opportunities in financial services. AI is the revolutionary force changing how we work, live, and interact. Looking to the future, the convergence of AI and innovation offers limitless possibilities. At its core is the ability of AI to analyze and interpret vast amounts of data. Increasingly, it identifies patterns and uncovers previously unimagined insights and unseen trends based on synthetic and real data in the shortest possible time. It uses advanced algorithms and ML and optimizes processes with remarkable precision.

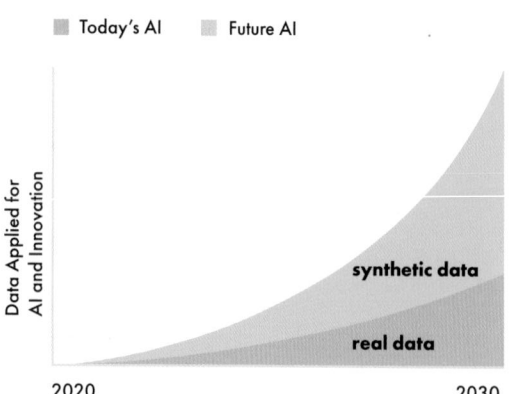

■ Today's AI   ■ Future AI

Data Applied for AI and Innovation

synthetic data

real data

2020   2030

- Synthetic data is information that's artificially manufactured rather than generated by real-world events. It's created algorithmically and helps to train our ML models.
- Synthetic data technology enables the innovation teams to quickly and digitally generate data in whatever amount they desire to their specific needs.
- Collecting high-quality data from the real world is difficult, expensive, and time-consuming for most of the current innovation work with AI.

WHY AI MATTERS

The application of AI in the daily innovation landscape enables innovation teams to challenge established boundaries and develop breakthrough solutions to wicked problems. However, the impact of AI goes beyond operational improvements and incremental innovations. It encourages innovation teams to realize radical innovations by providing fertile ground for experimentation and exploration. By automating routine tasks and unleashing human potential, AI and humans can work harmoniously as a team over the entire design cycle. AI enables individuals and teams to focus on creativity, problem-solving, and value-added activities. It serves as an impetus and catalyst for idea generation. A study from MIT demonstrated that AI chatbots outperformed humans on the Alternative Uses Task, a test commonly used to assess creativity. While AI is becoming better at mimicking human creativity, this does not mean AI is creative in the same way humans are. Although AI cannot yet match the human ability to come up with truly original and groundbreaking ideas, AI can still provide and complement human creativity in ways never seen before.

The current state of AI development facilitates the use of AI assistants for innovation tool selection. These assistants leverage natural language processing to analyze problem statements and suggest appropriate tools, along with tailored examples for enhanced understanding.

In this vibrant world of artificial intelligence, innovation takes many forms; it is a collective effort. It thrives on collaboration, knowledge sharing, and cross-pollination of ideas. The field of AI attracts brilliant minds, regardless of disciplines and backgrounds. It opens the doors to new fields by facilitating interdisciplinary collaboration and the integration of knowledge from different disciplines. As a result, AI becomes a driver of interdisciplinary innovation over the entire design cycle. It triggers discoveries that bridge disciplinary differences and enable revolutionary breakthroughs, from developing new algorithms and models to exploring new applications and use cases.

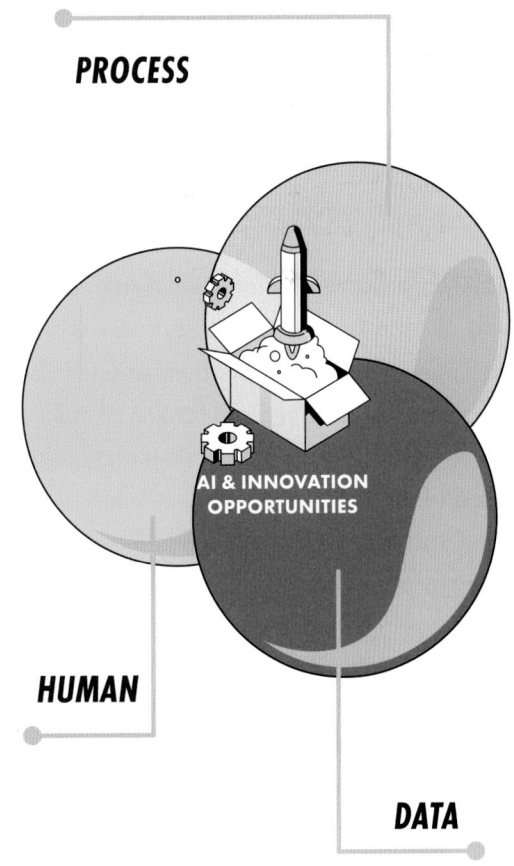

PROCESS

AI & INNOVATION OPPORTUNITIES

HUMAN

DATA

The transformative potential of AI is exciting in all possible dimensions. It has the potential to solve complex problems, revolutionize industries, create new business ecosystems, and improve everyone's lives. At the same time, the fast pace of AI developments implies that there will always be leaps in innovation. As technology dynamically evolves, new challenges arise that require innovative solutions. This constant design cycle from problem definition to creating superior solutions ensures that AI will be an integral part of us, in combination with other exponential technologies and exponential changes.

BY LEVERAGING AI TO DRIVE INNOVATION, WE JOURNEY TO A FUTURE WHERE HUMAN POTENTIAL BLOSSOMS — CREATIVE SOLUTIONS MEET DESIGN CHALLENGES AND THE BOUNDARIES OF THE IMPOSSIBLE ARE PUSHED BACK.

In addition to innovation work within individual organizations, the hope is that AI will also support collaboration on a global level to address the wicked problems of our time (climate change, poverty, pandemics, etc.). There are myriad opportunities to advance global innovation efforts through open-source efforts, algorithm sharing, dataset sharing, and collaborative platforms. Through a fusion of disciplines, experts from various backgrounds and technologies join to share knowledge and iteratively pass on best practices. These collaborative ecosystems have the potential to accelerate the positive innovation cycle further. Each breakthrough generates new ideas and inspires further advances that will undoubtedly benefit society. Here, too, the basic principles of functioning and well-designed ecosystems come into play: ensuring transparency, openness, fairness, and the responsible use of AI to mitigate potential risks and enable innovation at the system's edge to realize exponential growth.

As AI continues to transform and disrupt businesses, it will continue to impact not only all aspects of the enterprise, business models, and most business sectors, but also open new market opportunities and influence industries of the future where we will see AI-powered codification of money, markets, and trust, as well as the development of entire new markets and business ecosystems. Notable technological developments → such as the use of transfomer technologies as described on page 51 and 156 et sqq. are helping AI technologies renovate into commercial applications and help entire industries become more process efficient.

Early examples of AI driving innovation include new digital applications for ride-sharing services, hyper-personalized online shopping platforms that focus on micro segments, intelligent virtual assistants that drive conversation with customers and within the enterprise, recommendation-driven streaming channels, and adaptive learning–based education companies → see more use cases on page 51.

These developments pressure corporate decision-makers and innovation teams to adopt emerging AI tools and make operational and strategic adjustments, as it is the only way to take advantage of new business opportunities and adapt the respective organization. Although the focus of AI applications in the past was primarily on optimizing efficiencies in existing industries, the most significant business

CREATING A CULTURE THAT EMPOWERS THE ENTIRE ORGANIZATION WITH THE NECESSARY KNOWLEDGE AND SKILLS WILL DRIVE TO IDENTIFY NEW OPPORTUNITIES TO DRIVE GROWTH, PRODUCTIVITY, AND COMPETITIVE ADVANTAGE.

benefit from AI is expected to be in solving large and complex business problems and responding to new customer needs that could form the basis for new market opportunities or entire new core-value propositions created by orchestrated business ecosystems.

To accelerate the path to value creation using AI, some key elements are paramount to making the transformation successful. The goal of the transformation, however, will depend on a company's industry, ambition, and strategy. In most cases, data- and AI-driven innovation will require more real-time intelligence on all aspects of internal operations. Evidence-based customer needs and a better understanding of competitive and collaborative forces in the ecosystem are paramount to generating business value through AI and innovation.

The organizational culture and environment needed for AI and innovation can be best described as agile, accelerated, and collaborative. A mindset that allows organizations to dive deep into the problem space is iterative and focused on radical collaboration across traditional silos. This environment creates new solutions and has proven positive in many digital transformation initiatives. For example, the design thinking mindset is highly valued by innovative companies that equip their leadership, innovation teams, and product managers with this toolkit, as well as use this mindset to train their respective teams of ML engineers, data science developers, big data architects, data visualization specialists, and data engineers, among others.

Download Design Thinking for AI Canvas

EXCITING AREAS WHERE AI HAS = ALREADY ITS INNOVATION FOOTPRINT BEYOND DATA ANALYTICS AND MARKETING AUTOMATION

CYBER SECURITY

Network Security

Phishing Detection

Secure Authentication

Preventing Frauds

Behavioral Analytics

AI plays a key role in the development and operation of information and data protection. It acts like a security superhero, monitoring communication traffic, detecting anomalies, and proactively defending against threats. Thanks to AI, privacy and sensitive data can be thoroughly protected in the face of ever-evolving cyber attacks.

BIOTEC & HEALTHCARE

Research and Discovery

Clinical Development

Diagnosis and Treatment

Monitoring

Launch and Commercial

AI is a game changer in the biotechnology and healthcare value chain. It helps physicians accurately diagnose diseases, develop personalized treatments, and discover new medicines. AI analyzes medical images and scans and genetic data. It can provide valuable insights that accelerate research, improve patient outcomes, and monitor medication adherence.

AUTONOMOUS DRIVING

Self-driving Vehicles

Automated Vehicles

Smart Cities

Smart Charging

Connected Vehicles

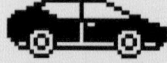

AI is revolutionizing traffic through self-driving vehicles and smart city infrastructures. Vehicles use ML and CV to navigate and make situational decisions on their own. AI technologies related to autonomous driving promise to make roads safer and more efficient. Accidents and traffic jams will be reduced.

NATURAL LANGUAGE PROCESSING

Lexical Analysis

Syntactic Analysis

Disclosure Integration

Pragmatic Analysis

Semantic Analysis

Conversational AI applications help to implement intelligent virtual assistants. This is the magic of NLP powered by AI. It enables computers to understand and communicate with humans through natural language. These language models feature translation, sentiment analysis, and speech recognition. They improve customer service and streamline a wide range of tasks.

PERSONALIZATIONS AND RECOMMENDATIONS

Product/Service Development

Distribution

Retail Insights

Customer Service

Customization

AI algorithms make personalized recommendations an everyday experience. Applications range from personalized online shopping, music streams, video snippets, and investment recommendations. AI analyzes users' preferences and behavior to suggest customized services, products, and content.

AUTOMATION AND ROBOTICS

Quality Control

Predictive Maintenance

Digital Twins

Supply Chain

Cost Optimization

AI has turned machines into intelligent assistants. They can perform complex tasks with minimal human supervision. Robots work seamlessly on factory floors and assemble products with incredible precision. AI has taken automation to a whole new level, providing increased efficiency and transforming industries such as manufacturing, logistics, and healthcare.

EVOLVING FIELD OF AI

We estimate that the investments in AI will continue to grow substantially, leading to over 10% additional GDP growth globally. By observing different technology trends and exponential technology developments, generative AI will play a critical role in driving innovation (see illustration Generative AI Acceleration). The innovation footprint on the previous double page depicts what has been achieved recently. AI technologies have expanded exponentially, starting with sophisticated language models such as GPT-3 and image-generation models such as DALLE-2. For a better understanding, the evolution of AI and the associated enabling technologies are briefly explained and will be revisited in depth in Chapter 3.

Contrary to popular belief, generative AI models have existed as a technology since the early days of AI. The history of generative AI models can be traced back to the 1950s when models, including hidden Markov models (HMMs) and Gaussian mixture models (GMMs), generated sequential data such as language and time series. With the beginning of deep learning, generative models experienced significant performance improvements.

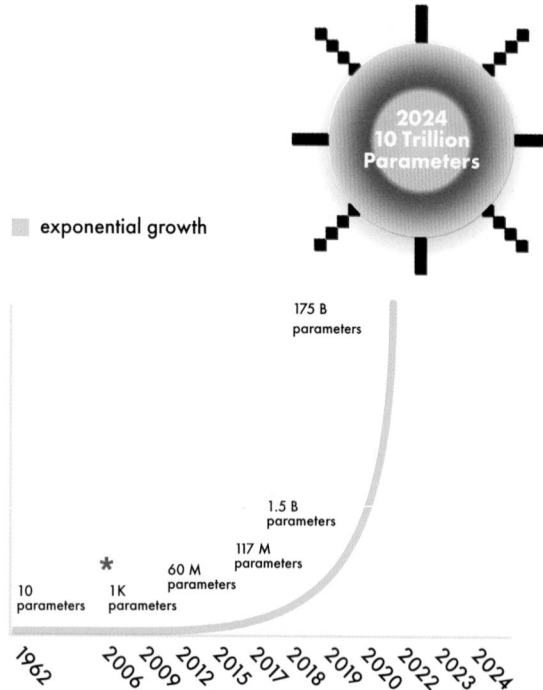

exponential growth

2024
10 Trillion
Parameters

175 B parameters

1.5 B parameters

117 M parameters

60 M parameters

10 parameters

1 K parameters

*

1962 2006 2009 2012 2015 2017 2018 2019 2020 2022 2023 2024

GENERATIVE AI ACCELERATION

When it comes to technology trends, growth is deceptively slow at first and appears to be decimal progress—just a dot on the horizon that no one really cares about yet. Generative AI has become exponential by 2018 and accelerated recently with broader use cases related to language processing.

*We see incremental progress in AI but not yet the great breakthroughs that people were predicting 30 or 40 years ago. (Expert opinion from Nick Bostrom, Director of the Future of Humanity Institute at the UK's Oxford University, 2006)

The current boost in generative AI originates from advances in NLP, a subfield of AI that deals with how computers process and analyze large amounts of natural language data. In NLP, the traditional method for generating sentences is to learn the word distribution using N-gram language modeling and then search for the best sequence. For example, this modeling can be used for disambiguation of the input.

The emergence of generative AI models in different domains has taken different paths, but the intersection emerged through the transformer architecture. A transformer model, which was introduced for NLP tasks in 2017 by Google, is a neural network that learns context, meaning by tracking relationships in sequential data such as the words in this sentence. Transformer models apply an evolving set of thematic techniques called attention or self-awareness to detect subtle ways in which even distant data elements in a series influence and depend on each other. Transformer was later applied in CV and then became the dominant backbone for many generative models in various fields. After the introduction of the transformer architecture, pre-trained language models have become the most prevalent choice in NLP due to their parallelism and learning ability. In general, these transformer-based pre-trained language models are categorized into two types based on their training tasks, subcategories, and variations tailored to use cases and research goals:

1. **Single-task Models:** These models are specifically trained for tasks or datasets, such as completing text or translating languages. They perform well in their designated task but may not perform well in others.

2. **Multi-task Models:** These models undergo training on various tasks and datasets, allowing them to handle natural language understanding and generation tasks. They offer versatility and adaptability across applications.

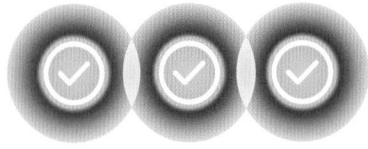

Despite being trained on large-scale data, these models may not always produce output that aligns with the user's intent. Reinforcement learning from human feedback (RLHF) is applied to fine-tune models in various applications and overcome the problem of aligning with user intent. Although these models are trained on extensive real data, the results may not always match the user's intent, as highlighted in the motivation of this book → on pages 12–14.

OVERVIEW UNIMODAL, CV & NLP

Natural language processing   Computer vision   Vision language

2012

N-Gram

2014

Show Tell   LSTM / GRU

GAN VAE Flow

2016

StyleNet StackGan   Transformer

BiGAN RevNet

2018

CAVP DMGAN VQ-VAE   ELMO BERT GPT-2

StyleGAN BigBiGAN   VisualBERT ViLBERT UNITER

2020

GPT-3 OPT BART 15   CLIP ALBEF BLIP VQ-GAN   DDPM ViT MoCo

Sparrow chatGPT   Jurassic   Lamda   DALL-E BLIP2 DALL-E 2

2022

ChatGPT   Claude 1.0   Cohere   Bloom   Galactica

Gemini   GPT4o   PaLM 2   Falcon   LLaMA3   Alpaco

Vicuna   30B-Lazarus   WizardLM   Guanaco-65B   Clause 2.1

2024

Ernie   Claude 3 Opus   Gemini Pro 1.5   Gemini Ultra

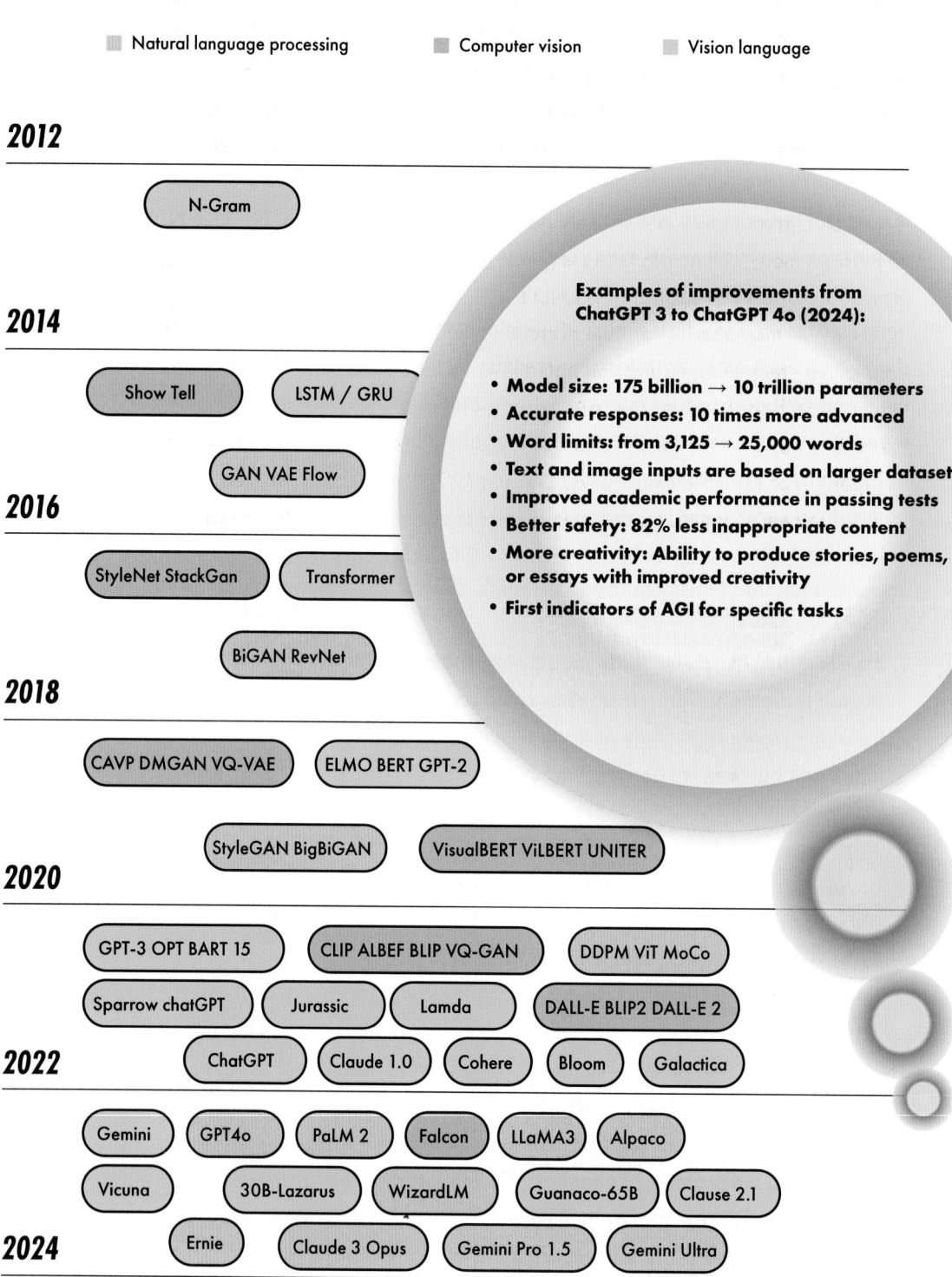

Examples of improvements from ChatGPT 3 to ChatGPT 4o (2024):

- Model size: 175 billion → 10 trillion parameters
- Accurate responses: 10 times more advanced
- Word limits: from 3,125 → 25,000 words
- Text and image inputs are based on larger dataset
- Improved academic performance in passing tests
- Better safety: 82% less inappropriate content
- More creativity: Ability to produce stories, poems, or essays with improved creativity
- First indicators of AGI for specific tasks

From 2023 onwards we have witnessed a surge in generative AI capabilities, blurring the lines between human and machine creation. From crafting indistinguishable human-quality text in various styles to generating high-fidelity images and videos, these advancements push the boundaries of creative expression. We've seen music composed by AI that rivals human-made pieces and 3D models with intricate details that revolutionize design and manufacturing. Even more exciting is the growing accessibility of these tools democratizing creativity for non-experts. Lately, we have observed leaps in generative AI from richer multimodal interactions to explainability and smaller models on personal devices.

Based on current trends, AI will likely be able to perform many of the tasks humans perform nowadays in a very accurate and more reliable way. AI may also be capable of creating radical new technologies that can potentially make significant advances and disruptions. Our hope is that the advancements also create a new era of peace and prosperity. For example, it may be applied to mediate conflicts between countries, to develop new economic models, and to create new forms of social organization.

IN THE FUTURE, AI WILL MAKE US SMARTER, AND WITH THE RIGHT TOOLS, THE FULL HUMAN POTENTIAL CAN BE REALIZED.

BEING AWARE OF TRENDS ON AI APPLICATIONS

In today's landscape, there's an insatiable hunger for AI-powered tools and applications. Organizations' demands for these tools continuously increase due to their potential to optimize and increase efficiency. The trend is moving toward organizations acquiring established AI systems as a service where they can modify them to their specific needs instead of organizations creating their own proprietary tools. An entire market of new and well-known providers offering AI as service models has emerged. These provide access to advanced generative AI tools and technologies that can be implemented with little effort and often deliver significant business impact. Such applications have quickly become the standard applications in all industries. They are often founded on cloud-based services and open-source platforms that make ready-made AI models and algorithms accessible to everyone. On this basis, more complex problems can be solved for specific use cases, decision-making can be improved, and new insights can be gained. At the same time, tech-savvy companies across all industries have decided to take the mission and invest in building more complex AI models to solve wicked problems. This trend is reinforced by new moonshot objectives driven by the transformative potential of AI for a variety of industries, as well as the increasing availability of data and computing power to train and deploy these models. Forward-looking decision-makers are struggling with competing goals of more computing power for AI and a better carbon footprint, not least because currently, the topic of green AI and architectures that boast sparsity and quantization have yet to fully mature. For example, the carbon footprint of all AI applications is estimated at 8% of all global emissions. The carbon footprint of AI models is a growing concern, as these models are becoming increasingly complex and demand more energy to complete the training process.

Clear ethical guidelines and standards are needed to evaluate business impact and the associated risks of AI. This includes, for example, principles such as privacy, fairness, transparency, accountability, and many others. Some regulations are established, while other areas are still being defined. With the increasingly realized potential of generative AI technologies, a global race for the best AI models is emerging, which, unfortunately, is leading to geopolitical tensions. It all comes down to a race for competitive advantages in the development, use, and added value of generative AI technologies for nations, economies, and societies.

Common application scenarios range from creating personalized experiences for customers to innovative manufacturing, enhanced well-being, and sustainable transportation. The attractiveness of each use case is to be defined and might relate to the business impact for the entire industry, the company, or single functions within the enterprise → see evaluating the business impact on pages 56–57. Other criteria to be applied may refer to scalability, feasibility, technological readiness, required resources, or the maturity of the regulatory landscape. In the context of this book and in selecting potential use cases for our clients, we take an optimistic stance that makes generative AI a potent force for innovation and progress in the targeted focus areas of each industry. Across broad sectors, we are sensing a growing acceptance of AI and its associated transformative impact. Depending on the industry, the fears and the need to elucidate the impacts of AI to stakeholders are different, as explained in the Use Case Healthcare example → provided on page 80 et seq. What seems important in all use cases is that AI applications are developed and deployed responsibly and ethical concerns are fully addressed. True moonshots and the associated missions make it possible to realize the market opportunities and ultimately improve the lives of all in a human-centric way. In this context, the proactive design of

THE TRANSFORMATIVE POTENTIAL OF GENERATIVE AI IS ENORMOUS, AND AS WITH ANY MOONSHOT, THERE ARE UNCERTAINTIES AND CHALLENGES THAT MUST BE ADDRESSED.

the business ecosystem takes on an increasingly important role, as cross-industry collaboration is necessary to solve complex problems or realize completely new customer experiences. Data and generative AI technologies become the enablers for aligned value streams and innovation.

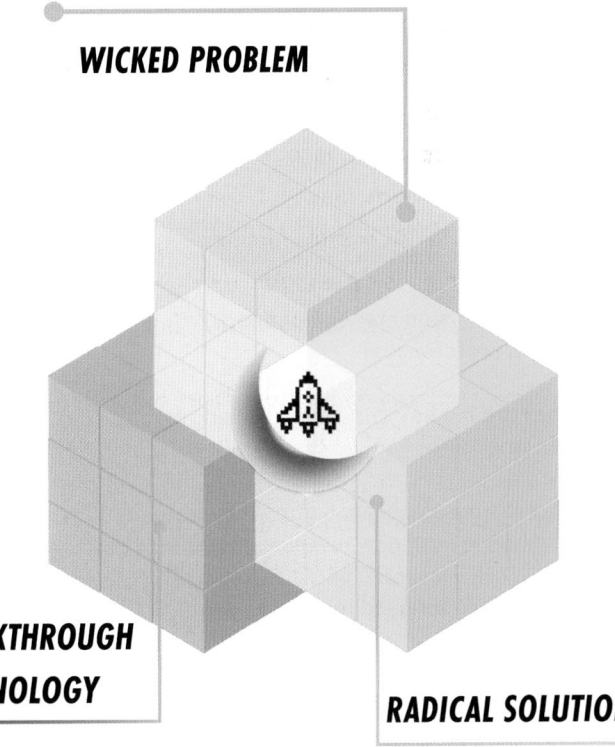

WICKED PROBLEM

BREAKTHROUGH TECHNOLOGY

RADICAL SOLUTION

EVALUATING BUSINESS IMPACT AND IMPLEMENTATION EASE

Once the trends in technology are understood, immediate questions arise: what is the business value? And how can we integrate AI activities into overall strategy? → See chapter 2, page 91 et seq. on AI Strategy, Capabilities, Ethics, and Regulation. Identified use cases can be discussed and positioned on the Impact Implementation Matrix to make initial assessments of the extent to which AI matters for specific functions, the entire company, or the industry. We recommend involving employees and other stakeholders in this assessment and making the activities transparent.

In addition, foresight activities and tools make sense as they help to navigate the rapidly evolving landscape of AI technologies and make informed decisions for the benefit of the business and society.

KEY QUESTIONS IN THE APPLICATION OF AI AND INNOVATION

- What are the top 10 revenue growth opportunities over the next five years?

- Which markets, technologies, and customers are the most attractive to place bets?

- Which technologies will be widely adopted in future?

- Which AI applications/use cases will be redundant in the next two to three years?

- What are customers' unmet needs/buying preferences?

- What are the key customer challenges/pain points?

- What are the competition gaps in their roadmap toward new revenue sources?

- How can AI be used to create new products and services?

- What is the cost of developing and deploying AI in the organization?

- What skills and resources are available to support emerging AI projects?

- How will organizations integrate AI with existing business processes and systems?

- How will AI models be managed and updated over time?

- What data is available to train AI models to be effective and accurate?

- What are the ethical implications of using AI?

- How will success from AI projects be measured?

Download Checklist Application of AI and Innovation

KEY QUESTIONS FOR COMPANIES
IN ADJACENT MARKETS

- How can AI be used to expand existing products, services, and experiences?

- What is needed to build and maintain trust with customers and partners?

- What is needed to stay ahead of the competition?

- What are the regulations surrounding data privacy and security?

- Which ML/AI approaches can be used to address data limitations so that AI models do not result in misleading insights or faulty predictions?

- How are companies handling machine bias?

- What will be the impact of cloud, Internet of Things (IoT), cyber security, and quantum on the AI market?

The Impact-Implementation Matrix for AI (see illustration below) can evaluate AI applications based on their potential business impact and implementation in three dimensions (function, company, and industry). By analyzing each dimension, decision-makers can prioritize AI applications with high business impact while considering the implementation required for a specific context. This matrix helps guide decisions for integrating AI into the company's strategic goals.

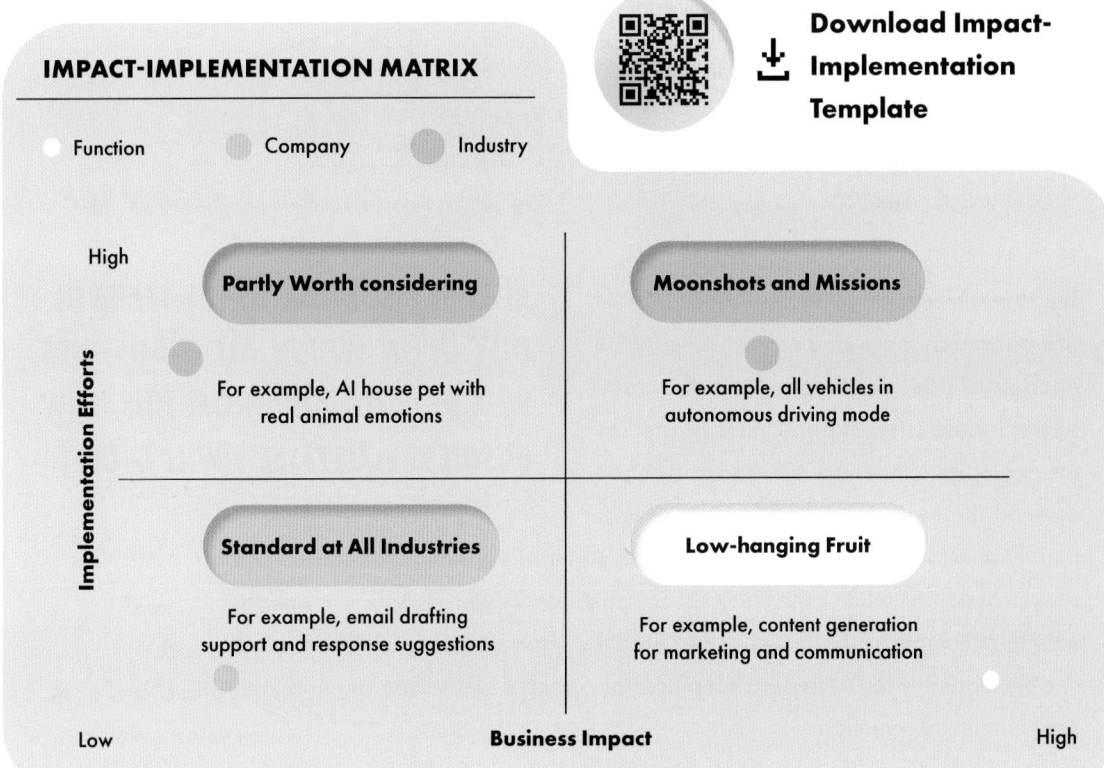

Download Impact-Implementation Template

IMPACT-IMPLEMENTATION MATRIX

Function   Company   Industry

Implementation Efforts

High

Partly Worth considering

For example, AI house pet with real animal emotions

Moonshots and Missions

For example, all vehicles in autonomous driving mode

Standard at All Industries

For example, email drafting support and response suggestions

Low-hanging Fruit

For example, content generation for marketing and communication

Low   **Business Impact**   High

AI AS A DRIVER FOR INNOVATION

As realized with the Impact-Implementation Matrix, AI has the potential to impact on many levels. Many use cases increase productivity, while in other cases, the mix of technology and use cases can unveil new market opportunities. In addition to humans as a mission-critical resource in the enterprise, AI is an emerging critical asset for innovation work, for example, to manage large-scale change with significantly reduced friction. In addition to AI's role in innovation, AI is a powerful enabler for overall business transformation.

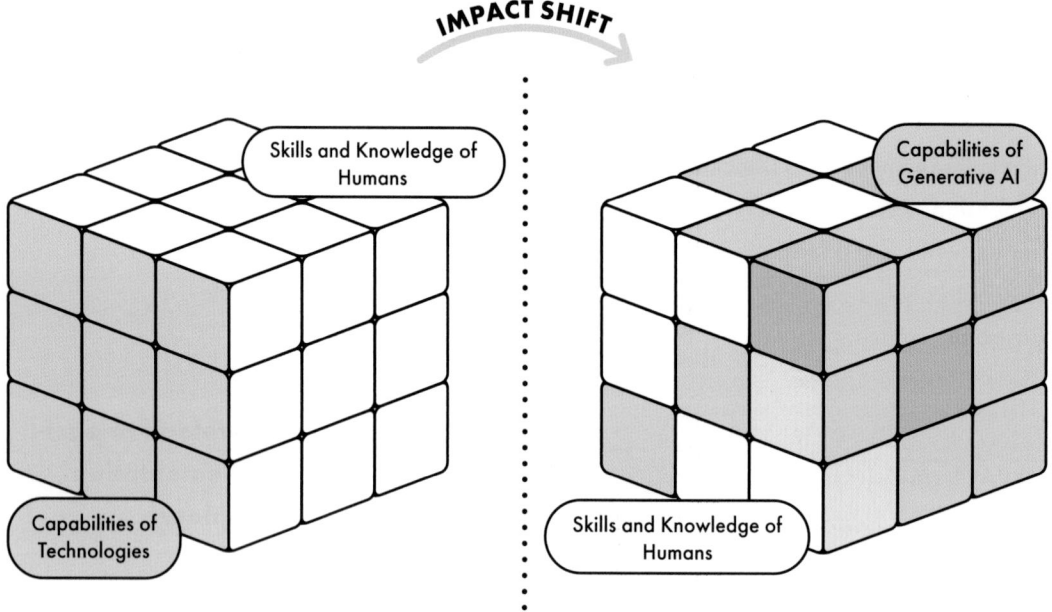

The driver trees of new technologies, like AI, are becoming more and more robust. With each additional technology leap, the possibilities for use cases expand, as illustrated by the examples of financial services and healthcare on the next page. In the past, AI was

AI IS THE FOUNDATIONAL TECHNOLOGY UPON WHICH ALL INDUSTRIES WILL BE BUILT, AND FROM THIS, NEW BUSINESS ECOSYSTEMS WILL EVOLVE.

merely a technological wave. However, as AI matures, it will inevitably create new professions while rendering others obsolete. Fewer people are needed now to accomplish jobs that once required the effort of many, and we already see the tendency for AI to perform pieces of complex innovation requiring minimal human intervention.

AI OPPORTUNITIES FOR INDUSTRIES AND NEW BUSINESS ECOSYSTEMS

HEALTHCARE
→ see Industry Case on page 80

BANKING, FINANCIAL SERVICES, AND INSURANCE
→ See Industry Case on page 131

RETAIL
→ See Industry Case on page 79

MANUFACTURING
→ See Industry Case on page 78

SPACE EXPLORATION
→ See Industry Case on pages 224–229

OTHERS

- Intelligent Health
- Patient Experience
- Coordinated Care
- Administrative Efficiency
- Proactive and Preventive Care
- Early Disease Detection
- AI-powered Diagnostics and Treatment
- AI-powered Home Monitoring
- Risk Stratification
- Mental Health Support
- Virtual Assistants and Chatbots
- Mental and Financial Well-being
- Fraud Detection and Prevention
- Advanced Risk Analytics
- Smart Claims Management
- Customer Experience
- Value-based Pricing
- Multifactor Authentication
- Biometric Authentication
- Fraud Analytics
- Predictive Underwriting
- Real-time Risk Assessments
- Auto Reconciliation
- Cognitive/Multilingual Chatbots
- Personalized Recommendations

REALIZING AI MARKET OPPORTUNITIES

Practical experience shows that realizing AI opportunities is easier for companies open to change and that have acted on it in recent years. So, once again, the mindset and the ability to find the appropriate problem are central to realizing innovation. Additionally, it is increasingly important to be aware of the signals of exponential technologies. Here, it helps to apply foresight methodologies to anticipate, understand, and capitalize on the evolving landscape of generative AI and other highly uncertain, complex topics. The results from the foresight activities help formulate and validate the assumptions of an AI strategy → see page 94 to leverage the transformative potential of emerging trends and technologies. In validating assumptions, adding additional data, including expert points of view, stakeholder consultations, and knowledge sharing with industry experts, is essential.

A company's well-defined North Star and AI strategy provide crucial guidance for the interdisciplinary teams to design market opportunities and effectively leverage new technology trends related to AI. The AI strategy should provide clear objectives, ethical considerations to consider, targeted markets and customer segments, and tools and frameworks to evaluate the potential risks

BEING PROACTIVE IS KEY. UTILIZE ALL INSIGHTS HELPING TO ENVISION HOW BUSINESSES CAN LEVERAGE NEW TRENDS AND TECHNOLOGIES TO GAIN A COMPETITIVE EDGE BECOMES IMPORTANT IN TIMES OF EXPONENTIAL CHANGE AND GROWTH.

and challenges. In hunting for the next market opportunity enabled by AI, it becomes essential to upskill organizations with new capabilities and skills. New skills might relate to problem-solving, awareness for mindset shifts in creating ecosystems, customized training to understand the fundamentals of disruptive technologies and trends, development of internal talent, or simply fostering a general culture of innovation.

The real innovation work starts after the mandate to innovate based on the AI strategy for teams is clear. In many cases, a facilitated design thinking workshop will help define the problem statement and measure success for teams and design challenges → see pages 181–183. Understanding the critical and unknown assumptions will help plan for the next activities. Collaboration between industry stakeholders, such as tech providers, research institutions, competitors, and other potential ecosystems partners, is essential to tap into the AI ecosystem as a driver for innovation. However, finding AI ecosystems partners to amplify innovation can be daunting, especially for more traditional companies that do not have experience and knowledge in business ecosystems design. A good starting point is to understand the organizational needs of ecosystems partners. Organizational needs are associated with data collection, validation or preparation, market and customer access and channels, AI model development or validation, integration or combination of offerings, and value propositions. Over the last few years, many business ecosystems and more specialized AI ecosystems have ripened. Therefore, we recommend searching for AI ecosystems that meet organizational and strategic needs and building an AI ecosystem radar to obtain information about the latest developments in

a specific industry and the technology community. Information can be obtained through benchmarking with other businesses that have collaborated or participated in a specific AI ecosystem or reaching out directly to the AI ecosystem orchestrator to obtain needed knowledge. Another strategy is to reach out directly to potential partners to learn more about their services and assess if they fit the articulated needs well. Once potential partners and their capabilities are understood, it is a good starting point to develop a collaboration plan to achieve the defined business and innovation goals. In the context of AI and innovation, many dimensions are essential, from defining an AI strategy to understanding the playing field for innovation and building new capabilities and skills.

Even traditional sectors, once slow to adopt emerging technologies, are now rapidly embracing the transformative power of AI and its associated capabilities. From automotive manufacturing to healthcare diagnostics, AI is being utilized to streamline processes, enhance decision-making, and deliver personalized experiences. Even those industries traditionally considered laggards, such as legal services and government, are recognizing the potential of AI to revolutionize their operations. As understanding of AI's capabilities grows, these sectors are poised to leapfrog early adopters like beauty, fashion, consumer electronics, gaming, and grocery retail, becoming leaders in the AI-powered era.

WHAT IF ...

To realize innovation, companies ask themselves, "What if..." concerning AI and the current possibilities and future advancements. AI and innovation work on two levels. Firstly, the burning question of startups and technology companies comes into play: what will be the radical innovation that will take the technology to a new level? Innovation usually comes from external sources and is not usually realized by the current players. There is currently an abundance of opportunities for new approaches to compete with dominant players such as Microsoft, Google, Facebook, Baidu, and their partially closed systems, as well as a multitude of choices for new business model patterns that allow for new ways of monetization and democratization of AI. Secondly, what problems arising from AI are targeted by companies to solve? Currently, many offerings aim to address issues relating to data quality, data/cyber protection, integration, and innovative products and services to help build the capabilities of tomorrow.

AI offers enormous innovation potential for companies → as already briefly presented on pages 48–49. Customer service is better, faster, and more personalized. Development cycles of new products, services, and experiences are accelerated, and data-driven innovation finally fulfills what it has taken years to realize. Innovation teams in companies across all

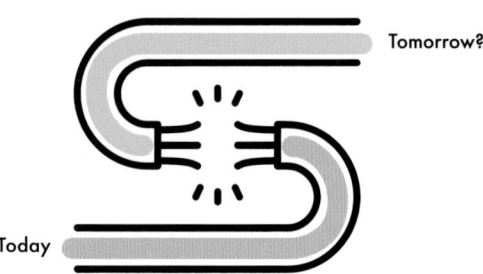

Tomorrow?

Today

sectors also leverage applications that provide support throughout the design cycle. Design thinking teams are incorporating AI to cluster insights faster and more accurately, outsourcing A/B testing to intelligent bots based on LLM-defined powerful HMW-questions, and comparing ideas from the past with their own new and future-focused visions – even if, at the time of this book's writing, we still have to admit that creative human imagination surpasses all AI models based on historical data and statistical probabilities.

While utilizing the benefits of AI to perform tasks more efficiently and to create new market opportunities is a crucial focus for organizations implementing this technology, another critical focus is brewing in the innovation community: how might we adopt our perspective of innovating radical new products, services, and experiences to address the emerging needs of humanity?

THE TECHNO-UTOPIANS ARE LOOKING FORWARD TO AN INEVITABLE, ECSTATIC FUSION OF HUMANS AND MACHINES TO IMPROVE HUMANITY. HOWEVER, AT THE SAME TIME, MANY FEAR THE LOSS OF HUMAN CONTROL.

A shift from human-centered design to designing for humanity might be needed to address the more significant problems. When organizations strategize about future opportunities and markets, it is essential to avoid getting anchored with the limitations of today's technologies, including the current state of AI maturity. Always adopt a foresight assessment and evaluate the progression of technology to determine the opportunities and limitations for the time period under assessment.

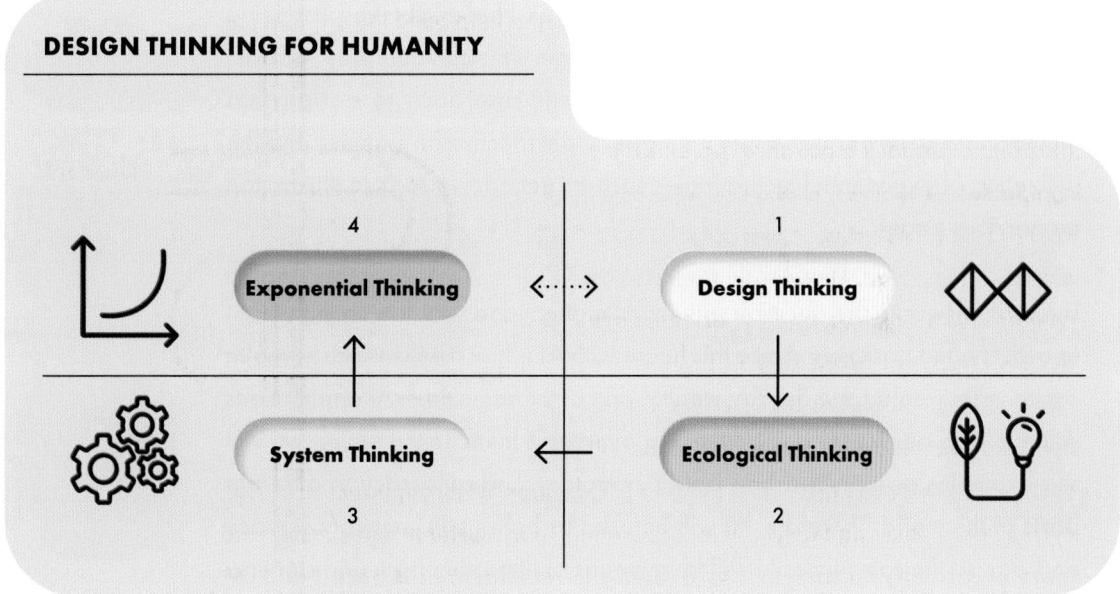

DESIGN THINKING FOR HUMANITY

4 Exponential Thinking

1 Design Thinking

3 System Thinking

2 Ecological Thinking

Download Design Thinking for Humanity Canvas

The hope is that AI will have the potential to revolutionize the way we design and build a better future for humanity. By using AI to identify and understand humanity's needs, develop new ideas and solutions, test and evaluate ideas and solutions, and communicate and share ideas and solutions, we can create a more equitable, sustainable, and prosperous world for all. Currently, we are already using AI to analyze large amounts of data, such as social media posts, news articles, and scientific studies, to identify and understand the needs of humanity and, for example, to enrich the first two phases of the design thinking process and to understand and observe with additional insights. Based on the different viewpoints, AI supports teams to develop new ideas and solutions to humanity's challenges related to sustainability, climate change, and the environment. AI, for example, is used to create new social and economic systems based on millions of data points. Once the most appropriate and effective behavioral changes are identified and tested, AI can communicate and share ideas, solutions, and customized stories with a broad audience; this can help build support for new ideas and accelerate the adoption of new solutions.

At the heart of design thinking for humanity lies the belief that design can be a powerful tool for addressing complex challenges and fostering positive change on a global scale. This paradigm shift pioneered by Michael Lewrick calls for a broader and more holistic approach to design that incorporates behavioral change, a long-term perspective on systems, and the utilization of exponential technologies such as generative AI (see illustration on previous page).

The best answer to the question of why AI matters and why it is so important to actively and positively shape this future with AI is that it will increase wealth, concentrate wealth, and destroy wealth – all at the same time. AI applications will reinforce our biases and be used to overcome them. In the future, we will see examples of AI supporting both democracy and autocracy in different parts of the world. Therefore, AI will be used as both an instrument of peace and war. At the same time, AI will be a means of liberation from and subjugation to various forms of labor. And it will help heal the planet, but it will also intensify our consumption of resources. AI will be used to tell us the truth and to lie to us.

WHAT IF AI...

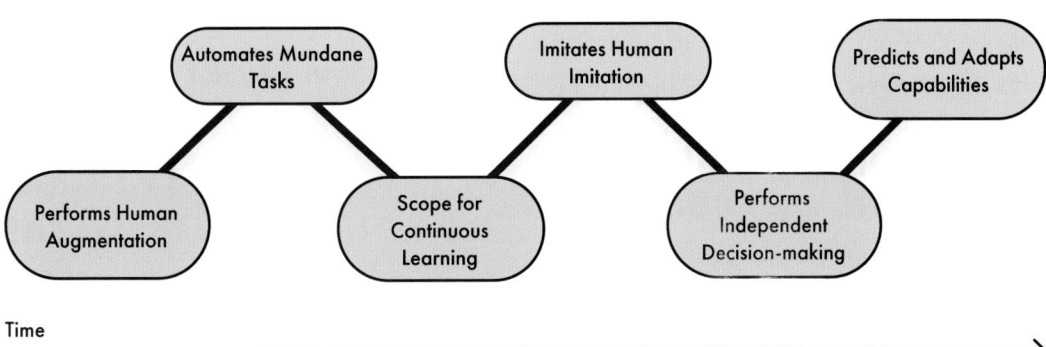

Time

Generative AI is not entering into our businesses and everyday lives in a neutral way. Its emergence will depend on our cultural values, economic systems, and collective imagination of generative AI as described at the beginning of this chapter. The key issues regarding ethics, regulation, and how we integrate generative AI into our operating model are central and need attention now:

→ Is human work drudgery or dignity?

→ What shouldn't be outsourced to generative AI even if we can?

→ What are the impacts of generative AI on retirement and future economic models?

→ What do we owe each other, anyway?

→ Should generative AI or humans decide what the future should look like?

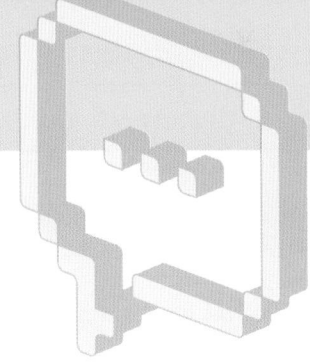

How we answer these questions – and whether we ask them at all – gives a clue to the tasks we might assign to generative AI and the considerations that will guide and constrain its emergence.

In the near future, generative AI will be used to expand the range of problems we can solve with computers and invent new problems that we didn't even think of as problems before. Over time, many of these gimmicks have become even more important to us than the serious applications of computers that they have long since replaced. We are seeing a shift from pure computation to its successors in the form of measurement and prediction. As we equip the world with more and more sensors, generate more and more data, and analyze it with more and more powerful algorithms, the cost of measurement is falling. As a result, many more factors than ever before can be measured and enrich companies' operating models → see comparison Traditional vs. Future Operating Model. As more of these factors can be observed, we will produce a growing supply of indicators and move from a retrospective understanding of the world around us to a more complete real-time understanding. It becomes evident that humanity will be overwhelmed by AI; it will be enhanced and strengthened by it, and in some areas, it will even surpass it.

THE AGE OF HUMAN DOMINANCE IN SOME AREAS WILL COME TO AN END, AS IT ALREADY HAS IN MANY AREAS OF LIFE. THIS IS A CAUSE FOR CONCERN BUT ALSO FOR CELEBRATION BECAUSE WE HUMANS ADMIRE EXCELLENCE, AND WE LOVE TO LEARN. THE RISE OF AI WILL PROVIDE AMPLE OPPORTUNITY FOR BOTH.

As a result, generative AI will provide us with answers we could not have arrived at any other way. We can ensure a humane future with AI by doing what we do best: ceaselessly asking questions, imagining alternatives, and reminding ourselves of the power that lies in our choices.

TRADITIONAL OPERATING MODEL — VS — FUTURE OPERATING MODEL

TRADITIONAL OPERATING MODEL	FUTURE OPERATING MODEL
• A top-down chain of command and decision based on evidence from the past	• Data-driven and generative AI support for effective decision-making, optimization, and prediction
• Multiple initiatives and priorities without alignment and multi-strategic objectives	• Decentralized chain of command and decision-making by humans and AI as a team
• Data and information silos confined to individuals, software, and departments	• Alignment through a defined North Star as well objectives and key results (OKRs)
• Quarterly and annual reviews based on traditional set of key indicators	• Continuous reviews linked to the problems to solve, validation, and continuous optimization

SHIFTING TOWARD NEW OPERATING MODELS

As highlighted on the previous page, a new mindset and a more flexible operating model are needed. A future operating model in exponential change and technologies needs a portfolio of existing and evolving business models to overcome seismic changes. A flexible operating model is key to managing exponential change and driving growth through the use of AI. A future framework for AI innovation management requires a state-of-the-art operating model and an appropriate mindset to realize the full potential of collaboration between AI and humans.

The principles of the operating model for companies must include new ways of thinking in terms of design thinking, systems thinking, exponential thinking, alignment, scalability, innovation culture, and a balanced portfolio between exploration and exploitation. Putting the customer at the center of everything the company does remains paramount; this means understanding customers' needs, wants, and problems and developing products, services, and experiences that meet those needs.

Traditional	Future

• Siloed and functional	• Integrated and networked
• Singular view on Business Models	• Multiple views on business models
• Rigid functional capabilities	• Dynamic coevolutionary growth
• Slow decision-making	• Adaptive and expandable
• Fixed mindset	• Growth mindset
• Waterfall	• Agile (if applicable)

Agility becomes key to responding quickly to market and customer needs changes. A flatter organizational structure, shorter decision cycles, and a willingness to experiment support the desired activities to increase the desired agility. At the same time, it is important to create a culture in which employees

DITCH THE OLD STRATEGIC CONSULTANCY PLAYBOOK – EMBRACE DESIGN THINKING, EXPONENTIAL THINKING, AND SYSTEMS THINKING TO WIN THE FUTURE.

are encouraged to be creative and take risks. Here, investments in skills training and new AI technologies are part of the change. When developing more complex solutions and products, collaboration between different departments and functions within and across the organization benefits innovation success. In the context of data analytics, using AI, data-driven decision-making, and support is a link between the mindset and the operating model to better understand customer behavior, market trends, and business performance in a more evidence-based way.

Future operating models will be characterized by integrated and networked structures, multiple business models, dynamic growth through coevolution, adaptability and scalability, a growth mindset, and an agile approach. → The key questions to be answered regarding the future operating model and AI can be found on page 143.

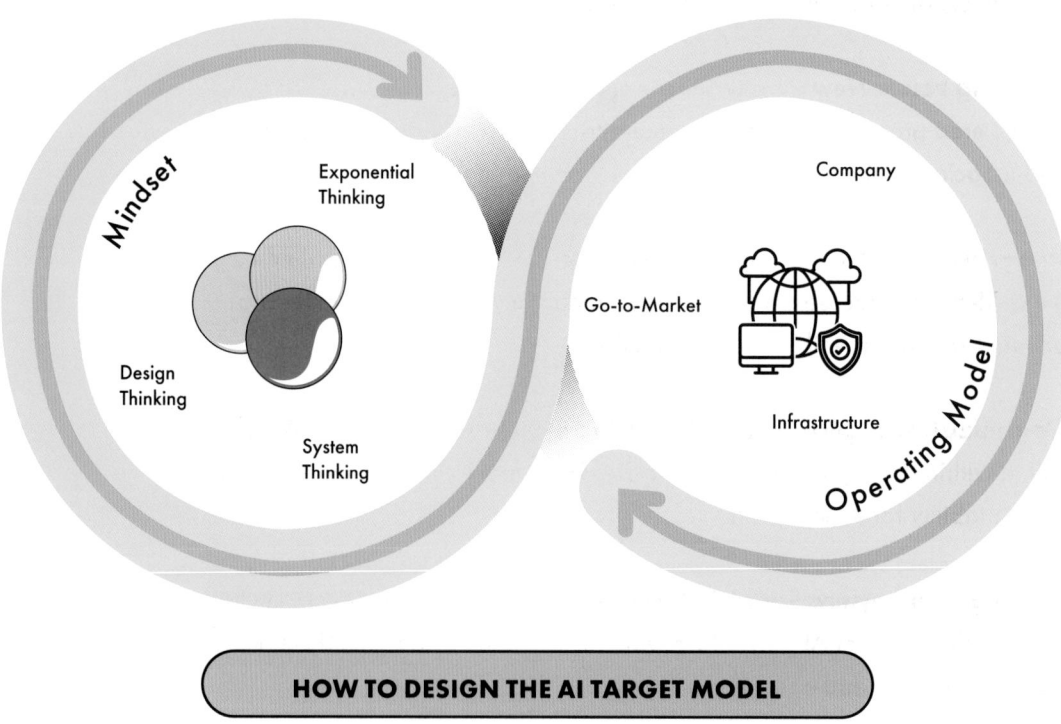

Mindset

Exponential Thinking

Design Thinking

System Thinking

Company

Go-to-Market

Infrastructure

Operating Model

HOW TO DESIGN THE AI TARGET MODEL

THE AI TARGET OPERATING MODEL

In the context of this book, the question immediately arises as to what the AI target operating model should look like based on the requirements of the future operating model presented. The core objective might mean leveraging generative AI to generate business value through innovations and projects or just identifying the appropriate use cases. These can encompass a range of goals, from boosting efficiency and enhancing customer experiences to creating entirely new products, services, or experiences for customers.

A well-defined AI target operating model acts as a roadmap, guiding the organization toward successful AI strategy execution. By addressing key questions upfront, the initial design phase paves the way for a smooth implementation. Here are some critical questions this initial design can help to answer before tapping into Part 2 of this book, which focuses on the creation of the AI strategy.

New capabilities: The model should identify the new capabilities that need to be integrated into the existing process flow. This might involve data analysis techniques, ML expertise, or specific AI tools.

Evolving roles: New roles will likely emerge to manage and execute these AI-powered processes. The design should outline the skillsets and responsibilities associated with these roles.

Integration with existing frameworks: The model should explore how these AI-driven processes will seamlessly integrate with existing or future operational frameworks within the organization.

Organizational placement: It's vital to identify where the new AI roles will fit within the organizational structure. This ensures clear ownership and accountability for AI initiatives.

Strategic and operational AI location: The design should determine the optimal placement of AI within the organization, both strategically (in terms of decision-making) and operationally (in terms of day-to-day execution).

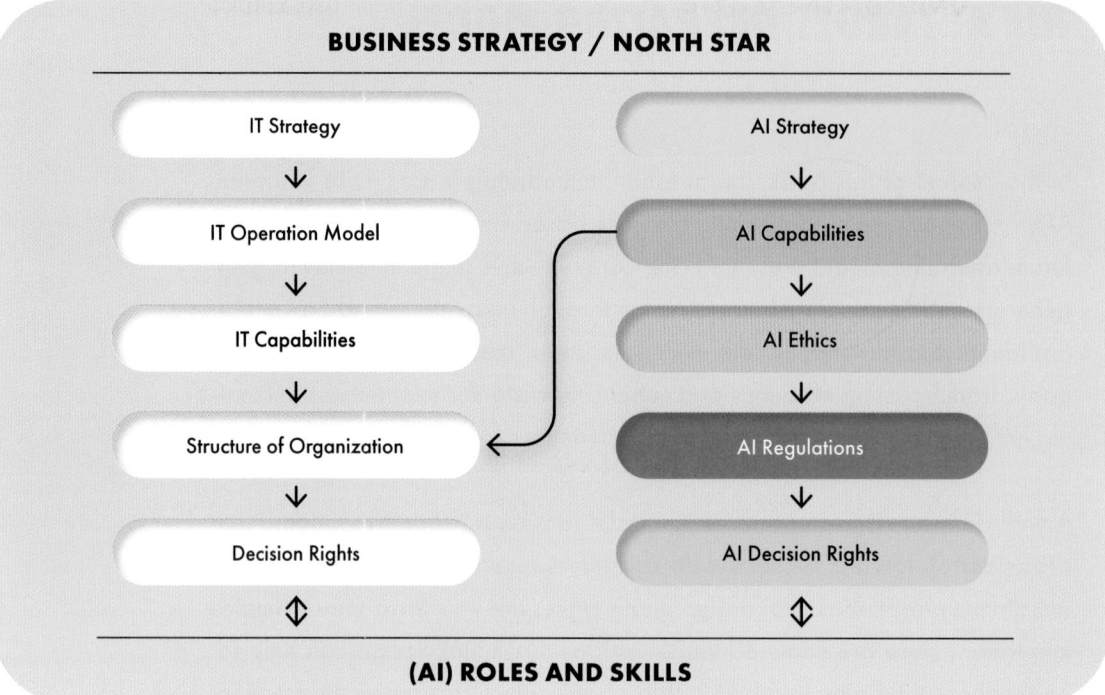

BUSINESS STRATEGY / NORTH STAR

IT Strategy	AI Strategy
IT Operation Model	AI Capabilities
IT Capabilities	AI Ethics
Structure of Organization	AI Regulations
Decision Rights	AI Decision Rights

(AI) ROLES AND SKILLS

→ We recommend to understand first your business, IT, and AI strategy before designing the entire AI target operating model.

MASTERING THE BALANCE BETWEEN GUIDANCE, SUPERVISION, AND OWNERSHIP

The governance model for AI operations isn't a one-size-fits-all solution. The ideal approach depends on several factors specific to your organization, including size, existing capabilities, goals, culture, and AI maturity. Broadly speaking, there are three main governance models that range from centralized control to complete regional autonomy. A centralized governance model offers a single point of control and decision-making for all AI initiatives. This can be beneficial for smaller organizations or those with limited existing AI expertise. However, it may become cumbersome and inflexible for larger organizations with diverse needs. A balanced governance model fosters shared responsibility between a central unit and regional or departmental entities. This approach allows for more tailored AI implementations while still maintaining centralized oversight for areas like ethics and compliance. Finally, independent governance models grant regions or units significant autonomy in their AI operations. This is best suited for mature organizations with well-established AI capabilities and a strong central AI strategy to ensure alignment with overall business goals and ethical principles.

UNIFIED/CENTRALIZED

BALANCED

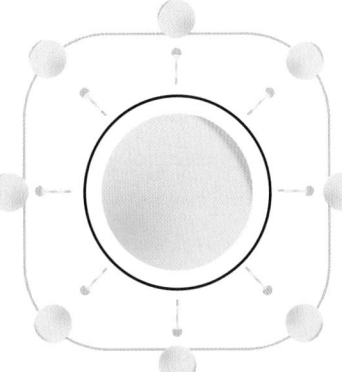

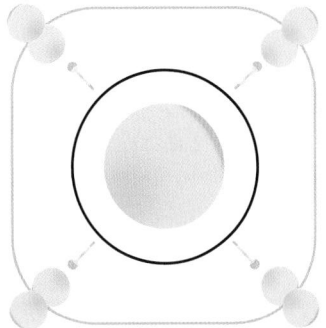

INDEPENDENT

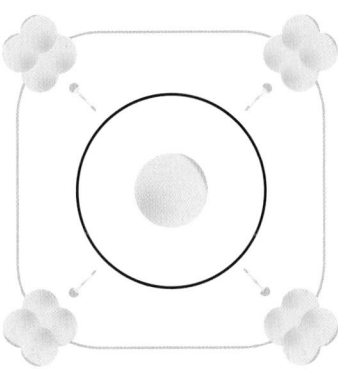

While the governance model dictates the overall structure of AI oversight, guidance and supervision from top leaders remain crucial for successful implementation. This leadership plays a vital role in defining the AI strategy, which encompasses not just the technology but also data strategy and management, as well as fostering a culture of digital and AI-driven innovation. Additionally, top leaders should champion the design, testing, and implementation of the entire business ecosystem.

However, supervision takes center stage in areas critical to responsible AI development. Leaders must ensure adherence to data privacy regulations, ethical considerations, and transparency in AI decision-making processes (often referred to as "black box" models). Staying abreast of evolving regulations and applying appropriate oversight to the leadership of the AI ecosystem are also essential aspects of effective supervision. This dual focus on guidance and supervision ensures both strategic direction and responsible execution within the AI operating model.

MINDSET REQUIREMENTS TO HANDLE UNCERTAINTY AND AMBIGUITY

In the course of the transformation toward a future operating model, uncertainty and ambiguity will be an integral part of design challenges and innovation projects. Innovation experts have mastered dealing with the unknowns – unknowns in creating offerings new to the market and new to the customers. However, the natural human tendency is to prefer knowing over not knowing. Decision-makers and innovation teams facing AI and innovation will wrestle with ambiguity at some point, and it seems that is not a choice because it is inherent in achieving superior outcomes. Adopting a certain mindset is critical to dealing with the complexity associated with AI and innovation. As a leader, knowing what to do for de-risking is more important than predicting the future. How the leadership or innovation team frames the problem determines the alternatives an organization evaluates and considers. If organizations have built capabilities and skills to define the problem differently and more appropriately than other players, alternatives will become apparent, leading to radical innovations. The future offers no linear path, and current technology advances in AI have only increased uncertainty, lowered barriers to participation in many industries, and increased the pace of change. Without the right mindsets, tools, and methods, decision-makers and entire teams fall into maladaptive traps such as threat rigidity, unproductive brooding, premature certainty, and misjudgment. When dancing with ambiguity, there is no clear, correct answer. It allows for layers of meaning for everything. There is no absolute truth or fact. Decision-makers and innovation teams must remember that their minds are free to explore and imagine possibilities that are unknown or do not currently exist.

ONE REASON THE DESIGN THINKING MINDSET IS CENTRAL TO SUCCESSFUL AI TRANSFORMATION WITHIN MANY COMPANIES IS THAT THIS MINDSET PERMITS UNCERTAINTY. THE MINDSET OF ACTION REPLACES UNCERTAINTY WITH THE CERTITUDE OF PURPOSE: "LET'S GET STARTED!"

In today's times of exponential change and technologies, we observe good and bad ambiguity depending on how decision-makers and innovation teams interpret the problem space and the mindset applied in the solution space. It is essential to train teams and decision-makers not to fall back on vagueness as an excuse for velocity. Tolerance for ambiguity becomes critical, and dancing with ambiguity is a crucial success factor in sustaining a more flexible operating model.

NECESSARY SHIFTS TOWARD MORE TOLERANCE FOR AMBIGUITY

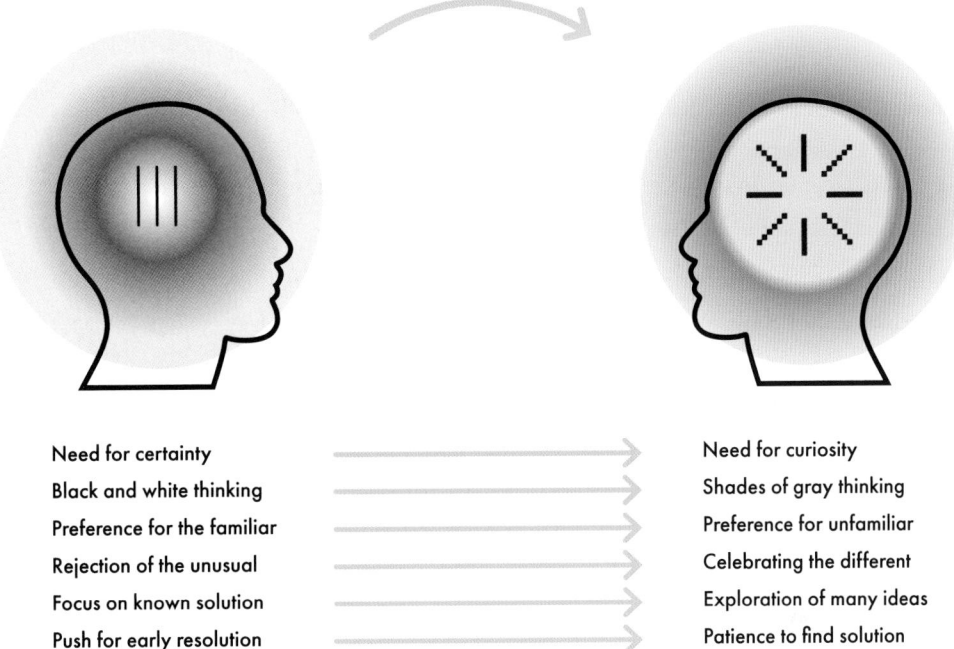

Need for certainty	→	Need for curiosity
Black and white thinking	→	Shades of gray thinking
Preference for the familiar	→	Preference for unfamiliar
Rejection of the unusual	→	Celebrating the different
Focus on known solution	→	Exploration of many ideas
Push for early resolution	→	Patience to find solution

Leadership teams that embrace ambiguity allow future AI value creation, even if we can't make it happen now. From our hands-on experience and teaching the design thinking mindset to numerous teams, we've learned that encouraging behaviors increases the likelihood of finding a path to innovation in the face of uncertainty. The starting point is defining the appropriate questions that decision-makers and teams must ask and allowing those questions to guide their choices.

IF YOUR COMPANY WANTS TO MAKE LEAPS WITH AI AND INNOVATION, AMBIGUITY WILL ARISE AT SOME POINT. DEALING WITH AMBIGUITY IS NOT A CHOICE BUT PART OF THE PROCESS THAT LEADS TO A GREAT RESULT.

COLLABORATION AND THE FUSION OF DISCIPLINES

AI innovation takes many forms and is a collective effort. It thrives on collaboration, knowledge sharing, and cross-pollination of ideas. However, we also know from our own experience that as team members in psychologically unsafe environments, we protect ourselves from embarrassment and other potential threats by remaining silent when we do not feel safe; this leads to a team culture that does not engage in collective learning behaviors, which in turn leads to poor team performance. Especially in creating new AI experiences and aiming for AI and human collaboration, companies must create an environment of psychological safety for their teams to support constructive interpersonal risk-taking. In short, companies should ensure that employees will not be punished or humiliated for speaking up to share ideas, ask questions, voice concerns, or point out mistakes concerning AI transformation. For a learning culture to thrive, all teams must feel safe to experiment. We learn through experimentation, but experiments fail frequently, and conducting good experiments means that the entire organization can learn as much from their failures as they do from their successes. First and foremost, we advise considering the eight core building blocks for a successful AI and innovation project outlined on the right. In this evolving landscape, where the rise of AI calls for humanity's adaptability, the pivotal role of proper organizational culture cannot be overstated. To illustrate this point, we refer to an interesting case: a fifth-generation traditional Japanese soy sauce maker, Yasuo Yamamoto. When asked how he produces one of the finest soy sauces in the world, he attributed his success to the environment. He said, "I don't make the soy sauce. The micro-organisms make it; I just create the environment where they can thrive." Whether we are creating an environment for micro-organisms to thrive or an environment for our corporate teams to succeed, the sentiment remains the same. Leaders within organizations must create spaces where empowerment and creativity can flourish and ensure individuals remain unburdened by fear or ridicule. In this way, we cultivate a fertile ground where innovation and imagination can bloom, ensuring our enduring relevance in the age of AI. We also observe a fusion of disciplines, which, in the context of this book, is an increasing integration of AI with other fields of study, such as engineering, computer

IN OUR INNOVATION PROJECTS, WE ALWAYS EMPHASIZE THAT AI IS NOT A DISCIPLINE IN ITS OWN RIGHT BUT A FUSION OF DISCIPLINES.

science, mathematics, statistics, economics, business, and the humanities. This fusion requires greater interdisciplinary collaboration and benefits from the development of new and innovative AI-powered solutions to a wide range of problems. For example, generative AI is being integrated with engineering to develop new and more efficient manufacturing processes → see examples on page 78, with computer science to develop new algorithms for machine learning and natural language processing, and with mathematics to develop new methods for data analysis and optimization. Generative AI is also being integrated with economics and business to develop new business models and to improve decision-making processes.

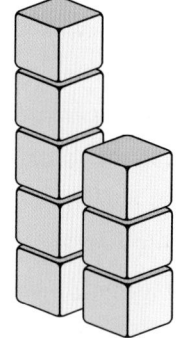

EIGHT CORE BUILDING BLOCKS TO SUCCEED IN AI AND INNOVATION

- **Involve relevant stakeholders:** Agree on stakeholder expectations to defuse communication and find effective communication channels. Ensure stakeholders communicate effectively, with a clear focus, and purpose-driven manner.

- **Ask powerful questions:** Asking "wh"-questions (why, where, what, who, and how) is a powerful tool for understanding and uncovering missteps and misunderstandings while raising awareness of the need for a moderated AI innovation journey.

- **(Re)frame the problem:** Many of the present problems are complex and ambiguous, and it is important to formulate the problem explicitly, preferably together with the customer/user involved.

- **Visualize information and apply storytelling:** Often, the problem to be solved cannot be described explicitly, in writing or verbally, which leads to communication problems. Applying methods from the design thinking toolbox (e.g. storytelling and visual thinking) will help to unite the team.

- **Identify critical assumptions and test hypotheses:** Innovation thrives on challenging assumptions. Expect 80% to be wrong, so focus on testing critical ones early to minimize risk and maximize success.

- **Articulate business value:** When defining AI use cases, reaching a common definition of business value is essential. Thus, the orientation on a vision and AI strategy is central to generating real added value within teams.

- **Facilitate ethical good decisions:** In an environment of vague regulatory guidance and differing ethical views, it is all the more important to address concerns, encourage teams to behave ethically, and guide, coach, and keep them informed of the latest developments.

- **The importance of foresight and vision:** An inspiring vision gives the innovation team direction and reduces uncertainty and ambiguity. Alternatively, teams can be tasked to leave existing paths and to think of radically new pathways. In both cases, leaders must be explicit about what is desired.

IMPACT OF AI: FROM EXPERIMENTS TO VALUE DELIVERY

Industries are moving from experiments with AI to value delivery in a number of ways. The opportunities of AI across the value chain are omnipresent and include functions related to product management, marketing, sales, and operations, as well as risk and compliance → as described on pages 48–49. The following example industry cases show how AI has transformed the manufacturing and healthcare industries. In manufacturing, AI is being used, for example, to improve product quality, reduce costs, and predict maintenance needs. In broader healthcare, AI is being used, for example, to develop new drugs and treatments, diagnose diseases, and personalize patient care. Meanwhile, sectors like retail use AI to improve customer recommendations, optimize inventory levels, and automate tasks like checkout. More traditional industries like banking see the value of AI primarily related to customer service automation and marketing while gradually realizing the value of generative AI across the entire banking value chain.

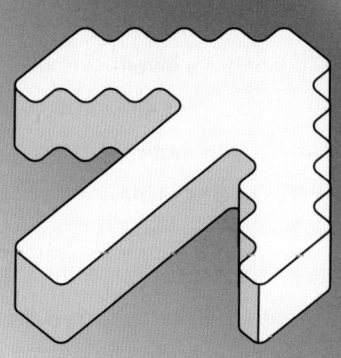

EXAMPLE INDUSTRY CASES SHOWING IMPACT OF AI ACROSS MANY SECTORS

THE IMPACT OF AI ACROSS MANY SECTORS

Organizations benefiting the most from AI solutions are constantly changing and adapting as the technology evolves and realizing the immense value of AI. Many industries are leveraging heavily on the capabilities of AI; among them is the manufacturing domain. For example, AI is being used to predict when equipment is likely to fail so that preventive maintenance can be performed and costly breakdowns and downtime can be avoided.

The German-headquartered multinational engineering company Siemens has been using AI to improve its B2B operations for years. Siemens uses AI to optimize its production lines, predict maintenance needs, and improve customer service. Siemens automation has experimented with AI solutions for process control systems, and the models trained are becoming increasingly intelligent. AI has kicked off the entire manufacturing industry, which is experiencing a tremendous transformation toward a real digital enterprise. To create their AI models, Siemens leveraged huge amounts of data to perform meaningful analysis. AI and ML helped to structure, analyze, and evaluate these datasets. This has been applied to the entire life cycle of a plant, including intelligent recommendations, generative design, anomaly detection, and predictive maintenance to optimize the way and speed with which products are designed and produced. AI takes over the tasks of factory personnel at all levels, starting with perception, thinking, and then action. For the first time in the long history of automation systems, the systems not only follow programmed instructions but also enable continuous optimization of the value chain in production inside and outside the factory. Siemens aims to use automation and cognitive technologies to merge. The assumption is that by improving connectivity worldwide and AI enhancements, automation will gradually replace the cognitive capabilities of humans by providing more speed, accuracy, and consistency. The long-term vision is that machines will be able to monitor the entire production. With the help of sensors, data will be collected that will help the machine train, optimize, and develop itself.

Another example of changing with AI industry standards is the multinational retail corporation, Walmart, which applies AI to improve its supply chain, personalize its customer experience, and develop new products and services. For example, Walmart uses AI to track inventory levels, to predict demand, and to optimize its shipping routes. Walmart also uses AI to develop new products and services. At an early stage, Walmart explored the potential of AI in two major areas with massive benefits: the warehouse and the Walmart Supercenter.

Walmart has, for example, implemented a conversational AI and assistant LLM solution called "Ask Sam," which helps Walmart and Sam's Clubs associates streamline various tasks. Walmart employees can ask the voice assistant for their work schedule or for information such as the location and cost of a product and general store sales information.

In 2023, the trained algorithm had 95% accuracy in distinguishing different brands and inventory positions. At the same time, AI supports alerts if the inventory of a product reaches a predetermined level, and the inventory room is automatically alerted so that the item can be restocked.

While implementing many solutions, Sam's Club recently launched its AI Labs team within its tech organization. Walmart's interdisciplinary teams research, explore, experiment, and innovate throughout all aspects of the clubs with both member and associate-facing technology. However, the most important design criteria remain in applying AI to find better ways to identify and satisfy customers' wants and needs.

For example, consider the implementation of a new AI-powered technology to streamline the checkout process. This AI system verifies purchases without needing a physical receipt check, resulting in a 23% faster exit for all members. Notably, Sam's Club designed and rolled out this technology themselves, making

RETAILERS LIKE WALMART WORK ON THE "STORE OF THE FUTURE" AND TEST GROUNDS FOR EMERGING TECHNOLOGIES, INCLUDING AI-ENABLED CAMERAS AND INTERACTIVE DISPLAYS, WHICH WILL CHANGE THE ENTIRE SHOPPING EXPERIENCE.

them the first retailer to widely deploy such an AI-based exit system at all Sam's Club locations to achieve a more convenient, better checkout experience for customers.

Ashley Hubka, senior vice president and general manager of Walmart Business, says that AI is no longer just a tool for efficiency and productivity but is becoming an integral part of daily workflows. She believes that AI will become a "true operational partner" for businesses of all sizes and that its ability to understand and answer customer questions will help businesses improve order placement times.

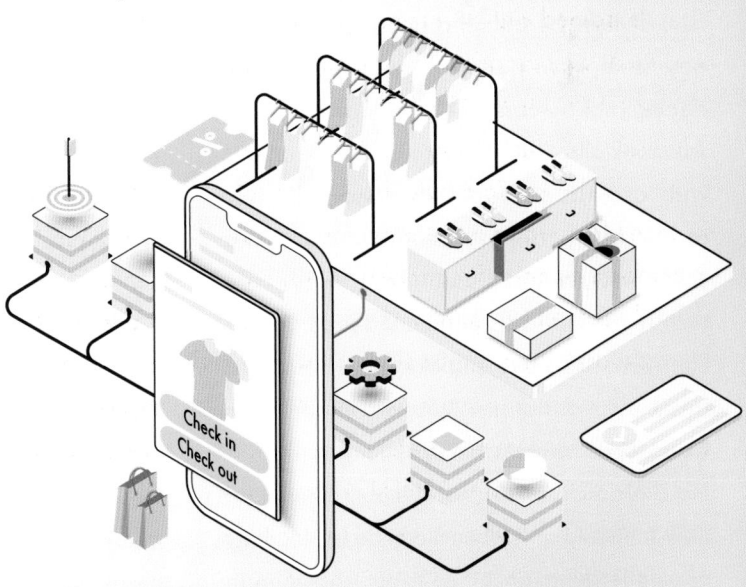

AI TRANSFORMING HEALTHCARE

Other sectors, like healthcare, are also benefiting from AI advancements. Especially at the current stage where healthcare systems face extreme global pressures, clinicians are burning out and considering leaving the industry.

According to the World Health Organization, there could be a shortage of 10 million health workers by the end of this decade. In this situation, AI applications have the potential to fill the gap and take over repetitive low-level tasks (e.g. administrative tasks, clustering information, or detecting patterns) to help clinicians focus solely on patients' care. On top of this, AI applications today can already detect potential risks of burnout.

GE Health takes advantage of this market opportunity with an aim to transform healthcare sectors by utilizing advanced technology to improve patient care options, experience, and outcomes. Newly developed AI solutions allow clinicians to provide patients with a more personalized and precisely targeted experience, ultimately improving outcomes. To find acceptance for the new tech revolution, building confidence among clinicians who are still skeptical about AI becomes mandatory. To overcome the barriers, GE is investing in upskilling and training clinicians to understand better where and how to use AI and when it can be trusted fully versus leaning on other tools and human expertise. Biotech companies are heavily

FROM HEALING HANDS TO AI MINDS, GENERATIVE POWER PAINTS A REVOLUTION IN HEALTHCARE, WHERE CURES DANCE WITH PIXELS AND BREAKTHROUGHS BLOOM AT THE INTERSECTION OF CODE AND CARE.

benefiting from AI to develop more efficient medicine. AI has been used, for example, in many ways to develop vaccines during the COVID-19 pandemic.

Pfizer created, for example, algorithms to predict how the virus might mutate and how vaccines might need to be updated. AI supported the design and optimization of vaccine candidates and tested their safety and efficacy. The major advantage of AI is that it can analyze large amounts of data to identify potential drug targets. This data often includes information about the genes involved in a disease, the proteins produced by those genes, and the molecules that interact with those proteins. AI has been instrumental in the understanding of protein folding. It achieves this by using deep learning algorithms to predict the three-dimensional structures of proteins. Impressive models like AlphaFold utilize datasets and neural networks to unravel the complex interactions and forces that govern protein folding, an essential aspect of biological function. With its ability to predict protein structures faster and more precisely than other methods, AI holds immense potential to transform drug discovery, enhance our understanding of diseases, and facilitate the development of innovative therapeutics, opening up avenues to tackle biomedical challenges.

In little to no time, new drugs can be designed that target specific drug targets by screening millions of compounds to find those that are most likely to be effective against a particular target. Trained algorithms can discover new drugs by automating the drug discovery process, involving tasks such as identifying potential drug targets, designing new drugs, and testing the safety and efficacy of those drugs.

For example, the collaboration of CeMM and Pfizer highlights the power of AI in drug design. By utilizing chemical proteomics, they tested thousands of small molecule interactions with human proteins, discovering new possibilities for drug development. This AI-powered approach not only identified previously unknown protein-ligand interactions but also enabled the creation of models to predict small molecule properties and target specific protein types.

The examples from Siemens, Walmart, and GE Health show the benefits of AI for these industries in various ways, including:

- **Improved efficiency:** AI can help automate tasks and improve decision-making, increasing efficiency.

- **Increased personalization:** AI can be used to personalize products and services, leading to increased customer satisfaction.

- **New product and service development:** AI can be used to develop new products and services, which can help to grow businesses.

- **Improved risk management:** AI can identify and mitigate risks, which can help protect businesses.

- **Cost savings:** AI can help to reduce costs by automating tasks and improving efficiency.

V.R. Ferose

→ Senior vice president and head of
SAP Academy for Engineering

PREPARING THE WORKFORCE FOR GENERATIVE AI AND HUMANS AS A TEAM

SAP has a long tradition in integrating technology with extensive industry-specific data and deep process knowledge to create powerful applications for everyday use. The SAP Academy for Engineering aims to combine the power of AI with the context of existing business data and process to enable innovation for the customers worldwide. As revealed already by the content of this book, generative AI has emerged as a transformative force, with the potential to revolutionize the way businesses operate. However, harnessing the power of generative AI requires a deep understanding of its principles, capabilities, and applications. This is where the SAP Academy for Engineering steps in, providing a comprehensive training program that equips engineers, managers, and data architects with the skills and knowledge necessary to solve real-world business problems using generative AI.

The SAP Academy for Engineering's AI training program delves into the fundamental concepts of generative AI, providing participants with a solid understanding of its theoretical underpinnings. The program also covers practical applications of generative AI, equipping participants with the skills to develop and deploy generative AI solutions in real-world scenarios. At the academy, we aim to work interdisciplinary, bringing together engineers, managers, and architects to generate common understanding about the technical aspects of AI, the business value proposition for different use-case scenarios, as well as concepts to implement, for example, data architectures to support AI applications. The SAP Academy for Engineering's generative AI training program leverages the SAP platform to provide participants with hands-on experience in developing and deploying generative AI solutions. Participants gain proficiency in SAP Cloud Platform AI services, enabling them to build and deploy generative AI models within the SAP ecosystem. This approach equips participants with the skills to:

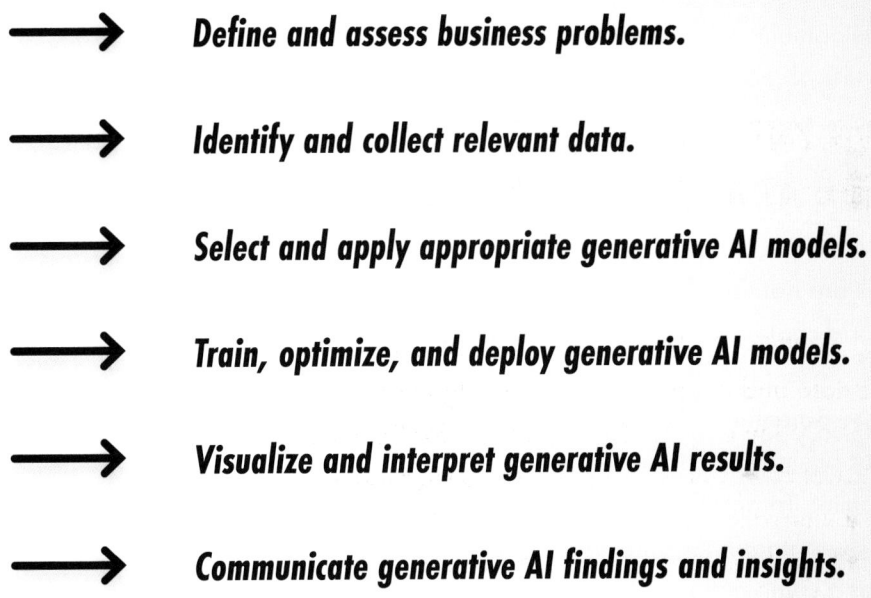

→ *Define and assess business problems.*

→ *Identify and collect relevant data.*

→ *Select and apply appropriate generative AI models.*

→ *Train, optimize, and deploy generative AI models.*

→ *Visualize and interpret generative AI results.*

→ *Communicate generative AI findings and insights.*

However, the SAP Academy for Engineering is not just about theoretical learning; it also emphasizes hands-on experience. Participants are given the opportunity to work on real-world projects that allow them to apply their knowledge to practical problems. This hands-on approach ensures that participants gain the skills they need to succeed in the workplace.

Further, the SAP Academy for Engineering draws upon SAP's rich history of applying design thinking to create innovative solutions. Design thinking emphasizes an empathetic approach, focusing on understanding the intricacies of the problem space before devising solutions. This human-centered approach is crucial in the context of AI, as it ensures that

AI-powered solutions are tailored to the specific needs and requirements of users and stakeholders. Design thinking helped to make many well-known SAP applications AI ready – for example, to create compelling job descriptions and interview questions within SAP SuccessFactors. AI helps, in this use case scenario, the hiring manager to write compelling job descriptions, attract top talent, and quickly generate interview questions tailored to the candidate and the role. Also, the interaction of Joule (the AI copilot from SAP) has been developed iteratively to empower entire teams to complete tasks using natural language and receive relevant in-application help from the "Copilot." Based on user needs, the solution navigates, streamlines tasks, gets smart insights on demand, and accesses tailored content to jumpstart the work of the teams. Consequently, we focus that the participants in our academy learn how to apply design thinking principles to the development of AI solutions, ensuring that they align with user needs and business objectives.

More than ever before, a human-centered approach to problem-solving plays a pivotal role in the successful implementation of AI. By focusing on understanding the needs and pain points of users, design thinking ensures that AI solutions are not merely technical exercises but rather tools that address real-world challenges and deliver tangible value.

AI holds immense potential to solve complex problems and unlock new opportunities for businesses. However, it is crucial to recognize that AI is not a magic bullet. To achieve optimal outcomes, AI solutions must be grounded in a deep understanding of the problem space. This understanding requires a combination of technical expertise, business acumen, and human empathy. Engineers must possess the technical skills to design and implement AI models, while managers and architects must understand the business context and the needs of their target audience. At the Academy, we foster a holistic approach to AI development, ensuring that participants gain a comprehensive understanding of the problem space before delving into technical solutions. This approach ensures that AI is not applied in a haphazard or uninformed manner but rather as a tool that addresses real-world challenges and drives meaningful business impact. The pipeline of new AI functions is reflecting this approach with improved solutions ranging from intelligent automation currently performed by humans to fraud detection, up to the next dimension of customer experience management, which aims to improve customer experience by providing personalized interactions, anticipating customer needs, and resolving issues quickly and efficiently.

JOULE, SAP'S AI CO-PILOT, EMPOWERS TEAMS WITH NATURAL LANGUAGE INTERACTIONS, STREAMLINING TASKS AND DELIVERING SMART INSIGHTS ON DEMAND.

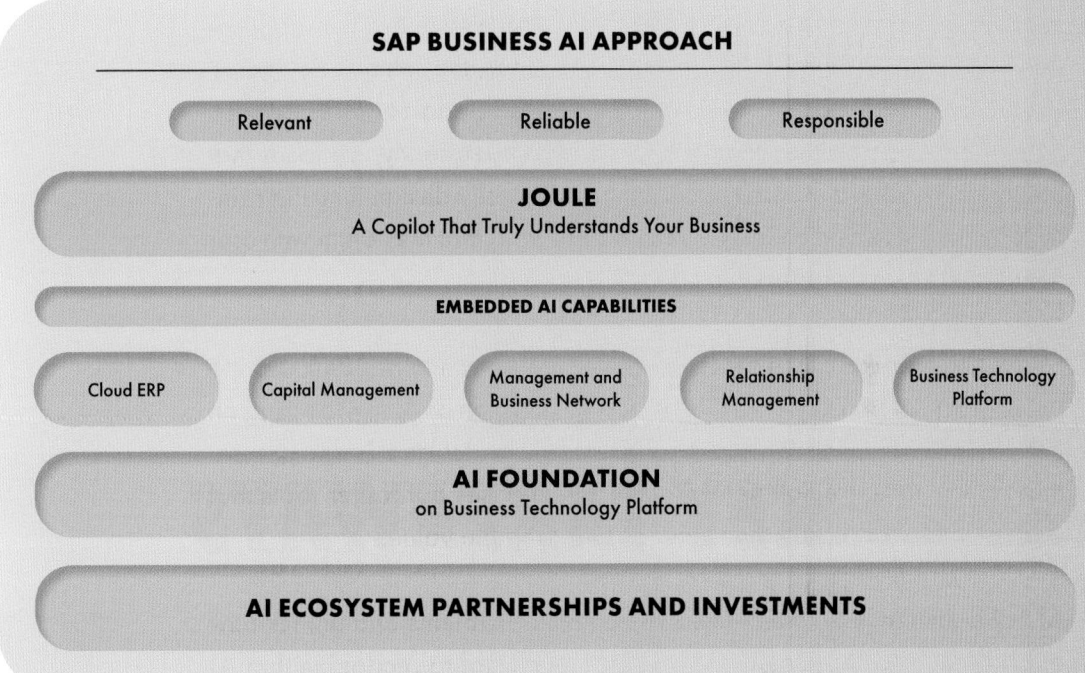

SAP BUSINESS AI APPROACH

Relevant   Reliable   Responsible

JOULE
A Copilot That Truly Understands Your Business

EMBEDDED AI CAPABILITIES

Cloud ERP | Capital Management | Management and Business Network | Relationship Management | Business Technology Platform

AI FOUNDATION
on Business Technology Platform

AI ECOSYSTEM PARTNERSHIPS AND INVESTMENTS

As AI continues to evolve, the SAP Academy for Engineering will remain at the forefront of innovation, providing the necessary training and support to enable organizations to harness the full potential of this transformative technology. By combining human-centered design with the power of AI, SAP is paving the way for a future where businesses can solve their most complex challenges with creativity and agility.

"JOULE AIMS TO KNOW WHAT YOU MEAN, NOT JUST WHAT YOU SAY."

KEY TAKEAWAYS

→ By leveraging AI to drive innovation, we journey to a future where human potential blossoms.

→ To accelerate the path to value creation with AI, key elements are essential, like real-time intelligence, understanding competitive and collaborative forces, mindset, culture, and team structures to make the transformation successful.

→ In a world of exponential change and uncertainties, a new mindset and a more flexible operating model are needed to achieve the desired activities and increase agility.

→ Across broad sectors, we can observe a growing acceptance of AI and its associated transformative impact. AI has already transformed manufacturing, healthcare, and retail, and more traditional industries are following.

→ In most application scenarios and use cases, the hope is that AI can revolutionize how we design and build a better future for humanity.

→ As AI evolves, a future generative AGI might solve some of the world's most wicked problems, such as climate change, poverty, and disease.

PART 2

HOW TO MAKE A DIFFERENCE WITH AI

AS ORGANIZATIONS AND LEADER- SHIP TEAMS LEARN MORE ABOUT HOW AI CAN BE USED TO SOLVE PROBLEMS, MANY OF THE QUES- TION MARKS AND UNCERTAINTIES DISAPPEAR.

WHERE TO PLAY AND HOW TO WIN

Business leaders, strategy and innovation teams, and managers at all levels need to understand the impact of AI from a non-technical perspective. Management teams require proficient skills in adoption and handling exponential change and growth. This includes the ability to craft a clear AI strategy that ensures future competitive advantage is maintained and possibly amplified. Traditional companies and industries must urgently embrace AI capabilities and ensure

THE DEVELOPMENT OF GENERATIVE MODELS HAS REVOLUTIONIZED AI, OFFERING THE POTENTIAL TO RESHAPE INDUSTRIES ACROSS ALL SECTORS. AS ORGANIZATIONS SEEK TO CAPTURE THE TRANSFORMATIVE POWER OF GENERATIVE AI, CRAFTING A ROBUST AI STRATEGY IS PARAMOUNT.

their workforce possesses skills and knowledge to implement them. It's also advisable to update future hiring plans to include expertise in AI that is currently lacking. In many cases, we recommended having distributed AI technology, which allows teams to innovate independently. The business model and the underlying operating model should be able to adapt and scale. Some prerequisites, like open access to good quality datasets for teams, are also essential to improve the accuracy of results and mitigate potential bias. This chapter discusses how to make a difference with AI based on four AI design principles: AI strategy, AI capabilities, AI ethics, and AI regulations.

KEY QUESTIONS TO BE ADDRESSED IN AN AI STRATEGY PLAYBOOK:

- What is the level of AI readiness (technical capabilities and infrastructure)?

- Where should the focus of AI investments be?

- How will AI deployment create value?

- What future capabilities are needed to execute the AI strategy?

- What kind of change management activities support the strategy?

- What systems will implement and manage AI?

- How will ethics be addressed, implemented, and monitored?

- What is the operating model and governance structure?

THE AI DESIGN PRINCIPLES
FOR BUSINESS LEADERS

⤓ **Download AI Checklist Principles for Leaders**

AI STRATEGY

Ambition	AI Use Cases	Adaption	Execution

Opportunity	Focus	Ecosystems	Culture	Risk Management	Monetization

AI CAPABILITIES

Exponential Thinking	System Thinking	Tech. Mgmt.	Governance

Design Thinking	Change Mgmt.	Operationalization

Foresight	Scenario Planning	Talent Management	Data Management

AI ETHICS

Data Ethics	Ethical AI	AI Ethics	Business Ethics

Data Protection	Law Enforcement	Safety and Certification	Justice and Equality	Displacement of Labor	Taxation

AI REGULATIONS

Transparency and Explainability	Fairness and Non-discrimination	Privacy and Security	Accountability and Liability

INTRODUCTION TO AI STRATEGY, CAPABILITIES, AND ETHICS

The AI strategy is the core to making a difference with AI, and it is the overall plan of how an organization will use AI to achieve its goals. The strategy should define the organization's AI vision, goals, and objectives and the steps it will take to achieve them. A well-defined AI strategy directs teams and reveals if resources are aligned to improve customer journeys, task automation, and product development or create radical new experiences. The strategy should also discuss the potential risks associated with AI and which capabilities are needed to evaluate and develop AI opportunities. We recommend setting specific goals for how the organization and responsible teams will achieve the missions related to AI activities. These goals should be measurable, achievable, relevant, and time-bound. In times of exponential change, applying a continuous loop for collecting feedback and adjusting the goals as needed by applying, for example, OKRs, becomes even more important. The biggest challenge in defining an AI strategy is keeping it up to date with the pace of technological change, further complicated by regulatory ambiguity. Additionally, the strategy should be in alignment with agreed AI ethics → see pages 132–137. The general shortage of skilled talent in the latest AI technologies is also something to consider, especially in evaluating AI technologies and implementation.

Besides the technical capabilities, the most important capability is to understand the problem that needs to be solved and the future of business and operating models. Business leaders must first figure out where and how they can apply AI to specific business problems across operations. To embrace this next wave of innovations, leadership teams should apply design thinking methodologies to achieve the cross-functional coordination and middle-management sponsorship required for enterprise adoption. Ultimately, the value of AI lies not in the AI operating models themselves but in the ability of companies to leverage them properly. The combination of exponential thinking, design thinking, and systems thinking → see page 23 supports an interdisciplinary cross collaboration that encourages employees to question, observe, network, and experiment in an environment that dismantles hierarchies, avoids egoism, challenges the status quo, and encourages intelligent risk-taking. Leadership teams that promote and build up such capabilities and mindset shifts can accelerate AI adoption, achieve organizational alignment, and foster commitment to their goals while reducing resistance to organizational change.

Ethical AI considerations should be understood holistically and from AI strategy design to capability building to the implemented operating model. It is important because AI has the potential to impact our lives in many ways, both positive and negative. For example, AI could be used to improve healthcare, education, and transportation. However, it could also be used to create autonomous weapons or to discriminate against certain groups of people in various capacities. Business leaders and decision-makers need to take on the challenge of developing an AI strategy that is ethical and responsible. This

→ AI is a tool. The strategic choice of how it gets deployed is ours.

means considering the potential risks and benefits of AI, as well as the ethical implications of its use. Corporate practice shows that it is useful to involve stakeholders, such as employees, customers, and regulators, early in the development of an AI strategy. This will help to ensure that the strategy is aligned with the values of all stakeholders.

The following pages present frameworks and detailed information about AI principles that help define a suitable AI strategy, to build up the corresponding capabilities, and, above all, to address important ethical principles. The various building blocks are based on the experiences and advice of companies from different sectors and industries that have embedded AI strategy as an important cornerstone of an overarching business, digital transformation, and IT strategy. The biggest challenge for the vast majority of companies was the comprehensive consideration of management, technology, and employee views that influence AI strategy. Additionally, the uncertainties regarding regulation were challenging, as complex assumptions had to be made for specific applications and use cases.

THE AI STRATEGY IS KEY FOR BUSINESS TRANSFORMATION. IT SERVES TO UNLOCK THE AI'S POTENTIAL ETHICALLY AND STAY AHEAD OF THE CURVE.

→ Further tools and methods supporting the AI activities can be found in Chapter 3 (see page 153 ff).

HOW TO DESIGN THE AI STRATEGY

AI STRATEGY			
Ambition	AI Use Cases	Adaption	Execution

Opportunity	Focus	Ecosystems	Culture	Risk Management	Monetization

This framework for creating an AI strategy is a great starting point for aligning stakeholders and ensuring that AI is used effectively and aligned with the overall business objectives. The ambition must be clear and range from improving efficiency to improving competitive stance by enhancing decisions and developing new products, services, and experiences. Once the ambition and focus of the strategy are clear, it becomes much easier to identify the opportunities and problems to be solved with AI → see AI Opportunity Map on page 98. However, not all problems are suited for AI solutions. Therefore, it is important to identify the use cases where AI can be leveraged to achieve the most significant impact; this may involve experimentation, conducting feasibility studies, or running pilot projects to test the viability of AI for a particular problem. To harness the full potential of AI applications and use cases, broader ecosystems must be taken into account, encompassing various foundational models, datasets, and algorithms. AI ecosystems provide totally new opportunities to realize innovations at scale → see AI Ecosystem on page 110. In addition, adaption and culture change are important elements of the strategy and for implementing AI solutions. Disruptive technologies change the way people work and interact with each other. Corporate practice shows successful organizations establish a culture that can cope well with exponential changes. Successful companies proactively prepare the organization by informing and educating employees about AI, creating a culture of continuous learning, and providing support for employees feeling displaced by AI.

In our experience, particular attention must be paid to risk management when formulating an AI strategy, as AI is a complex technology that can introduce new risks such as bias, privacy concerns, and security risks.

The execution of use cases and monetization of an AI strategy requires a comprehensive and well-thought-out roadmap to ensure proper AI adoption. The roadmap includes important elements related to the timeline for implementation, budgets, and a plan for training and upskilling employees. Finally, the viability of an AI strategy is important. Typical measurements regarding monetization of AI strategies, applications, and models are associated with direct revenues, indirect revenues, new revenues from innovation, cost savings, improved efficiency, and increased customer satisfaction. However, not all metrics are created equal. When choosing metrics to measure the monetization of AI, it is important to choose metrics that are relevant to the organizational goals and objectives. The application of the Basic AI Strategy Canvas addresses the most important questions.

UNLOCK HIDDEN INSIGHTS, UNLEASH INNOVATION, AND OUTMANEUVER COMPETITORS – AN AI STRATEGY IS YOUR KEY TO UNLOCKING EXPONENTIAL GROWTH.

Download Basic AI Strategy Canvas

BASIC AI STRATEGY CANVAS

Strategy	Opportunity	AI Solution
How is the AI strategy contributing to the overall business strategy?	What problem is the AI solution trying to solve?	What specific multi-modual) task(s) is the AI designed to accomplish?
Users/Stakeholders	**Use Case**	**Data/Ecosystem**
Who needs it? Who benefits?	How to describe the use case?	What are the model inputs?
Success Criteria	**Focus**	**Policies, Processes, Training**
How is success defined and measured?	What is the primary focus (for example, better productivity, increased efficiency, better decision-making, innovations, etc.)?	What else must be considered, trained, or changed?

EXPERT TIP: APPLYING AI IN STRATEGIC WORK

AI can be used to better construct and validate the strategy. It is especially powerful where vast internal knowledge and external data exist. In these cases, AI excels at untangling factors with high uncertainty and crafting insightful future scenarios. Furthermore, AI helps to produce strategy recommendations based on selected scenarios. For example, generative AI can provide a comprehensive view of business environments across multiple industries. The models can bring new points of view to the often-missing link to similar historical events and save time in collecting, clustering, and summarizing information. However, the real strategic work – the implementation of the strategy – will still be driven by human leaders communicating the North Star and explaining the purpose of adopting a given strategy.

WE CANNOT PREDICT THE FUTURE, BUT AI CAN HELP US TO IMAGINE AND UNDERSTAND THE MOST PROBABLE AND DESIRABLE PATH.

UTILIZING GENERATIVE AI IN CREATING STRATEGIC CHOICE

↧ **Download Template for Strategic Choice**

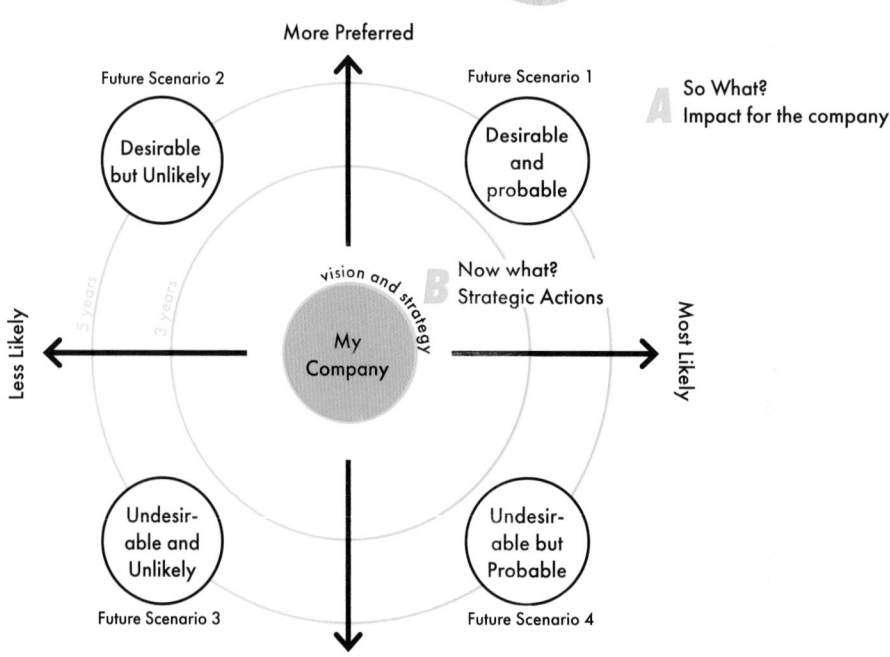

For companies that already use business intelligence and predictive analytics, the step toward AI-supported systems is the natural evolutionary step in strategy work. The interaction of humans and AI will help amplify informed and fast decision-making.

EVOLUTION OF STRATEGY WORK

Technique	Analytics	Human Intelligence → Artificial Intelligence		
		Insights	Decisions	Actions
Data Visualization	Descriptive: What happened?			
Business Intelligence	Diagnostic: Why did it happen?			
Predictive Analytics and Modeling	Predictive: What will happen?			
Machine Learning and Optimization	Prescriptive: What should I do?	Decision Support		
		Decision Automation		
Generative AI	Artificial Intelligence: How can I enhance or replace human reasoning?			

Practical experience applying AI for strategic work shows that AI powerfully enhances and complements human reasoning. Organizations can leverage different techniques to gain efficiency, including the following:

- **Data analysis and insight generation:** AI can analyze vast amounts of data quickly and precisely, identifying patterns, trends, and correlations that can inform decision-making.

- **Predictive analytics:** AI can predict the future using historical data; this can help organizations anticipate potential problems and take preventative measures.

- **Optimization of business processes:** AI can identify inefficiencies in business processes and suggest improvements, which can assist in resolving issues relating to cost, time, or quality.

- **Decision support:** AI can model complex scenarios and calculate the potential impact of various decisions.

- **Anomaly detection:** AI can identify anomalous data patterns or outliers that may indicate a problem.

- **Automation of routine tasks:** AI enables employees to devote more time to complex problem-solving tasks by automating routine tasks.

- **Enhanced collaboration:** AI tools can enhance collaboration by automating scheduling, facilitating document sharing, and even translating languages in real time.

THE AI OPPORTUNITY MAP

The fundamental question for business leaders in forming an AI strategy is knowing where the most significant AI opportunities lie. A common way to answer this question from business practice is to examine what kind of tasks and what complexity and accuracy of execution should be taken over by AI.

AI OPPORTUNITY MAP

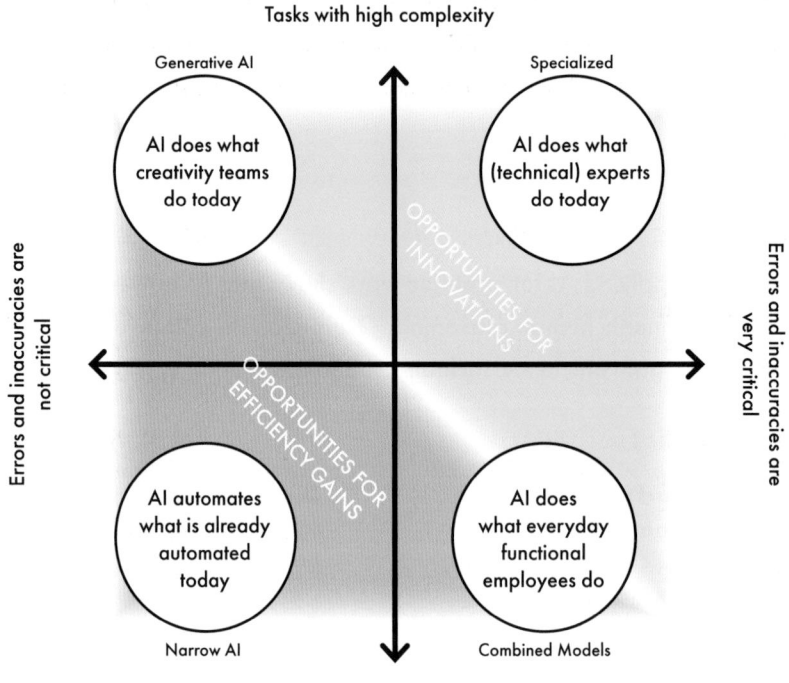

 ⬇ **Download AI Opportunity Map Template**

Generative AI may help create more appropriate value propositions, while specialized AI is creating breakthrough developments in drug design. Combined models allow the optimization and automation of in-house logistic transportation based on self-driving vehicles.

HOW TO IDENTIFY THE OPPORTUNITIES

Many playbooks for AI and innovation recommend defining the opportunity, creating the business case, building and deploying the solution, and measuring the impact. However, identifying opportunities requires more skills and capabilities than simply envisioning bright ideas about the future of business. One of the most important skills in this context is understanding the problem well enough to deliver potential solutions to resolve the concern. One reason why design thinking capabilities are one of the key skills in AI and innovation is because the mindset focuses on human-centered design. We can use design thinking to ensure, for example, that AI-enabled products and services are designed to meet the needs of users/customers and minimize the potential negative impacts.

STEPS FROM IDENTIFYING OPPORTUNITIES TO STRATEGIC INTEGRATION

- **Understand the problem:** What is the job to be done or the problem to be solved?

- **Create potential solutions:** What is the comprehensive solution to a complex problem?

- **Define the opportunity for AI:** What is the opportunity to address with AI?

- **Build the business case:** What is the business case for AI?

- **Select the right AI technology:** What AI technology is right for the application scenario?

- **Build the AI solution:** How do we build the AI solution?

- **Deploy the AI solution:** How is the AI solution deployed?

- **Measure the impact:** How is the impact of the AI solution measured?

The best framework to realize transformative opportunities will depend on the specific context of the organization and the problems to solve. However, the best advice at this point is to understand and properly frame the problem. Understanding and observing the key challenges and needs of users/customers helps to validate assumptions about potential opportunities. Additionally, being open to feedback and iterating on any AI solutions created is recommended. More problem-solving and innovation tools and frameworks for AI and innovation are described in Chapter 4.

FOCUSING ON REAL AI OBJECTIVES

AI solutions have different focus areas that can contribute to the AI strategy regarding productivity, efficiency, profitability, and innovation. AI can be used, for example, to automate tasks that are currently done mainly by humans, freeing employees to focus on more creative and strategic work. Typical application scenarios include AI-powered chatbots, which are used to answer customer questions, and AI-powered scheduling tools, which are applied to optimize the allocation of resources. However, AI is also applied to improve the efficiency of processes, such as by identifying bottlenecks and optimizing workflows. For example, AI-powered predictive maintenance systems can identify potential equipment problems before they occur, which helps prevent downtime. AI also has the potential to improve profitability by reducing costs, increasing sales, and improving customer satisfaction. However, AI-powered pricing algorithms don't just set prices, they optimize them to maximize profits. Similarly, AI-powered marketing campaigns go beyond targeting customers; they do so with laser focus for maximum effectiveness. Another important focus area in this book's context is AI's ability to generate new ideas and insights, which supports innovation and creative teams to innovate and stay ahead of the competition. For example, AI-powered ML algorithms can be applied to analyze large datasets to identify patterns and trends that would be difficult to spot with human eyes. The focus of AI may vary across industries. Manufacturing has embraced AI for tasks like quality control, where AI systems meticulously inspect products, and predictive maintenance, where AI analyzes data to predict equipment failures before they happen. In healthcare, AI diagnoses diseases, develops new treatments, and personalizes care. In finance, AI detects fraud, manages risk, and makes investment decisions. In retail, AI personalizes the shopping experience, optimizes inventory, and predicts demand. In mobility, the focus has been on applying AI to develop self-driving vehicles to optimize traffic flow and increase safety. In the following pages, the impact of different focuses will be briefly addressed before the need to increasingly involve the ecosystem in the formulation and implementation of AI strategies.

EMBRACE GENERATIVE AI AND WATCH YOUR PROFITS SOAR, YOUR SALES SKYROCKET, AND YOUR CUSTOMERS DELIGHT.

PRODUCTIVITY AND EFFICIENCY

The focus on productivity is associated with improvements due to significantly faster and more intelligent data processing. In particular, simple activities have a greater potential to generate quick wins and, at the same time, to create the basis for data-driven innovation and the development of better measurement systems. We expect productivity to increase by almost 40% in the medium term in the workforce with everyday functional work, and 20% of the workforce will either take on higher-value tasks or will no longer be needed for the original task. In addition, through the increase in data and the linking of AI models, we will have more opportunities to share knowledge in a targeted manner and to see whether all activities in the company pay off in terms of value creation, value delivery, and value capture. The efficiency gains will also impact the time-to-market in new products, services, and experience development. The application of AI in different industries shows that the average macro design cycle in product development will be half compared to traditional product development cycles without utilizing data capabilities, ML, and generative AI.

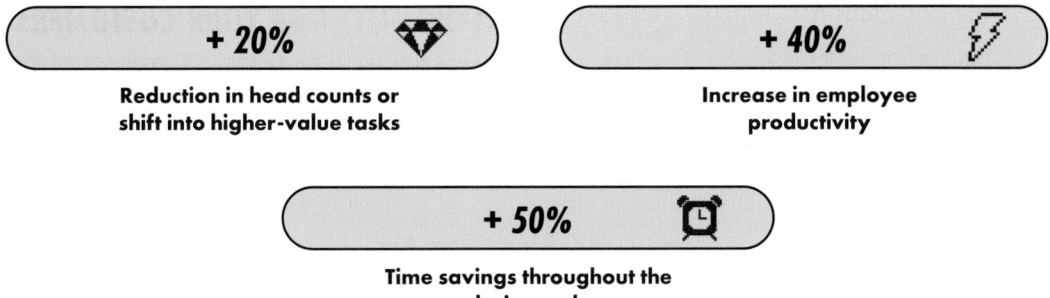

+ 20%

Reduction in head counts or shift into higher-value tasks

+ 40%

Increase in employee productivity

+ 50%

Time savings throughout the design cycle

Research on the first users of Microsoft's generative AI productivity service, Copilot for Microsoft 365, reveals that 70% of users said they were more productive and the time to complete common tasks was on average 29% faster with Copilot. However, generative AI for workforce productivity should be more than just unlocking efficiencies. We strongly believe that generative AI will have the ability to reshape collaboration and improve employee fulfillment and well-being. These benefits will be amplified as more power tools emerge like Gemini 1.5. These power tools will include faster response times, enhanced understanding of complex queries, or even entirely new functionalities. This will contribute to a better user experience and even increased productivity.

LONG-TERM PROFITABILITY OUTLOOK

As previously discussed, one primary driver for implementing AI is realizing better profitability. Automation and efficiency gains for specific tasks free up resources and provide competitive advantages. For example, AI-powered chatbots can answer customer questions and resolve issues 24/7. The collective learning and corporate knowledge capabilities of AI will create a knowledge base beyond human capability, resulting in superior services at scale and freeing up human customer service representatives to focus on more complex tasks. We observe similar profitability gains and phenomena as realized with the rise of the internet in the 1990s. Current estimates about value gains in global annual corporate profits reach more than USD 4 trillion. At the same time, labor productivity in conjunction with AI could increase annually by up to 1% within this decade. Comparatively, the internet has created approximately USD 16 trillion in val-

GENERATIVE AI WILL AFFECT ALMOST 40% OF JOBS AROUND THE WORLD, REPLACING SOME AND COMPLEMENTING OTHERS. WE NEED A CAREFUL BALANCE OF POLICIES TO MAXIMIZE ITS POTENTIAL AND CREATE A FAIR AND INCLUSIVE FUTURE FOR ALL.

ue gains for global corporate profits since its conception. AI seems to be more transformational, and some scenarios predict that in the next 25 years, half of the current workforce might be replaced by automation and AI. According to a report by Goldman Sachs, 300 million jobs could potentially be lost due to AI. Especially in current cycles of recession in which companies experience decreased revenue and profitability due to reduced demand for their products or services, current AI and generative AI in the future will help to increase revenue efficiency by automating tasks, interacting with customers and pricing and developing processes in companies around the globe.

Once again, monetary policy measures are unlikely to save the economy. Still, salvation may be found through innovative companies that actively address major issues of digitalization and invest in and democratize AI technology.

APPLYING AI IN INNOVATION WORK

Another critical factor for a flourishing economy and thriving businesses is their ability to innovate. Currently, AI is changing the familiar frameworks used in innovation work and thus completely changing companies' innovation management. In line with the exponential change of technologies and the interaction of AI with creative teams, new innovation approaches have emerged that permit the exploration of new market opportunities with unprecedented efficacy. When reflecting with management teams about innovations in the VUCA (volatility, uncertainty, complexity, and ambiguity) world, all agree that we face a volatile and changing environment, increasingly competitive global markets, competing technologies, and dramatically shifting political landscapes. With this comes an exponential increase in available information and knowledge. For many companies, validated information, insights, and existing knowledge are the foundation of their problem-solving and innovation capabilities across organizations.

Modern and contemporary approaches and paradigms such as design thinking, Lean Startup, and ecosystems design attempt to solve even the most complex problems iteratively, minimize risks, and reduce development costs. But despite this, innovation efforts remain high and subject to constant scrutiny in times of uncertainty. Consequently, finding

GENERATIVE AI HAS THE POTENTIAL TO RESHAPE OUR WORLD, NOT JUST BY MAKING TASKS MORE EFFICIENT BUT BY ENHANCING HUMAN CAPABILITIES AND CREATING A MORE EQUITABLE SOCIETY.

ways to apply AI and ML to corporate innovation processes should greatly interest all relevant functions up to top management. On one hand, this has the potential to provide companies with better ways to respond to their increasingly competitive environment and manage the growing amount of information around them, becoming even more evidence based. On the other hand, recent years have shown that AI support for the innovation process can create real value for companies by reducing the risks and costs of the innovation process in addition to the design and innovation paradigms described above.

AI systems can automate, replace, augment, or help validate assumptions in human decision-making. In the context of this book, AI and innovation can be divided into two broad capability levels that mirror the types of information processing capabilities (expansion and automated) described on the next page.

WHAT IS THE EVOLUTION OF AUTONOMY INNOVATION LEVELS OF AI SYSTEMS ?

Almost all industries and sectors are recognizing the transformative potential of generative AI and are actively exploring its applications to enhance customer experiences and open new revenue streams. While the adoption of generative AI may initially be gradual, its long-term impact on product and service offerings is undeniable. With regard to expansion, businesses are leveraging generative AI to create personalized experiences, automate customer interactions, and develop innovative products and services. At the same time, generative AI itself is undergoing rapid advancements, paving the way for a broader range of applications and expanding the impact of AI automation across industries. At the forefront of these advancements are improvements in AI application frameworks, enabling seamless integration and interoperability of generative AI models. Prompt stores, prompt caching, prompt translation, and other platforms are simplifying the development and deployment of generative AI applications, enhancing their consistency and performance.

The trend toward developing smaller, more efficient generative AI models is gaining traction, with medium language models (MLMs) and small language models (SLMs) emerging as promising alternatives to LLMs. This shift is driven by the need to optimize performance while minimizing resource requirements, making generative AI more accessible and scalable.

Retrieval-augmented generation (RAG), a technique that combines retrieval with generation, continues to gain popularity and will help to overcome "hallucinations" of LLMs. RAGs are a practicable complement to LLMs that rely extensively on the relevance of retrieved documents. Corrective retrieval-augmented generation (CRAG) was developed later to improve the robustness of generation. CRAG represents significant new advancement in AI and NLP, offering new possibilities for improving the accuracy and effectiveness of language models across a wide range of applications. CRAG is producing more reliable and contextual content. CRAG is also plug-and-play and can be seamlessly coupled with various RAG-based approaches.

1. Expansion based on human-designed AI systems

Simple information processing capability means that the AI system can support human innovation managers and design thinking teams in processing much more significant amounts of information and knowledge than they could on their own. AI systems can extend the entire design cycle by generating new ideas and possibilities or overcoming constrained search routines to find more sophisticated solutions. AI systems can expand beyond human intellect and substantially complement their skills and capabilities. Organizations using AI will process significant advantages over those that don't. At this capability level, AI systems work with humans as a team.

2. Automated AI systems with high autonomy

A higher level of automation allows AI systems to break new ground in the innovation process and across the entire design cycle. These types of AI systems can handle more advanced and difficult tasks in the innovation process and are therefore able to support human design thinking and innovation teams and even replace them to a certain extent. These automated systems can also transverse across multiple domains and compile more robust capabilities. In Chapter 4, a target picture is derived from our daily AI and innovation work for the future of AI in the context of innovation management and current future autonomy levels.

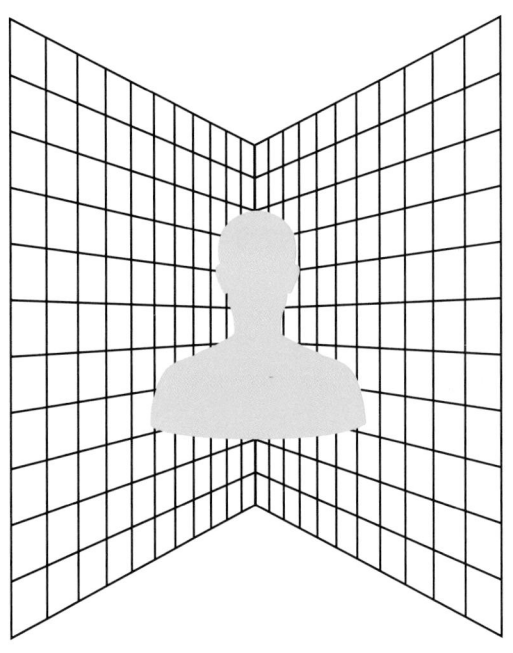

Human-designed AI Systems

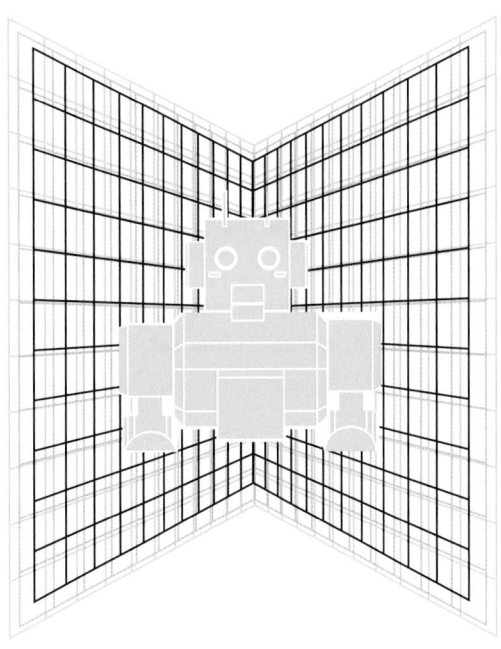

AGI Systems with Increasing Machine Autonomy

STRATEGIC RESPONSE TO SET FOCUS

The strategic response to the set focus (e.g. productivity, innovation, etc.) varies in the respective industries and in how products, services, and experiences are provided (physical vs. digital). In addition, the degree of digitization is often decisive, which influences rapid AI integration and how offerings are received by customers and users today. Digitalization is not just a technology; it's a business culture change across the entire organization. The High-Level Focus Areas – AI Strategy Matrix (see next page) can, therefore, only provide an orientation as to how the respective response to an AI strategy is typically structured. Adopting standard AI applications is sufficient for many industries, while other industries are forced to rethink their entire business model to stay competitive. In many digital services as well as experiences, the integration of AI is feasible. Some digital companies are forced to pivot their entire offering, adapt their business models, or even consider an exit if offerings are not creating value for customers anymore.

WHERE TO PLAY, HOW TO WIN, AND CONFIGURE IS COMPRISED OF:

- **Understanding** the objectives that drive the organization.

- The **performance** measures of employees within the organization.

- Identifying **use cases** to enable the organizations' objectives and improve the performance metrics set.

- Identifying the right **technologies** to address the use case.

- **Preparing** a roll-out program with tech support, change, and communications.

While the advent of powerful AI tools like ChatGPT has made it easier than ever to integrate AI into business operations, a successful implementation requires a well-defined strategy that goes beyond simply adopting AI tools. Organizations that rely solely on these tools without a comprehensive plan are likely to face challenges in achieving their desired outcomes in the set focus.

BY ADOPTING A COMPREHENSIVE AI STRATEGY THAT GOES BEYOND TOOL SELECTION, ORGANIZATIONS CAN MAXIMIZE THE VALUE OF AI AND ACHIEVE SUSTAINABLE SUCCESS.

106

EXAMPLE OF HIGH-LEVEL FOCUS AREAS – AI STRATEGY MATRIX

WHERE TO PLAY?

Response →

Focus ↓

	Products		Services		Experiences	
	Physical	Digital	Physical	Digital	Physical	Digital
Productivity and Efficiency	Efficiency gains in product development	Diverse (high) efficiency and productivity gains	Augments workforce and efficiency gains	Replacement of large parts of employees	Efficiency gains in processes	Improved automation
Profitability	Less development costs and higher prices for individualized products	Quicker time-to-market, less costs with data-driven innovation	Less costs from labor-intensive routine work	Optimized and less costly customer interactions	Optimized and less costly customer interactions	Automated coding, testing, and deployment with less labor costs
Innovation	AI influence on design, customization, and life cycle management	AI integration in products, processes, maintenance	AI supports route planning, utilization, and automation for settlements	AI integration over the entire digital customer journey and beyond	AI supports prediction of purchasing behavior and movement patterns	AI integration as well as influence on personalized customer interaction

HOW TO WIN AND CONFIGURE?

	Leverage	Integrate	Follow	Pivot	Follow	Pivot/Exit
Response to AI Strategy	Apply AI for sustaining or inventing products and leverage operational efficiency gains	Create a key feature of the product related to AI capabilities or/and automate development	Adapt and use standard AI tools to increase efficiency	(Re)design business models and strengthen value proposition	Adapt and use standard AI tools to increase efficiency	Adapt business model or exit if digital offering is not competitive anymore
Relevant Industries	• Pharma • Manufacturing • Agriculture • Construction	• Software • Hardware • Sensorics/IoT	• Health-care-Well-being • Tourism • Legal	• Telecom Digital Marketing • E-Commerce	• Hospitality • Events • Sports • Retail	• Gaming • VR/AR • Mobile Apps, Social Media

ADAPTION AND CULTURAL CHANGE TO THRIVE AI

A thriving AI culture should include elements related to encouraging curiosity, risk-taking (within a defined AI ethics framework), and continuous learning. These elements prioritize data-driven decision-making and empower employees to apply design thinking to explore the problem space, test assumptions, and embrace failure as a stepping-stone toward success. Great value will only emerge by embracing some measured risk. Practical experience shows that successful innovators are those companies that have embraced a culture of experimentation, leading to remarkable results. By empowering their employees to experiment, these organizations have disrupted industries, optimized user experiences, and continuously improved their offerings. The key here is being proactive; being reactive will diminish the organizational strategic advantage and cause the organization to fall behind its competitors. However, many traditional companies still operate in different silos, hindering the aggregation of data and impeding the full potential of analytics and AI. A good starting point is to break down the silos and encourage collaboration between teams to foster the exchange of diverse perspectives, skills, and expertise. This collaborative environment facilitates innovation and ensures comprehensive experimentation across different aspects of the organization. This collaboration should transcend the organizational barrier and extend across various industries.

THE DEMOCRATIZATION OF AI IS IN FULL SWING. THERE'S NO BETTER TIME THAN NOW FOR COMPANIES OF ALL SIZES TO EMBARK ON THEIR OWN TRANSFORMATIVE AI JOURNEY.

However, many companies have started small by setting up centers of excellence or focus groups within business units experimenting with AI. At the same time, employees at all levels and functions have started to get involved with recent LLMs ChatGPT, Gemini, or Ernie. In many cases, businesses utilize LLMs without implementing specific organizational guidelines around trust and accountability or defining the areas where AI can and should be applied.

This kind of use of AI runs smoothly in companies where a culture has already been established, where employees take ownership of projects and ensure that the company's purpose, goals, and compliance requirements are not violated. In many cases, ChatGPT, Gemini, and Ernie are used in the working environment as an extension or integration of the preferred web browser to gather information or receive impulses. As long as no negative consequences result from the knowledge gained, this has become part of everyday work that, from our point of view, does not require further adaptation and cultural regeneration. Adaptation and cultural change, however, are bigger issues that only a few companies have faced in the past; in this context, it's about ensuring humans and AI work as a team. This new relationship is triggering questions about the adaption of humans interacting across all functions with AI. AI is the new coworker joining the team with all their advantages, skills, and potential bias to live with. So the question is how to stay competitive, thrive with this new setup of capabilities and skills, and decide which changes need to be made from product, service, and experience perspectives. More importantly, from the perspective of culture and employees, those who are in a position to make progress together with AI. If these important elements are addressed first, organizations will be well on their way to becoming learning organizations, thriving in a digital economy, and redefining the market in which they operate. Embracing a culture that is open to leveraging these AI tools is more important than the tools themselves, as these tools will evolve, and new ones will emerge with higher capabilities and potential for transformation.

BUSINESS LEADERS ARE INCREASINGLY RECOGNIZING THE IMPORTANCE OF CREATING A CULTURE OF EXPERIMENTATION AND LEARNING WITHIN THEIR ORGANIZATIONS, PARTICULARLY AS IT RELATES TO AI TECHNOLOGIES.

AI x CULTURE

FORGET "MAN VS. MACHINE." THRIVE WITH AI! BUILD A COLLAB CULTURE WHERE HUMANS AND AI TEAM UP TO CONQUER THE FUTURE.

Practical observation shows that AI-fueled organizations typically do more than trust data; they are willing to quickly turn insights into action and rapid experimentation. However, when applying organizational design, it is recommended to keep in mind that the most successful transformations typically take some time and are based on employees' consent and buy-in. Adding support where behaviors aren't taking hold and celebrating achievements along the way is vital to ultimately arriving at a culture that can thrive.

UNLEASHING NEW VALUE ACROSS INDUSTRIES

We face an accelerated shift toward ecosystems thinking. Based on the leap of natural languages and the speed of diffusion of AI technology, all established concepts of information management and how we realize digitization are changing. The new AI ecosystems provide totally new opportunities to realize innovations through the orchestration of AI systems and their collaboration to achieve a common goal. In most cases today, the common goal is mechanization through AI. The groundwork for this revolution and shift is based on all efforts to collect and organize data over the last decades. One of the many significant advantages of implementing the AI ecosystem over standalone AI is the ease of data refinement in the network. However, the innovation work in the AI ecosystems has just started; new market roles will be defined, and different players will take the lead in orchestrating the dynamic ecosystem landscape. Ecosystem-fueled innovation will demand open collaboration, where data and intentions are shared clearly, fostering responsible development and ethical solutions that benefit all. It's not just about the technology, it's about building a future where humans and AI thrive together.

SIMILAR TO HOW A SYMPHONY ORCHESTRA COMBINES THE TALENTS OF DIFFERENT MUSICIANS INTO A HARMONIOUS WHOLE, REALIZING THE FULL POTENTIAL OF AN AI ECOSYSTEM REQUIRES THOUGHTFUL INTEGRATION OF TECHNOLOGIES, DATA, AND HUMAN EXPERTISE.

AI x ECOSYSTEM

- EXTENSIBILITY
- INNOVATION & CO-CREATIONS
  ↑ ↓
- AI ORCHESTRATOR
  ↓ ↑
- AI MODELS
- DATA
- AI INFRASTRUCTURE

110

Building a successful AI ecosystem with multiple models requires expertise in orchestrating models, data, infrastructure, and operations into a system of initiate, orchestrate, and adapt. The virtuous design loop explores which complementary AI models to use and what resources are required for appropriate governance to create real value in the domain. For example, with the appropriate methodology and tools from business ecosystems design, we can develop an optimal AI environment that also addresses important ethical implications. The following questions for AI ecosystems are considered helpful from practical experience to create robust, dynamic systems. Orchestrators are equipped with the appropriate principles to guide such initiatives in the right direction:

- What is the right AI framework and infrastructure to support model deployment, monitoring, and updating?

- What expertise, capacity, and skilled AI resources for training, fine-tuning, and validation are needed?

- Which of today's and tomorrow's specialized AI and generative AI models can work together to support and challenge each model?

- What architecture, training, processes, and procedures are appropriate to promote modularity and improve collaboration between models?

- What are the appropriate datasets to minimize bias and maximize accuracy, fairness, and certainty of results?

- What methods and validation sets are used to achieve the desired results and reduce the risk of errors such as hallucinations?

- Where is continuous human oversight needed across the system to autonomous components?

 ↓ **Download AI Ecosystem Design Canvas**

Decision-makers must embrace open collaboration to unleash new value across industries. Sharing expertise and data across internal and external partners unlocks innovation potential, but this requires breaking down silos and prioritizing data accessibility. However, this openness needs ethical and secure governance. Ecosystem actors' selection based on talent, technology, customer reach, and shared values ensures responsible and trustworthy innovation in this AI era.

By considering these elements, AI ecosystems are able to revolutionize industries. Smart cities with optimized traffic flow and healthcare offering AI diagnostics are just the beginning. Self-driving cars, personalized learning, and AI tackling climate change are exciting possibilities for the future.

RISK MANAGEMENT IN AI WORK

Alongside its positive effects, some AI applications raise legitimate concerns and risks. AI ethics is a multidisciplinary and multistakeholder field that aims to define and implement technical and socio-technical solutions to address these concerns and mitigate the risks → see table on the next page. For example, there are risks and associated challenges with generative AI that may drive second-order costs. These risks are now well understood and include data hallucinations, bias, cybersecurity, and copyright issues. However, many companies we work with have only realized the scope of these risks as they have begun to scale with AI.

TO MAKE THOUGHTFUL INVESTMENTS IN AI THAT HAVE THE GREATEST IMPACT, IT IS IMPORTANT TO THINK THROUGH THE STRATEGY AND TECHNOLOGY APPROACH, UNDERSTAND THE ALTERNATIVES, AND BE PREPARED TO PIVOT QUICKLY.

Observed risks relate to the trustworthiness of AI systems and contextual norms and values. For examination of risks, different methods and taxonomies might be applied. Many companies have included the recommendations from the OECD, EU AI Act, EO 13960, into applied AI ethics frameworks to address them.

Some companies we work with have also created their own risk tiering for AI with categories indicating unacceptable risks to minimal risks on a scale from 1–4. Other AI-related risks are caused by the external business environment, such as disruption from startups or tech-savvy competitors. In this case, companies urgently need to rely on generative AI to develop new offerings and value propositions. Often, however, these are mainly horizontal use cases that are less strategic. Nevertheless, companies are advised to prioritize them carefully, accounting for the level of investment, ROI, and risk, among other factors.

We recommend a proactive approach to AI risks. For many decision-makers, the current question is whether the previous considerations are sufficient or if there is a need for further considerations. Often, standard AI solution providers already have integrated offerings related to managing risk. However, no company will fail to regularly review and test the AI systems in use to ensure accuracy, regulatory compliance, and the absence of bias. The important principle here is to reduce the risks to customers so as not to lose their trust in the age of AI. Thinking in terms of "privacy by design" and other basic data and AI principles supports these activities.

MINIMAL RISKS

No intervention, AI systems represent only minimal or no risk for citizens' rights or safety.

- Use of applications such as AI-enabled video games or spam filters.

LIMITED RISKS

Dealt with specific transparency obligations.

- For AI systems such as chatbots, users should be aware that they are interacting with a machine.

HIGH RISK

Subject to strict obligations before coming to market with risk mitigation, oversight, and documentation.

- AI used in critical infrastructures, educational training, essential private/public services, law enforcement, migration, border control management, etc.

UNACCEPTABLE RISK

Poses a threat to the safety, livelihoods, and rights of people and will be banned.

- System that manipulates human behavior to circumvent users' free will.
- Systems that allow "social scoring" by governments.

SUMMARY OF RISKS AND CHARACTERISTICS

	Technical	Socio-Technical	Principles
OECD AI Recommendation	• Robustness • Security	• Safety • Explainability	• Traceability to human values • Transparency and responsible disclosure • Accountability
EU AI Act	• Technical robustness	• Safety • Privacy • Non-discrimination	• Human agency and oversight • Data governance • Transparency • Diversity and fairness • Environmental and societal well-being • Accountability
EO 13960	• Purposeful and performance driven • Accurate, reliable, and effective • Secure and resilient	• Safe • Understandable by subject matter experts, users, and others as appropriate	• Lawful and respectful of our nation's values • Responsible and traceable • Regularly monitored • Transparent • Accountable
Summary	• Accuracy • Reliability • Robustness • Resilience or ML security	• Explainability • Interpretability • Privacy • Safety • Managing bias	• Fairness • Accountability • Transparency

MONETIZATION OF AI

In terms of monetizing AI, there are countless perspectives and possibilities. We would like to focus on two interesting aspects. First is the AI vendors' perspective on AI business value and AI business transformation. The other is the monetization and savings opportunities for companies that use generative AI. The easiest approach is to create products or software that uses AI to solve a specific problem or enhance a specific service; for example, implementing AI chatbots using common LLMs or AI integration in apps for additional customer value. In addition, there are countless opportunities to sell so-called AI-powered services, such as customer support services, cybersecurity and fraud detection services, and social media content or consulting services. Implementing AI in this way can boost eCommerce sales or create more customized offerings.

THE INTRICATE NATURE OF AI'S VALUE PROPOSITION NECESSITATES INNOVATIVE MONETIZATION APPROACHES THAT TRANSCEND TRADITIONAL PRICING MODELS. SUBSCRIPTION-BASED SERVICES, PAY-PER-USE STRUCTURES, AND DATA-SHARING PARTNERSHIPS OFFER AVENUES TO EXPLORE REVENUE STREAMS THAT ALIGN WITH AI'S UNIQUE CHARACTERISTICS.

For larger companies that are active in the AI domain as vendors, the question is where the current and future focus lies on the possibilities between being an AI product vendor, an AI platform vendor, an AI software as a service (SaaS) product vendor, or tapping into more of the value creation as an AI tech and management advisor (see excerpt of characteristics on the right). It is exciting for companies to imagine how they will position themselves to be the next AI x ecosystem initiator and orchestrator in the future and realize another dimension of monetization for themselves.

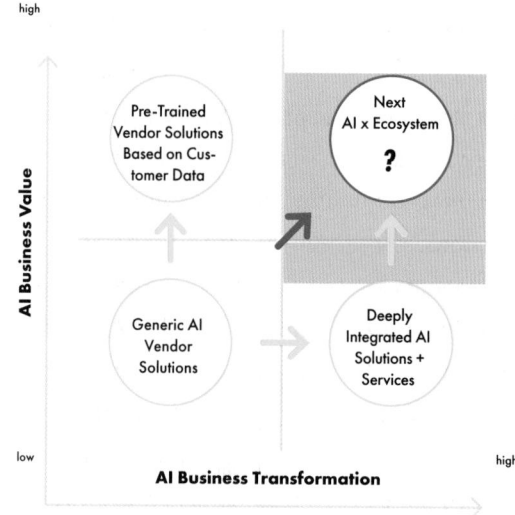

AI VENDOR TRANSFORAMTION – VALUE MATRIX

The business models in AI ecosystems will go beyond the currently observed blend of specialization, data monetization, and outcome-based pricing.

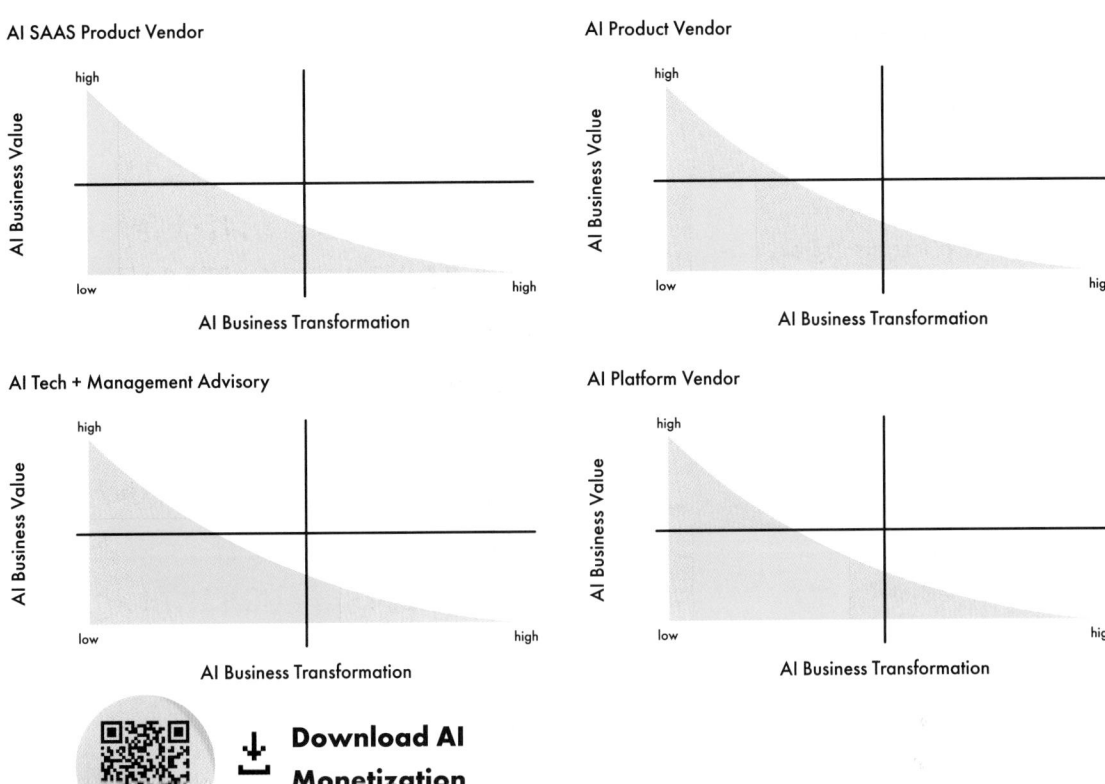

AI SAAS Product Vendor

high — AI Business Value — low

AI Business Transformation (low → high)

AI Product Vendor

high — AI Business Value — low

AI Business Transformation (low → high)

AI Tech + Management Advisory

high — AI Business Value — low

AI Business Transformation (low → high)

AI Platform Vendor

high — AI Business Value — low

AI Business Transformation (low → high)

↓ Download AI Monetization Template

For many traditional, non-tech companies, the first option of monetization is realized cost savings. AI can be used to automate tasks and improve efficiency, which can lead to reduced costs. For example, AI can be used with low investments to automate customer service tasks, or more complex AI solutions and integration can optimize supply chain activities. For customer service automation, investments are typically related to the costs of utilizing, for example, ChatGPT API, SW adjustments, developments, and deployment, as well as cost for training and maintaining specific AI models. The returns and benefits include increased revenue from new products and services (value creation), reduced costs from automation and efficiency improvements, improved customer satisfaction, and better competitive advantages. Regarding business models, a growth in number of customers/users, increased engagement, and new monetization techniques are often realized. The operating model usually benefits from AI/ML-driven improvements and innovations.

A DIVERSE RANGE OF MONETIZATION PATTERNS CAN BE EMPLOYED TO CAPTURE THE VALUE OF AI INVESTMENTS, ENCOMPASSING TRADITIONAL STRATEGIES LIKE CREATING NEW PRODUCTS AND SERVICES, AS WELL AS EMERGING APPROACHES LIKE REPACKAGING EXISTING FUNCTIONALITY AND LEVERAGING AI AS AN UNDERLYING PLATFORM.

HOW TO DEVELOP AI CAPABILITIES

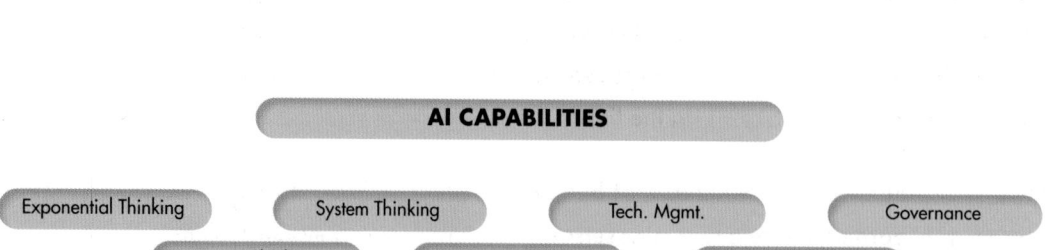

The constant evolution of AI demands constant upskilling. Mastering emerging capabilities becomes essential for harnessing the true power of the latest AI technologies and applications, ensuring organizations don't get left behind. Many companies know how important it is to constantly develop the skills and abilities of their employees, as the average half-life of qualifications is just 4 years; in some technical areas, such as ML engineering, it's only two and a half years. This is especially true when dealing with exponential technologies, such as AI. It becomes apparent that new skills are not only needed for technical implementation, but also how they are best used, up to radical changes of entire job profiles and tasks of functions in the organization.

Consequently, AI capabilities are related to technical capabilities → see page 124 as well as management capabilities → see page 120. Additionally, different thinking types → see page 23 ranging from exponential thinking and design thinking to systems thinking are in high demand to help companies understand, design, and deploy AI. For AI, capabilities that deal with data and technology management are also of great importance and are usually covered by technical capabilities. A good starting point is to embark on a discovery phase to analyze which capabilities are already available in the organization today and what capabilities are missing that would provide value beyond what currently exits. By understanding the status quo and AI capabilities needed, leaders can make informed decisions about how to better deploy AI and what kind of skills and capabilities are needed to build, develop, and maintain AI solutions.

A rule of thumb is to allocate between 1–3% of total budget on training and up-skilling annually, depending on the level of education and industry, to fill the gaps in critical capabilities. However, we recommend a higher percentage of the total budget be repurposed for that. Given the rapidly changing landscape of AI, adaptability is of paramount importance to ensure that the organization and workforce remain agile. For this reason, technology players such as Amazon have launched initiatives such as the Machine Learning University, where thousands of employees who initially had little experience with ML have become experts in the field.

Many companies have realized that building AI capabilities goes hand in hand with learning the relevant mindsets (e.g. design thinking, systems thinking, and exponential thinking). Since 2023, there has been a real boom in the desire for AI and design thinking offerings. The reason is simple: learning about AI and relevant mindsets at different levels leads to better employee morale and engagement. At the same time, building and developing new capabilities are cornerstones of a successful future of work strategy. Applying a robust capability build and learning framework for an AI strategy is essential. A carefully adapted strategy for AI should include concrete steps and a way to measure progress along the way and implement a proper feedback loop to make adjustments as needed. In times where

BY LEVERAGING DESIGN THINKING, ORGANIZATIONS CAN HARNESS THE COLLECTIVE WISDOM OF THEIR STAKEHOLDERS TO IDENTIFY AND IMPLEMENT AI SOLUTIONS THAT DRIVE INNOVATION AND BUSINESS SUCCESS.

well-educated employees are in short supply, it becomes a strategic imperative to develop the existing workforce. This enables companies to quickly build a competitive advantage by fostering talent that is not readily available in the marketplace and closing skills gaps that are critical to achieving, for example, strategic AI goals faster and better than rivals.

In many of the capability-building programs we have initialized at companies, it has become a requirement to closely link the business and AI strategy with reskilling. This includes, for example, the initial systematic definition of critical skills related to AI strategy, which correspond to a series of accelerator programs, design thinking skill journeys, and skill shifting objectives. Most of which are dedicated to transforming industry-specific experts into AI and data science experts. Often, the programs were closely timed with the rollout of OKRs, which contributed to cultural change of autonomous teams and new way of work practices.

A proper capability build system should be much more than just reskilling employees. It requires an organizational framework that fosters success and positive reinforcement. For this reason, the mindset becomes central across all organizational levels, as it helps to shape the appropriate behavior of both employees and managers. In this context, a capability build system is better described as a broad and deep change management program that requires a focus on many different tasks at the same time.

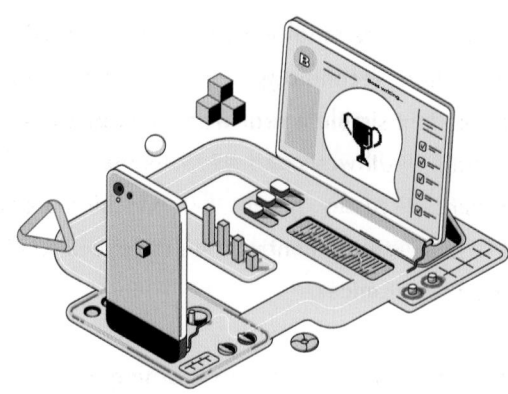

FOR EVERY EMPLOYEE IT IS NO LONGER JUST ABOUT A DEGREE OR BEING QUALIFIED; IT'S ESSENTIAL TO HAVE AN ADEQUATE CULTURE AND MINDSET SHIFT.

Corporate practice shows that many organizations globally have started mapping a general skills taxonomy to future roles and functions to identify skills available internally and externally, as well as the skills needed to succeed. Working with a general skills taxonomy is an effective way of starting the assessment because around 80% of the skills in an organization are common while 20% are unique, so this taxonomy will do most of the heavy lifting for most organizations. The big challenge, however, is to predict the future and what impact exponential changes will have on digitalization and the required skills of the workforce. This is one reason why there is a lot of emphasis on exponential thinking in this book series, as it is the cornerstone for interpreting future scenarios and taking the necessary measures in a timely manner.

Operationally, this means that exponential thinking and a skills taxonomy promote responsiveness and agility, as employees can be easily redeployed. And in most cases, a critical skills gap will not catch the company unprepared.

However, the transformation in corporate training is ongoing. In the short term we see a shift from passive, information-based methods to dynamic, experiential learning. In the face of rapid technological advancements and an increasingly dynamic business landscape, traditional corporate training methods, which often relied on lectures, presentations, and static materials, are no longer sufficient. Employees need to be able to learn and adapt quickly in order to keep pace with the changing demands of the workplace. This is driving a shift toward more dynamic and experiential training approaches, which focus on hands-on learning, problem-solving, and collaboration.

In addition, technology and community will play a pivotal role in this transformation. Technology is enabling the creation of immersive learning experiences that simulate real-world scenarios, while also providing personalized learning pathways and adaptive feedback. Community, in the form of online forums, discussion groups, and coaching programs, is fostering a collaborative learning environment where employees can learn from each other and share their experiences.

The evolution of corporate learning is not just about adopting new technologies or methodologies; it is also about creating a culture of continuous learning and development.

As a result, employee development must also adapt to the new velocity. The start is often personalized development and learning paths based on the skills taxonomies described above.

EVOLUTION OF CORPORATE LEARNING IN TIMES OF EXPONENTIAL CHANGE

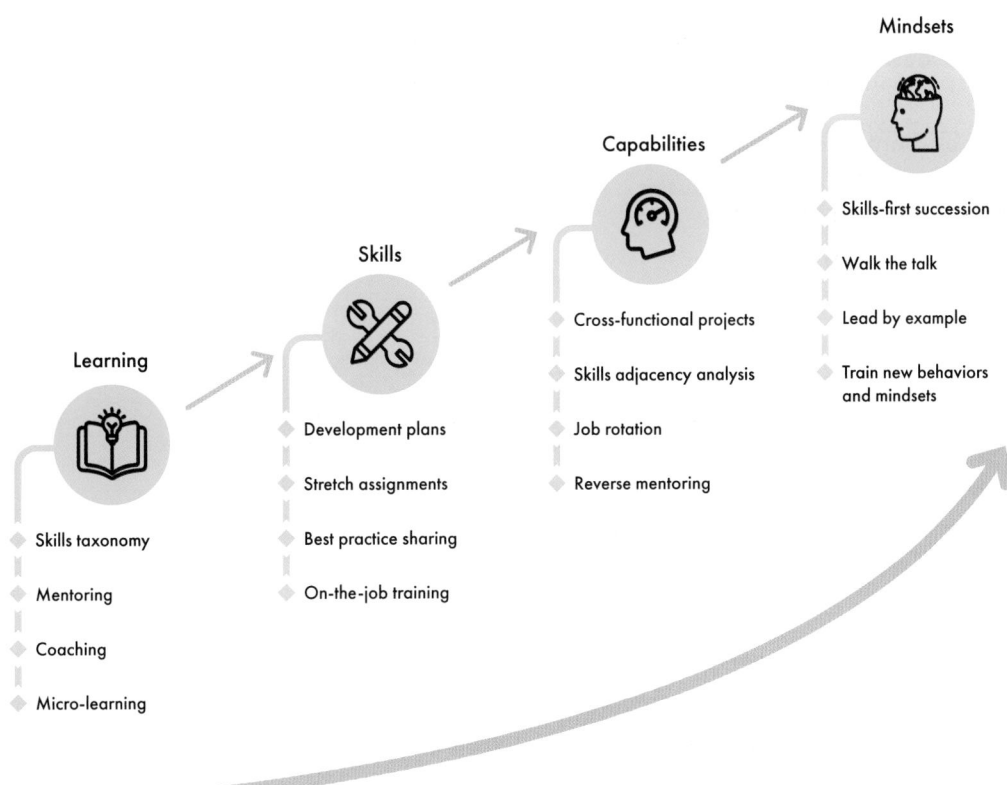

Mindsets
- Skills-first succession
- Walk the talk
- Lead by example
- Train new behaviors and mindsets

Capabilities
- Cross-functional projects
- Skills adjacency analysis
- Job rotation
- Reverse mentoring

Skills
- Development plans
- Stretch assignments
- Best practice sharing
- On-the-job training

Learning
- Skills taxonomy
- Mentoring
- Coaching
- Micro-learning

EXAMPLE OF DEVELOPING IT MANAGERS INTO AI PRODUCT MANAGERS

The application of skills taxonomies for many functions and roles would fill a whole book, and therefore, we would just like to present one concrete example often seen in many organizations worldwide: a shift and learning path from the traditional IT manager to an AI product manager. This recently emergent role is best viewed as a role that encompasses tasks related to overseeing the development, implementation, and maintenance of AI-powered products and services. Working in this role requires a blend of technical expertise, strategic thinking, and business acumen to successfully navigate the intersection of AI and product management.

In the context of this chapter, as AI is a strategic imperative for companies to gain a competitive advantage, the role of the AI product manager becomes increasingly important. These product managers have the expertise to align AI initiatives with broader business objectives, identify new

IN THE ERA OF AI-DRIVEN INNOVATION, THE EMERGING ROLE OF SKILLED AI PRODUCT MANAGERS PLAYS A CRUCIAL ROLE IN DRIVING THE SUCCESS OF AI PROJECTS.

and unforeseen opportunities for AI adoption, and lead the development of AI-enabled products that meet new market needs. Their ability to bridge the gap between technology and business needs makes them an invaluable asset to any organization.

AI product managers use data-driven and human-generated insights and agile methodologies to make informed decisions. They work closely with cross-functional teams, including data scientists, engineers, design thinkers, and business stakeholders, to define AI product strategies, prioritize features, and iterate based on user/customer feedback. At the same time, AI product managers need the ability and awareness about continuous learning and professional development to keep up with the latest AI advancements.

At the same time, AI is birthing new roles like AI ethics, who ensure responsible development and deployment, and AI explainability specialists, who translate complex algorithms into understandable terms for stakeholders. These emerging roles work alongside the described AI product manager to bridge the gap between AI capabilities and business needs.

CURRENT ROLE: IT MANAGER

- Adaptability
- Business Development
- Computer Science
- Business Case Development
- Business Strategy
- Consulting
- Customer Analysis
- Management
- Performance Assessment
- Prototyping
- Scrum
- Working Collaborative
- DevOps

TRANSFERABLE SKILLS

Personalized Development and Learning Path

Identify and decide on the skills to train...

- Data analytics tools
- Design thinking tools
- Product management frameworks
- Customer experience management
- Systems thinking methods
- Agile tools and methods
- Data discovery tools
- Business and stakeholder communication
- Product strategy tools

- Team of teams methodology
- Ethical frameworks and principles
- Applied data management
- Foresight thinking tools
- Prioritization tools and methods
- Change management framework
- Team management
- ...
- ...

NEW ROLE: AI PRODUCT MANAGER

Specific Skills

- Monitoring and iterating AI products
- User-centric design and experience
- Ensuring ethical and responsible AI practices
- Managing data and model development
- Collaborating with cross-functional teams
- Opportunities and defining AI product roadmap
- Bridging between AI technology and business

Technical Skills

- Understanding of ML algorithms
- Knowledge of AI concepts and technologies
- Data analysis and statistics
- SW developing skills
- Data management and infrastructure
- Data science and design thinking tools
- Understanding AI ethics and regulations

Domain Knowledge

- Understanding user needs
- Translating business requirements
- Guiding product strategy
- Effective stakeholder communication
- Anticipating industry challenge
- Identifying opportunities for innovation
- Building credibility and trust

Leadership Skills

- Effective stakeholder engagement
- Bridging tech and non-tech teams
- Clear and concise documentation
- Leadership and team management
- Decision-making and prioritization
- Adaptability and change management
- Influencing and negotiation

121

The previous example has shown that AI strategy development and strategy execution do not need totally new teams hired from outside of the organization. The continuous digital transformation accelerated by AI is people and workforce transformation at its core. The key questions are related to:

- Who can be up-skilled from the existing workforce?

- Who can get on a totally new level?

- Which traditional roles need a development path into new roles?

- Which capabilities are in the future more AI enabled?

- What capabilities and skills are needed to handle the technology debt?

- How to measure the digital and AI transformation?

- What are the new skill-based compensation models?

As a complex workforce transformation, digital transformation accelerated by AI cuts across all functions and roles, meaning that the processes, systems, and mindsets need to be continuously reworked across the entire organization. What needs to be done can be quickly defined, but the question now is "how do we do it?" Here, tools and methods are needed that ensure effectiveness, independent of the latest technological developments. In Chapter 3, we have therefore provided additional tools and methods to help you get started and to steer AI transformation in successful directions. In the path of learning, the leadership team is not exempt. It may take a quarter or two to understand the most important terms from the world of AI and what the difference is between a data scientist and a data engineer, or why there will be more need for AI product managers than IT managers in the future. Other questions might need to be asked, like "why are transformer technologies so important?" and "how is an AI ecosystem defined and best used?" It is most important to develop a common language in the organization, which is part of a cultural change and a new common mindset that is understood by everyone in the team.

IT IS APPARENT THAT DIGITAL TRANSFORMATION IS A CONTINUOUSLY EVOLVING PROCESS THAT WILL NEVER BE "DONE." IT'S MORE LIKE A MUSCLE THAT NEEDS TO BE CONSTANTLY EXERCISED, AND EVERYONE MUST KEEP ADAPTING THEIR TRAINING PLANS FOR CONTINUOUS IMPROVEMENT.

Business leaders need to become technology leaders as well. AI transformation will most likely be faster and more successful when boards are equipped with tech-savvy team members and not where IT competence is simply limited to the CIO. CEOs must become the orchestrator of new processes, systems, and mindsets. CEOs enable the learning path to a changed mindset and focus on learning in an environment of unknown-unknowns. In addition, it has become the CEO's task to align the entire organization on a business-led technology roadmap.

Moreover, AI enablement of knowledge workers is just beginning, and generative AI will increasingly change the workplace and employee experience. AI enablers will benefit in the future from the knowledge of global and corporate foundation models and other approaches that will lead to the next AI advancements → see page 155.

THE TYPES OF AI ENABLEMENT FOR KNOWLEDGE WORKERS

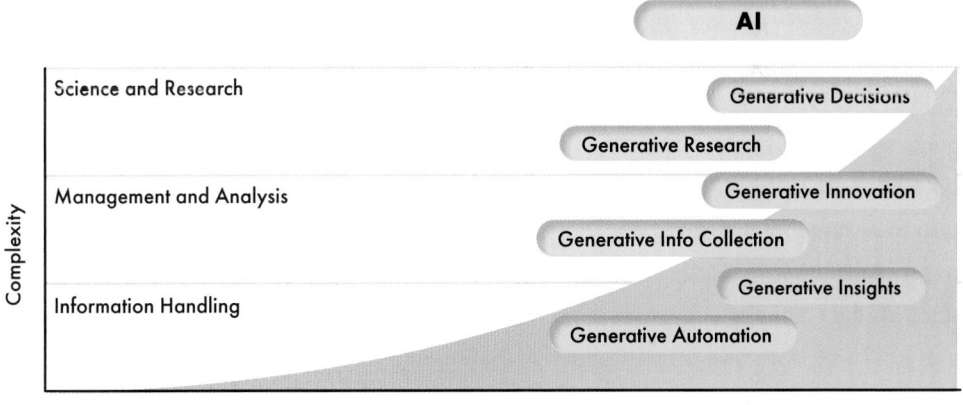

To realize the enablement in the short term, companies will prioritize maintaining the flow of work for knowledge workers by driving automation and fostering a culture of integration. Knowledge work automation will streamline processes, reduce manual tasks, and empower knowledge workers to focus on higher-value activities. Simultaneously, organizations will invest in integrating their business systems to break down silos and enable seamless data flow, enabling AI to provide its full potential. By prioritizing automation and integration, organizations will boost productivity, enhance collaboration, and harness the power of AI to drive growth and innovation.

REQUIRED TECHNICAL AI CAPABILITIES

Very often, technical AI capabilities already exist in organizations. Typical technical roles include data engineers, ML engineers, data analysts, and roles bridging the gap between the business and the data world (mainly associated with the role of the data scientists). Other roles like prompt engineers and AI ecosystems designers emerged in the early 2020s. These profiles have different skills needed to operate successfully in the current and future AI environment. The overview on the next page displays the technology and soft skills currently required in the fields of ML and AI.

However, not all roles with technical AI capabilities are the same. For example, some data scientist are at the very top of their field, while others have focused too much on learning pure data analytics tools. In the training and further development of these important roles, care must be taken to ensure that they not only have the breadth of tools needed but also to ensure they master them. They should

DATA SCIENTISTS AND OTHER AI-RELEVANT ROLES ARE AFFECTED BY UP-SKILLING. SOFT SKILLS, PROBLEM-SOLVING TECHNIQUES, AND LEADERSHIP AND TEAM TRANSFORMATION TECHNIQUES ARE INCREASINGLY IMPORTANT.

become the thought leaders in this space, with extraordinary problem-solving skills. At the same time, they need the freedom to develop real working products based on data and create impact. In the training and capability programs we offer for data scientists, it is a core component to master, for example, design thinking or to develop new AI products, services, and experiences in the artful combination of AI, data analytics, and design thinking. In addition, there is a strong focus on our capability to build programs that recognize complex interrelationships in the AI ecosystem and analyze them by breaking them down into subsystems and developing them further in a targeted manner to create more business value. These expanded and strategically relevant tasks are also important because AI will also automate many activities and tasks of data scientists. An expansion of skills is, therefore, also important for the AI-related functions in the company.

A prompt engineer (see illustration on the next page) should, for example, possess expertise in NLP, the ability to design and implement prompts, strong programming skills, attention to detail and problem-solving skills, and creativity and experimentation.

DATA ENGINEER

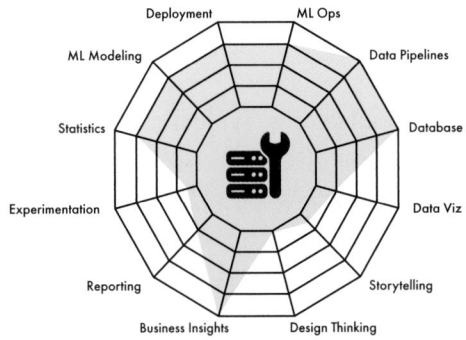

ML ENGINEER

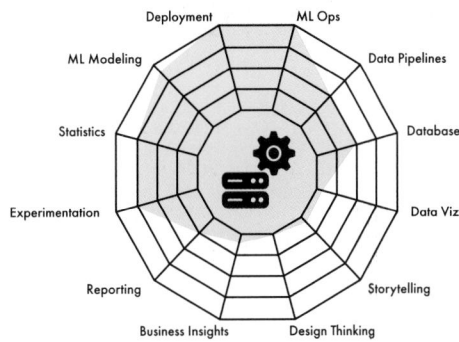

DATA SCIENTIST

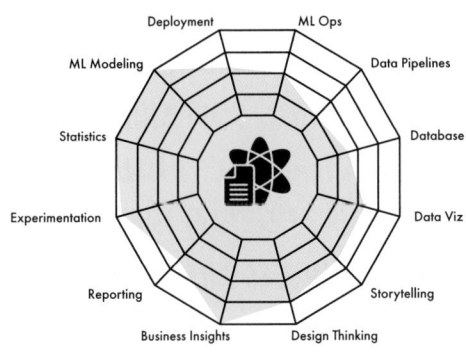

DATA ANALYST

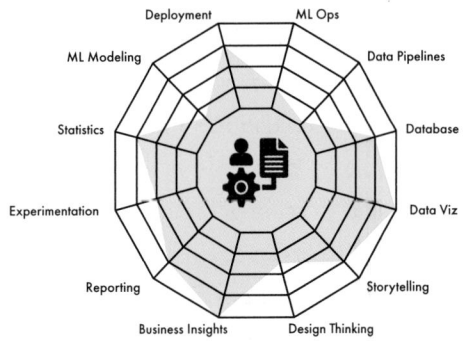

PROMPT ENGINEER

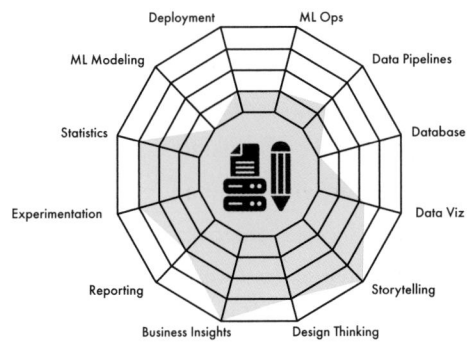

AI ECOSYSTEMS DESIGNER

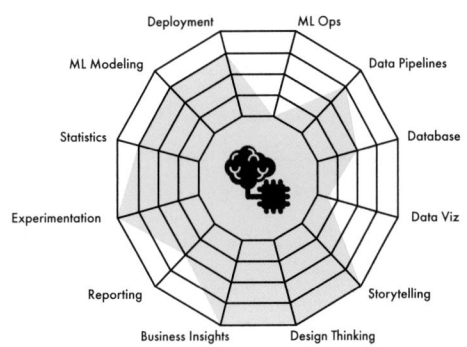

Download AI Capability Assessment Template

→ The specific skillset needed can vary depending on the industry and requirements for a specific job description.

SKILLS AND AI: THE NEW TEAM FORMATION

The future of work hinges on a new skillset, according to research institutes and the World Economic Forum (2023). Forget rote tasks – problem-solving (think Design Thinking), self-management (think resilience), and collaboration superpowers (think radical collaboration) are the keys to thriving alongside technology. While automation takes over repetitive functions, humans will lead with their uniquely human abilities to learn, adapt, and work together – leveraging AI tools for maximized productivity. The future workplace is a dynamic feedback loop of technology, jobs, and skills, and those who master these essential skills will be at the forefront of this exciting transformation.

WORKING WITH PEOPLE AND INTELLIGENT SYSTEMS

- Radical collaboration
- Idea conceptualization and rationalization
- Feedback loops
- Listening and dialogue operating in team-of-teams

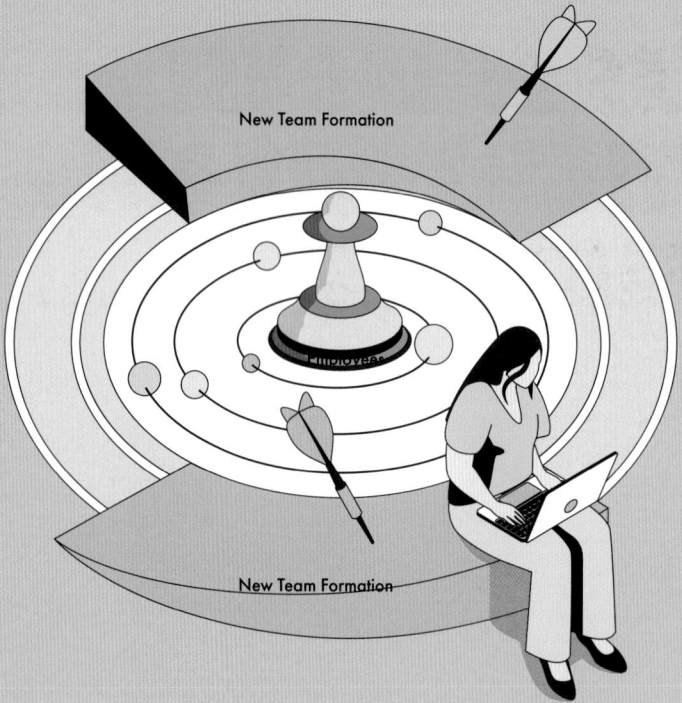

New Team Formation

GENERAL SKILLS

- Design thinking
- Analytical thinking
- Systems thinking
- New mindsets
- Cross-cultural skills
- Understanding of ethics and principles
- Resilience

New Team Formation

TECHNOLOGY USE AND DEVELOPMENT

- AI
- Technology design, use, monitoring, and control
- Technology programming
- Utilizing intelligent and autonomous systems

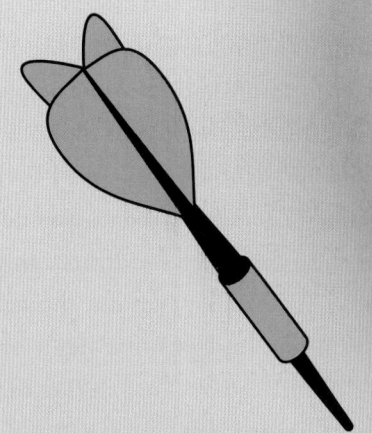

EXAMPLES OF INDUSTRY CASES ACTIVELY BUILDING NEW CAPABILITIES FOR AI

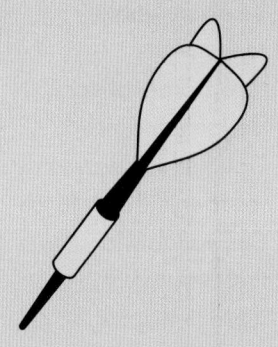

LEARNING, APPLYING, AND LIVING-UP AI PRINCIPLES

Many technology companies are launching programs for their own employees and the wider public to get acquainted with the skills needed to build and deploy AI. Some technology leaders, like Amazon, even expanded their well-known leadership principles to strong statements highlighting that "Success and Scale Bring Broad Responsibility," initiating a program that provides almost 30 million people with access to free new skills and capability training by 2025; science, technology, engineering, and math (STEM) education programs for young learners, including Amazon Future Engineer, AWS Girls' Tech Day, and AWS GetIT; and many other programs with universities. Since 2021, Amazon SageMaker Studio Lab has the ambition to make it easy for anyone to quickly set up an ML development environment for learning and experimentation at no cost. The initiative includes an AI and ML scholarship aiming to help underrepresented and underserved high school and college students learn foundational ML concepts and prepare them for careers in AI and ML. In addition to no-cost access to dozens of hours of free ML model training and educational materials, over 2,000 qualifying students from underrepresented and underserved communities are eligible for a scholarship for the AI Programming with Python Udacity Nanodegree program, which is designed to give scholarship recipients the programming tools and

techniques fundamental to ML. Google started its high-impact AI Principles training in 2019 for employees globally, including the very popular four-part Tech Ethics self-study course and a one-part deep dive based on Googler feedback. In respect to responsible innovation, thousands of Google employees have been engaged over the last years in a series of engaging online puzzles, quizzes, and games

AI at Google

7 Principles

1. Be socially beneficial
2. Avoid creating or reinforcing unfair bias
3. Be built and tested for safety
4. Be accountable to people
5. Incorporate privacy design principles
6. Uphold high standards for scientific excellence
7. Be available for uses that accord with these principles

to raise awareness of the AI Principles and measure at the same time employees' retention of important ethical concepts, such as avoiding unfair bias → see more principles of Google in the graphic on the previous page. Other internal Google programs, like the Principles Ethics Fellow Program, have been educating both Google employees and senior leaders globally. These principles are also incorporated in the exploration, building, and testing phase of new AI applications at Google to ensure responsible AI innovation. In 2023, Google also launched a great variety of free learning courses accessible to everyone. These courses cover topics such as introduction to generative AI, LLMs, and image generation.

Traditional sectors and industries also allow their employees to obtain the necessary skills in a timely manner. Most programs we observe for our clients are twofold. First, they help employees stay up-to-date on the latest AI technologies. Second, they help employees develop the skills they need to use AI to improve their work. For example, Johnson & Johnson runs an AI Academy to train its employees on the basics of AI and how to use it to improve patient care. The academy offers courses on topics such as AI for drug discovery, AI for medical imaging, and AI for personalized medicine. Other sectors, like financial service companies, are active as well. The Bank of America operates, for example, an AI Center of Excellence to help its employees learn about AI and how to use it to improve the bank's products and services. The center offers courses on topics

AS AI PERMEATES EVERY FACET OF OUR EXISTENCE, ITS TRANSFORMATIVE POWER IS UNDENIABLE. BUT THE TRUE IMPACT AI WILL HAVE ON THE WORLD LIES IN THE HANDS OF HUMANITY — IN OUR COLLECTIVE CHOICES AND ACTIONS.

such as AI for fraud detection, AI for risk management, and AI for customer service. Industry giant GE invites employees to the AI Learning Lab, which supports the learning journey about AI and how to use it to solve business problems. The lab offers courses on topics such as AI for manufacturing, AI for customer service, and AI for marketing. The retailer Walmart calls it AI Academy, a place that trains employees on the basics of AI and how to use it to improve their work. The academy offers courses on topics such as ML, NLP, and data visualization.

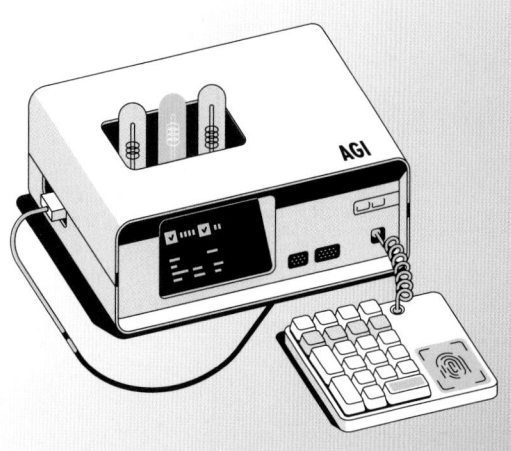

IMPORTANT SKILLS BEYOND AI AND ML

Meaningful and ethically responsible AI solutions require more than skills in ML, AI, and dealing with ethical issues. Pretty much all technology consultancies and tech-savvy industrial companies also rely on the soft skills and capabilities that allow them to understand the problem in the best possible way. Some companies, such as IBM, have made the design thinking mindset their central starting point for all technology-related questions, including AI, with the slogan "To design for a relationship with AI, we need to know ourselves first." Designing for AI at IBM includes, for example, new considerations and new ways of thinking. Especially when it comes to unfamiliar territory (working with the unknown-unknowns in finding solutions), the best way to begin is by applying human-centered design, the true purpose of any innovation: to improve the quality of human life. AI work at IBM is based on three lenses related to purpose, value, and trust.

PURPOSE
The reason for the user/customer to engage with the system. It will evolve as the user/customer and system grow with each other.

AI DESIGN BASED ON DESIGN THINKING AT IBM

TRUST
The willingness of a user/customer to invest in an emotional bond with the system. This trust is predicated on security of the system's data, the feeling of human control, and the quality of the results the system provides.

VALUE
The augmented capabilities provided by the system that tangibly improve the life of the user/customer.

IBM'S AI INITIATIVES ARE GUIDED BY A THREEFOLD COMMITMENT TO PURPOSE, VALUE, AND TRUST, ENSURING THAT AI IS DEVELOPED AND DEPLOYED RESPONSIBLY TO ADDRESS CRITICAL CHALLENGES AND ENHANCE HUMAN WELL-BEING.

Technology consulting firms like Accenture also apply skills beyond pure mathematical, computing, and developer skills for designing and implementing powerful AI. For successful designing and deploying AI at clients, consultants at all levels need to know about organizational behavior and corporate environment dynamics. Problem-solving skills and the ability to collaborate radically are of paramount importance. In addition, Accenture has realized the positive reinforcement between AI and innovation, which is asking for an inquisitive mind with the ability to think outside the box. In other words, to succeed in AI, it is necessary to explore new ways and ideas to deal with business and customer problems, which is the groundwork needed to create innovative solutions.

Accenture's latest technology, Vision, predicts that AI will revolutionize human–computer interaction, making it more natural and intuitive, potentially transforming the technology landscape as profoundly as previous waves like the mouse, cloud, and mobile. Businesses should prepare for this shift by modernizing their data systems and investing in human talent with the necessary skills and capabilities.

The design thinking mindset is typically used to empathize with users/customers of a potential AI solution. Understanding their needs, pain points, and jobs to be done is essential for defining the appropriate problem the AI solution is trying to solve → see more about applying Design Thinking for AI on page 181. The problem space takes the lion's share of the time before the team starts to brainstorm, sketch, and prototype potential solutions, which are tested with the potential customer/user afterward. Over the entire design cycle and multiple iterations, the aim is to improve the solution. Over time, a more concrete and well-defined solution based on the feedback from users/customers emerges. The final prototype provides, In many cases, the requirements for more validation based on an MVP (minimum viable product). As a result, applying design thinking is a must skill for data scientists working on the next level of automation via AI → see Skills Diagrams of Data Scientists on page 124.

By understanding user needs and pain points through interviews, observation, and workshops, organizations can identify where AI can truly add value.

DBS BANK HAD ALREADY DEVELOPED MORE THAN 600 AI/ML MODELS AND 300 USE CASES BY 2023.

DBS Bank, for example, used design thinking to address customer frustration with loan applications. Immersing themselves in the customer journey, they pinpointed the tedious document verification process as a prime candidate for AI automation. This resulted in their "Instant Loan" powered by AI, streamlining the process and boosting customer satisfaction. Design thinking doesn't just identify problems, it inspires solutions that leverage AI's potential to enhance both human experience and business outcomes.

ACCENTURE USES DESIGN THINKING TO HELP BUSINESSES DEVELOP AND IMPLEMENT AI SOLUTIONS. THEY HAVE HEAVILY DEDICATED TEAMS OF DESIGN THINKERS WHO WORK WITH BUSINESSES TO UNDERSTAND THEIR NEEDS AND DEVELOP SOLUTIONS THAT ARE BOTH INNOVATIVE AND USER-FRIENDLY.

HOW TO ADDRESS AI ETHICS

AI ETHICS			
Data Ethics	Ethical AI	AI Ethics	Business Ethics

Data Protection	Law Enforcement	Safety and Certification	Justice and Equality	Displacement of Labor	Taxation

The ethical discussion about the application of AI is the biggest challenge since many elements have to be taken into account, starting from the national legislation, the cultural context, and the organizational culture, up to the individual perception of each employee and decision-maker. However, there is always a balance between over-regulating ethical frameworks and stifling innovation. We recommend that each organization define an AI ethics framework to ensure that AI-powered solutions and innovation work are developed in a way that minimizes the risk of harm to relevant stakeholders. The framework must ensure that the AI technology being developed has appropriate characteristics and guardrails, for example, related to fairness, robustness, and explainability and that all employees (technical and non-technical) have the right tools and training to easily incorporate these characteristics into their activities. Every organization must ensure that the risks in the use of AI, in all dimensions (including internally, for other companies, and in collaboration of actors in an AI ecosystem), are adequately mitigated.

We recommend applying a multidisciplinary view in defining AI ethics, including technical AI knowledge and perception, ethical considerations, social science, familiarity with technology law, and business strategy know-how. Larger organizations might consider establishing an AI ethics board, led by the topic owner of AI ethics, with representatives from all the company's divisions and with decision-making power, visibility, and governance authority fully supported by the leadership team and senior manager.

Many companies have already initiated such boards in the past for the implementation of big data/analytics initiatives and can build on this approach, learnings, and principles. However, such a board should not only focus on risk mitigation but also encourage AI to be seen as a source of value and a strategic differentiator and not just a set of guardrails to be adhered to.

CORNERSTONES OF AI ETHICS FRAMEWORK

- Ensure to assess, audit, and mitigate risks related to AI holistically

- Work with interdisciplinary teams to consider all points of view

- Decide and communicate an AI ethics framework to all stakeholders

- Educate and guide employees at all levels and functions

- Leverage the AI ecosystem to plan, build, deploy, and manage AI

- Apply design thinking for AI adaption, change, and innovations

- Ensure that AI as a discipline is applied and perceived as fair, explainable, transparent, empowering, privacy-preserving, and robust

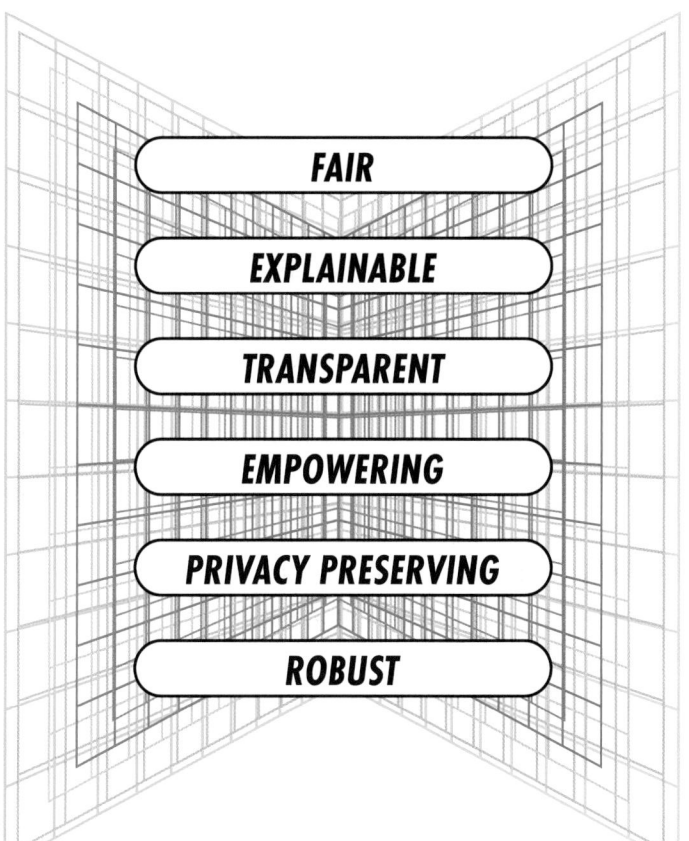

96% OF BUSINESS LEADERS USING GENERATIVE AI ARE PROACTIVELY BUILDING ETHICAL FRAMEWORKS FOR RESPONSIBLE AI USE (IBM STUDY).

- AI Ecosystems Ethics
- AI Ethics
- Data Ethics
- Business Ethics
- Ethical AI

NAVIGATING BIAS IN AI

One of the key concerns in AI ethics is bias. Bias can occur in AI systems when they are trained on data that is not representative of the population; this can lead to AI systems making unfair or discriminatory decisions. The consequences can be far-reaching, affecting everything from hiring processes and customer service to financial and medical decisions. The multifaceted aspects of bias in AI within organizational settings are complex and transversal. Therefore, decision-makers have to understand the implications and consequences properly. There is a multiplicity of biases derived from AI. The data upon which these systems are trained may be at the core of AI bias. AI algorithms can unwittingly perpetuate biases present in historical data. For example, we evaluated one of the most common AI image-generating systems to assess inherited biases. We created a prompt that creates an image for a variety of professions. We used the same prompt multiple times for each category, and the results were consistent. When prompted to generate an image of a nurse, for instance, the created image was always of a female, while for a doctor, the vast majority of generated images were for men. The same was true when prompted for a CEO; almost in all cases, the generated images depicted white men. The same bias permeated throughout the results relating to other professions and attributes, like maids, the unemployed, and many others.

EXAMPLES OF COMMON AI BIAS

Prompt: Doctor

Prompt: Maid

Prompt: CEO

Prompt: Unemployed

Another domain in which bias could present itself is in hiring. If past hiring decisions have favored certain demographics, an AI model trained to make hiring decisions may inadvertently favor those same demographics when screening new resumes, thereby perpetuating systemic bias. The same could apply when assessing merits and bonus systems in organizations. The significance of AI bias is perhaps most pronounced when applied to AI-assisted medical decision-making or in medical care, where the implications are substantially amplified.

The issue of bias in facial recognition systems is another issue that has become a prominent and concerning topic, gaining much attention recently. These systems are designed to identify and verify individuals by analyzing their unique features. These systems have been found to exhibit bias in various ways. One significant manifestation of bias is prejudice, which becomes evident when these algorithms struggle with recognizing individuals with darker

TO HARNESS THE FULL POTENTIAL OF AI WHILE MITIGATING ITS INHERENT BIASES, DEVELOPERS AND USERS MUST PRIORITIZE A PROACTIVE APPROACH, ENSURING DIVERSE TEAMS, DIVERSE DATA SOURCES, AND ETHICAL DATA COLLECTION PRACTICES.

skin tones. This bias can lead to misidentifications and can have a disproportionate impact on marginalized communities. Gender is another aspect of prejudice that's relevant to facial recognition technology. Many facial recognition algorithms exhibit diminished accuracy when processing the faces of females, especially when individuals are of color or present nonbinary gender expressions. Addressing bias in facial recognition systems is a challenge that requires implementing data collection methods that promote transparency in algorithmic processes and consider ethical implications. There are emerging initiatives aimed at improving the fairness and accuracy of these systems by diversifying the datasets used for training and developing inclusive algorithms. As face recognition technology continues to advance, it is essential to ensure that it is accompanied by a commitment to minimizing bias and upholding principles of fairness, equality, and safeguarding individual rights.

AI algorithms can also compound existing biases in other domains, even if the initial dataset is unbiased. This occurs when algorithms, through their design or optimization process, inadvertently favor certain outcomes. For instance, algorithms used to predict crime rates might disproportionately target minority communities if not calibrated appropriately.

However, to ensure that AI serves as a force for good, stakeholders from industry, government, and academia must collaborate to develop human-centric and equitable AI strategies, mitigating biases, managing automation's impact, and fostering a smooth transition into an AI-augmented future.

Another element is the choices users make within AI systems, which can introduce bias. Recommendation algorithms, like those on social media platforms, tend to show users content that aligns with users' existing beliefs and preferences. This can create and reinforce cognitive biases.

Addressing bias in AI requires an approach that covers crucial aspects. As a start, organizations need to examine their training data, looking out for any indications of bias. It is vital to use representative datasets to ensure the training of AI systems. Moreover, transparency in algorithms is crucial. AI models and algorithms should be designed with transparency and interpretability in mind, enabling examination and the ability to make adjustments to prevent unintended biases. Additionally, fostering diversity within AI development teams is essential as it brings a range of perspectives that can help mitigate bias. Regular audits of AI systems should be conducted proactively to identify and rectify any emerging biases. Establishing feedback mechanisms would also enable users to report behavior so that corrective action can be taken swiftly. In addition, adhering to defined frameworks should guide the entire process of developing and deploying AI systems while emphasizing fairness and equity in their applications.

THE RAPID ADVANCEMENT OF AI TECHNOLOGIES AND THEIR INCREASING INTEGRATION INTO VARIOUS ASPECTS OF SOCIETY NECESSITATE THE DEVELOPMENT AND IMPLEMENTATION OF ROBUST AI BIAS MITIGATION FRAMEWORKS. THESE FRAMEWORKS ARE CRUCIAL TO ADDRESS THE INHERENT BIASES THAT CAN BE EMBEDDED IN AI SYSTEMS AND ALGORITHMS, ENSURING THAT AI IS USED IN A FAIR, EQUITABLE, AND RESPONSIBLE MANNER.

Organizations need to remain watchful, constantly examining data, algorithms, and results to guarantee that their AI systems function as impartial, equitable tools. By embracing openness, inclusivity, and ethical values, organizations can leverage the potential of AI while mitigating any effects. Tackling bias in AI goes beyond being an obstacle; it is a duty and a societal necessity for future-oriented organizations.

A POTENTIAL AI BIAS MITIGATION FRAMEWORK

Awareness	"Fair Test"	AI Ethics Assessment	Implement	Monitoring
• Individual prejudices • Societal prejudices	• Test in closed environment • Ensure quality data check • Test in open environment with "Fair Test"	• Run Bias Impact assessment • Consider, for example fairness, explicability, transparency, empowering, and privacy preserving	• Implement in real-world environment • Prepare for monitoring	• Detect bias • Apply compensation measures when damage is detected • Feedback of the results of the monitoring into the awareness phase

The major and predominant AI players try to address bias with ethical frameworks. Google AI has, for example, developed a tool called Fairness Indicators, which helps identify and

A NEW AND ITERATIVE APPROACH TO DEALING WITH DISCRIMINATORY BIASES IN AI IS NEEDED.

mitigate bias in AI systems. Other players, like Microsoft, created a set of AI principles that guide the development and use of AI within the company. At the same time, IBM addresses the issue of bias with the IBM AI Ethics Guidelines, which are based on the principles of trust, transparency, accountability, fairness, and inclusion. For further developments in generative AI, it would be desirable to establish mandatory systems and an effective framework for bias mitigation.

Data cleansing, counterfactual comparisons, and fairness-aware algorithms are all tackling bias at its source. Explainable AI sheds light on decision-making, while federated learning protects privacy during collaborative learning. However, human oversight remains crucial, but these advancements offer promising tools to build trustworthy and equitable AI systems.

To mitigate the risks posed by scientific and pervasive uncertainties, model developers should work closely with the organizations that use them. Therefore, teams should ensure regular model updates and test and recalibrate model parameters against updated representative datasets to meet business objectives while maintaining desired performance targets and acceptable bias levels. Ensuring such a framework can only be done through voluntary adherence to the approach by the relevant players or strict regular frameworks, similar to those from other regulated industries.

HOW TO HANDLE AI AND DATA REGULATIONS

AI REGULATIONS

Transparency and Explainability	Fairness and Non-discrimination	Privacy and Security	Accountability and Liability

The capabilities of AI models are a big issue for governments, researchers, decision-makers, policymakers, and individuals. Governments around the world have enacted AI regulations. The European Union's AI Act, Canada's Artificial Intelligence and Data Act (AIDA), the US AI Bill of Rights and State Initiatives, and China's Algorithm Transparency and Promotion of AI Industry Development have been subject to show how the AI question is discussed in the context of their respective cultures, laws, and assumptions made.

The different approaches to AI regulation reflect the different views on the risks and benefits of AI. Some countries believe that AI poses a significant risk to society and that strict regulations are needed to mitigate those risks. Other countries believe that AI has the potential to be a powerful force for good and that regulations should not stifle innovation. While the AI Law focuses on a risk-based approach to the use of AI in both the private and public sectors, the AI Bill of Rights targets specific use cases. In 2023, the Chinese government began to enact a law regulating the use of algorithms for consumer marketing. It becomes evident that the scope of AI regulations varies from country to country. Some regulations only apply to certain types of AI, such as facial recognition or autonomous vehicles. Other regulations apply to all kinds of AI. However, the most significant difference in AI regulations globally is the level of detail and specificity. Some countries, such as those in the European Union, have adopted comprehensive regulations that address a wide range of issues. Other countries, such as the United States, have adopted more general regulations that leave more room for interpretation.

Amid the rapid evolution and adoption of AI tools, AI regulations and regulatory proposals are spreading almost as rapidly as AI applications, and it is recommended to keep an eye on the latest developments for a specific region and globally. The table below provides a snapshot of AI regulations and regulatory proposals in 2024.

AI REGULATIONS AS OF 2024

Region	Focus	Examples of policies/Laws
US federal	AI risk assessment	• **Algorithmic Accountability Act** • **Deep Fakes Accountability Act** • **Digital Services Oversight and Safety Act**
	AI bill of rights	• **White House Blueprint for an AI Bill of Rights**
	AI framework	• **NIST's AI Risk Management Framework**
US state and city	AI regulations	• **California, Connecticut, Texas, Illinois, Colorado, NYC are among states and cities with laws or bills to regulate AI**
Global	High-risk AI applications	• **European Union's Artificial Intelligence Act**
	Generative AI regulation	• **China's proposed Administrative Measures for Generative Artificial Intelligence Service**
	Risk mitigation, transparency	• **Canadian Parliament's Artificial Intelligence and Data Act**
	Developing regulations	• **At least eight other countries across the Americas and Asia**

Based on 2023 AI regulations, researchers at Stanford University and the Institute for Human-Centered Artificial Intelligence extracted twenty-two requirements from the EU AI Act, categorized them, and then created a five-point rubric for twelve of the twenty-two requirements. Overall, the researchers noted that there was quite a bit of variability in model compliance across providers, with some providers scoring less than 25% (AI21 Labs, Aleph Alpha, Anthropic) and only one provider scoring at least 75% (Hugging Face/BigScience) at present being compliant with the applied regulatory framework. The research findings show that vendors and users of generative AI technologies still have a long way to go. Legislators, system developers, governments, and organizations must work together to address these important issues. In addition, to support environmental, social, and governance (ESG), a standardized framework for measuring and reporting energy consumption should likewise be established. Above all, AI systems must be secure, respect privacy, and uphold human values.

IMPACT OF AI REGULATION ON BUSINESS AND INNOVATION SUCCESS

The impact of regulation on companies is twofold. On one hand, clear legislation and regulatory frameworks help guide the development of AI applications and the realization of use cases. On the other hand, the effort for compliance, data management, and other privacy concerns is increased.

According to experts we have been working with, burdensome regulations on AI technology could stifle innovation, benefit big tech companies, and hinder the widespread benefits of AI to society. Instead of regulating AI as a whole, many of the experts advocate for a case-by-case approach, focusing on regulating the outcomes or effects of AI in specific sectors. While some suggest the need for a standard set of AI-specific rules, others emphasize the importance of governing the underlying processes and data in AI systems to ensure fairness, accountability, and safety. However, the overarching goal for all of them is to ensure AI is used responsibly and ethically, maximizing its potential to address global challenges and improve people's lives.

Since 2023, we have observed some impact of AI regulations related to the complexity of business, compliance costs, vendor selection, and internal coordination efforts to provide the appropriate guidance and policies for employees. For many companies, it was extremely challenging to understand how old laws applied to new algorithms. In many cases, companies had to hire and get advice from AI law specialists to ensure compliance in the workplace and interactions with customers and users. We recommend keeping up to date on the increasing regulation of AI worldwide. Regulation of AI is increasing globally, and interest in AI oversight will continue to grow over time. When developing new AI systems, companies should anticipate the constraints that may arise from upcoming regulations, such as conditional market access, increased liability, or data use. Companies should be prepared to adapt to increasing restrictions as more regulations are enacted and new causes of action are created or recognized in some jurisdictions.

A well-defined AI strategy and defined ethical principles help companies stay focused on their innovation missions. While coaching teams in AI projects, it has also become mandatory to ensure that everyone in the team perceives AI with clear eyes and without being seduced by the hype of ChatGPT, Gemini, and Ernie.

CREATE TRANSPARENCY ABOUT RISK LEVEL TO INNOVATION TEAMS

Based on national and global regulations, risk levels might be defined to guide teams – for example, not allowing to engage with any social scoring initiatives governments are running or creating AI to harm or kill human beings. Risks aligned to the EU regulations might include products already covered by specific EU product safety legislation, such as machinery, toys, radio equipment, cars and other types of vehicles, and medical devices, or used in certain contexts, such as safety in the management and operation of critical infrastructures, human resources, and creditworthiness assessments. Other risk levels might be categorized with minimal risks, using, for example, LLMs for creating AI-enabled video games. Certain low-risk AI systems, like deepfakes, might be subject to harmonized transparency rules in the near future and need readjustments from time to time.

EXAMPLE OF DEFINED RISK LEVELS

MINIMAL RISKS

- Permitted with no obligations
- e.g. spam filter, AI-enabled video games

LIMITED RISKS

- Permitted subject only to transparency obligations
- e.g. deepfakes, chatbots

HIGH RISK

- Permitted subject to conformity assessment and obligations
- e.g. recruitment, credit scoring, safety components in critical infrastructure

UNACCEPTABLE RISK

- Prohibited
- e.g. unethical application of social scoring beyond core social benefits

WHEN AI RISKS REARED THEIR HEADS, COLLABORATION – NOT SOLITUDE – PROVED THE KEY TO UNLOCKING SOLUTIONS. CERTIFIED VENDORS AND TOP-NOTCH LEGAL MINDS, HAND IN HAND, BECAME THE DE-RISKING SHIELD.

 **Download AI Regulation Canvas**

CHECKLIST REGULATION

As your company explores incorporating AI applications, it's crucial to delve deeper than the potential benefits and ask the hard questions that ensure responsible and ethical implementation. This means looking beyond technical feasibility and understanding the impact on data privacy, legal implications, potential biases, and employee well-being.

- What are the specific AI applications that your company is considering or using?
  _____
  _____

- How will the AI applications be used?
  _____

- What data will be used to train and operate the AI applications?
  _____

- Who will have access to the AI applications and the data that they use?
  _____

- How will the AI applications be monitored and controlled?
  _____
  _____

- What are the legal implications of using AI?
  _____
  _____

- How will the company mitigate the risks associated with using AI?
  _____

- What are the policies and procedures for dealing with AI-related incidents?
  _____
  _____

- How are employees informed/trained about risk levels/regulatory boundaries?
  _____
  _____

- How are modifications to applicable laws and regulations monitored?
  _____
  _____

- How do we ensure that AI applications in use are not biased or discriminatory?
  _____
  _____

- What is the accountability for actions created by AI applications?
  _____
  _____

- How can AI be used to explore new products, services, and experiences and not just used to replace jobs?
  _____
  _____

IN THE AGE OF AI, DECISION-MAKERS MUST RISE TO THE CHALLENGE AND ASK THE BOLD QUESTIONS ACROSS THE ENTIRE OPERATING MODEL THAT WILL UNLOCK THE TRANSFORMATIVE POWER OF AI FOR BUSINESS SUCCESS.

 ⬇ **Download AI Regulation Checklist**

SUMMARY: AI FOR BUSINESS LEADERS

To make an impact with AI, many layers of a future operating model must be considered, and the appropriate frameworks must be applied to leverage AI for innovation. Regardless of the framework, strategic approach, and industry specifics that are chosen, the following summary of questions is of relevance to decision-makers and innovation and AI teams. Within the operating model, technical tools, algorithms, and skills are equally important to AI strategy, culture, and the applied mindset to build the solutions themselves. Once an updated and more flexible operating model emerges, it becomes a game changer that revolutionizes traditional approaches through data-driven innovation, automation, and scalable processes. The shift in management dynamics has proven to unlock efficiency, improve decision-making, and accelerate growth. In many cases, employees take on new roles as they design and collaborate with a software-automated and algorithm-driven organization.

Company		
	Strategy	What is the AI strategy?
	Leadership	What is the communicated vision for AI innovation?
	Capabilities	What capabilities and skills are needed to execute AI strategy?
	Culture	Is the organization's culture supportive of AI innovation
	Consequences	What are the potential consequences of AI innovation?
	Risks	How to mitigate potential risks?
	Collaboration	Who are the stakeholders needed to collaborate with?
	AI Ecosystem	What are potential AI ecosystem actors?
	Measure	How is the impact of the AI opportunity measured?

Go-to-Market		
	Problem Definition	What is the problem that you are trying to solve with AI?
	Customer Needs	What are the customer/needs?
	Prototyping	What are potential ideas and solutions?
	Define Opportunity	What is the solution provided with AI?
	Data Collection	How is the data collected to address the problem?
	Build the Model	How is the model built to solve the problem?
	Business Case	What are the benefits and costs?
	Deploy the Model	How to deploy the model?

Infrastructure		
	AI Technologies	What kind of AI Technology is most appropriate?
	Data	What kind of data from which systems are needed?
	AI Value Chain	What foundation models, applications, and services are needed?
	Processes	What processes are automated?
	Functions	How are functions be scaled to accommodate future growth?
	Interoperability	How is the AI system interacting with existing infrastructure?
	Data Management	How is data accessed, processed, and stored for AI learning?

Much evidence has been outlined showing that AI provides a competitive advantage across all industries, and a well-defined AI strategy, including discussions about capabilities and ethics, should be at the forefront of any business transformation. However, having everything in place is not a guarantee for success, but addressing the appropriate questions will significantly improve the likelihood of realizing new market opportunities.

Transformation leaders must establish an organizational structure that ensures the AI ethics, AI ambitions, and corresponding datasets are understood and the benefits are clear. The ultimate objective of using AI should be to increase business value faster by optimizing solutions and processes, improving decision-making, or unleashing skilled resources to focus on more valuable activities.

Implementing a company's vision for AI requires a framework that, at its core, drives innovation through a mechanism to understand the problem space, develop ideas, prioritize, test concepts or fail, and select (MVP) toward a program of transformation and industrialization. The mindset that we are most familiar with from the design thinking and lean startup spheres is particularly suitable for this purpose.

EFFECTIVELY HARNESSING THE POWER OF AI DEMANDS A HOLISTIC APPROACH THAT EXTENDS BEYOND SIMPLY LICENSING AI-POWERED TOOLS LIKE MICROSOFT COPILOT. BUSINESSES MUST EMBRACE A STRATEGIC FRAMEWORK THAT INTEGRATES AI INTO THEIR OPERATIONS AND CULTURE TO DRIVE EFFICIENCY GAINS, INNOVATION, AND SUSTAINED BUSINESS SUCCESS.

As we focus on exploration work for AI and innovation, the important innovation work must also be provided with capabilities that improve decision-making to create value, momentum, and credibility; this is the only way to ensure that stakeholders and budgets are not diverted to other urgent priorities to just use AI for efficiency gains (exploit). However, the best framework to apply AI for innovation will depend on the specific context of the organization and the innovation challenge that it is facing. All of the frameworks and recommended tools mentioned in this book can provide a valuable starting point for organizations that are looking to use AI to drive innovation. Nevertheless, these recommendations should be adapted to the respective circumstances, culture, and other prevailing conditions.

Dr. Saeed Aldhaheri

→ Futurist, AI ethicist, and thought leader
Director, Center for Futures Studies,
University of Dubai
President, Robotics and Automation
Society of the UAE

THE FUTURE OF PRIVACY, AI ETHICS, AND RESPONSIBLE AI

How impact has been generated with AI in the last 10 years and which benefits can be realized through a strong AI strategy in the future have already been described in detail in this chapter. One topic that particularly concerns us at the Center of Future Studies is how to deal with the ethical issues to ensure AI's positive impact on society, which includes privacy and data protection. A Gartner survey (2023) shows that 40% of organizations have experienced an AI privacy breach, with only 25% being malicious. With the current move into generative AI, privacy and ethical incidents are expected to more than double, according to the 2023 AI index report from Stanford University. It seems that current AI systems that were developed with little oversight to assess the impact on privacy and other ethical issues might suffer major consequences once AI regulations become more established.

At the same time, increased expectations about transparency and consumer demand for user rights drive the need for a centralized privacy user experience (UX). AI tech developers must bring together all aspects of the privacy UX, such as notices, cookies, consent management, and subject rights request handling, into one self-service portal. Also, new privacy-enhancing computation (PEC) techniques – protecting data in use – are a growing trend that could provide a solution to privacy issues in the future. Implementing true "privacy by design" in AI and having responsible data governance practices have the potential to reduce AI privacy-related problems. Responsible data governance is essential to address the privacy issue and prevent societal harm.

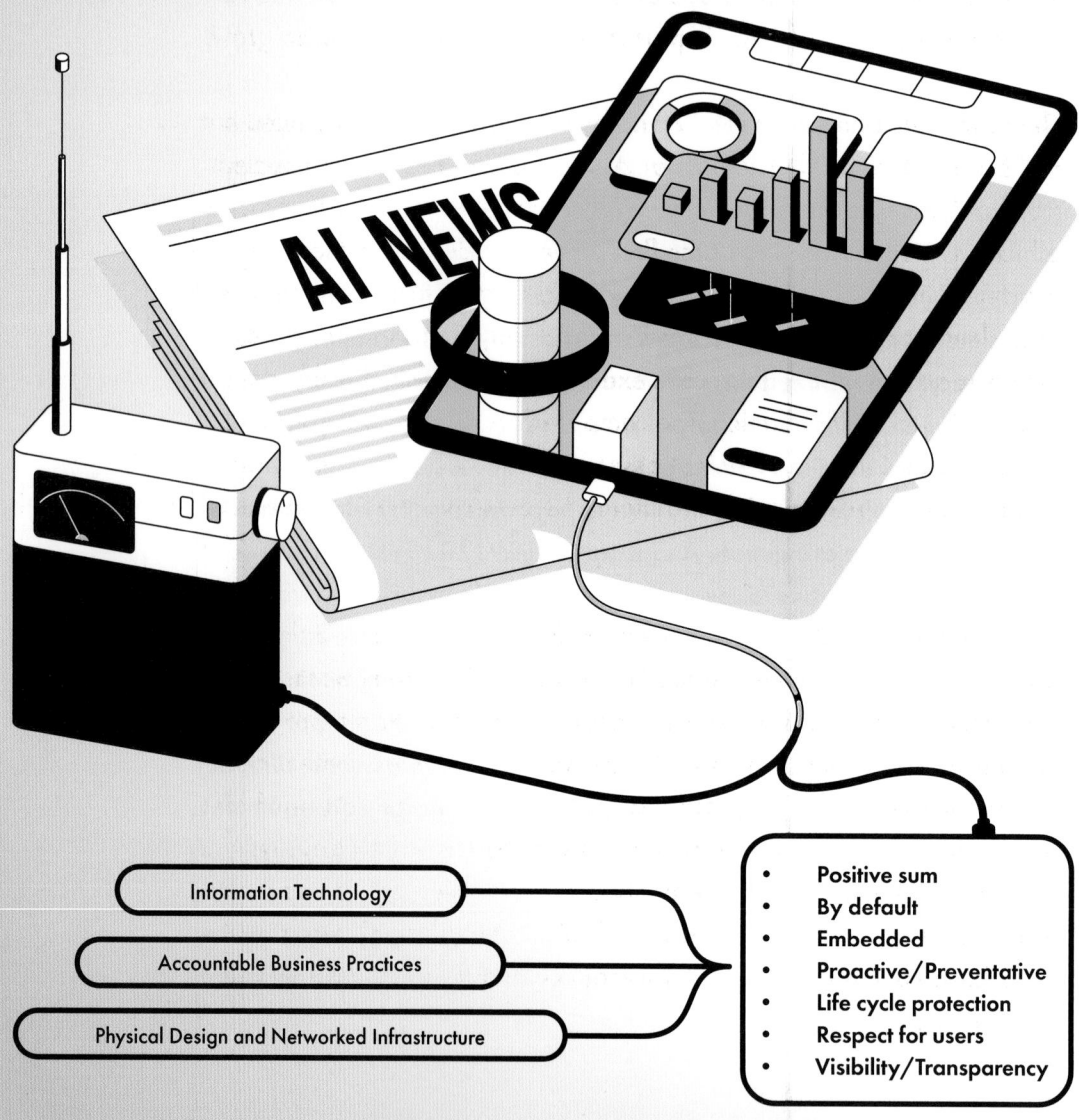

Information Technology

Accountable Business Practices

Physical Design and Networked Infrastructure

- Positive sum
- By default
- Embedded
- Proactive/Preventative
- Life cycle protection
- Respect for users
- Visibility/Transparency

We have learned from the most recent studies that AI and generative AI pose many risks to individuals and society at large. These include bias and discrimination, privacy and data protection, generating harmful content, misinformation and fake news, hallucination, human manipulation, copyright infringement, and risk of unemployment and workforce displacement due to automation. The latest report from Europol (2023) estimated that as much as 90% of online content may be synthetically generated by AI by 2026. This adds to the rise of disinformation that undermines public trust in AI, which the United Nations raised a concern about. The increasing prevalence of risks associated with AI is already causing harm in society, with numerous cases being registered in courts worldwide.

As AI becomes more widespread and algorithms are integrated into various aspects of our lives, the importance of AI ethics continues to grow.

The aforementioned concept, "ethics by design," is rarely practiced but will be a differentiating factor for AI technologies in gaining societal trust and acceptance in the future. This concept is intended to prevent ethical issues from arising in the first place by addressing them during the development stage rather than trying to fix them later in the process. Tech developers can achieve this by proactively using the principles as system requirements. A good case example is the responsible-by-design approach used by Telefonica. The company trained its people on AI ethics, developed impactful ethical assessment practices, and established responsible AI governance and thought-leadership endorsement and responsible AI culture.

Tech companies such as IBM, Accenture, Microsoft, Google, Salesforce, and many others have developed their own AI ethics frameworks, which are based on principles of fairness, privacy, transparency, interpretability, security, and accountability. UNESCO also developed recommendations on the ethics of AI that represent a global agreement on AI principles that need to be operationalized in the development and deployment of AI technologies to achieve trustworthy AI. These ethics codes and frameworks are good but not a silver bullet without compliance practices embedded in responsible AI governance and enforced by policy and regulations.

Technical assessment toolboxes and platforms covering ethical assessment now exist and have become more widely available to support responsible AI development. What is lacking, however, is adequate governance mechanisms that empower ethics teams, emphasize responsibility and accountability, engage third-party auditing, implement red-teaming exercises to uncover unforeseen issues, and have leadership endorsement. BCG's Responsible AI Study (2023) found that the failure rate of AI systems was reduced by 9% in companies that achieve significant responsible achievements before scaling compared to those that don't. Tech firms and decision-makers that invest and establish responsible AI governance will reap the benefits in the future.

The Partnership on AI and the Global Partnership on Responsible AI are examples of a multi-stakeholder approach that fosters collaboration among governments, industry, academia, and civil society to address AI challenges responsibly. The adoption of available AI ethical standards by tech developers will be another differentiating factor for acceptance and use by corporations and government organizations. Few standards exist now for adoption, including the NIST AI Risk Management Framework, ISO standard on Trustworthiness in AI, and IEEE Standards Project.

However, it is not only the decision-makers' and developers' but also the users' responsibility to use AI ethically and maturely, especially in this era of generative AI. Organizations are now developing comprehensive generative AI use policies to address the ethical and safe use of generative AI to prevent any future mishaps. The World Economic Forum (WEF) also stresses on educating and reskilling the workforce and improving public AI literacy to make AI basics and ethics part of curricula in schools and organizations' core training agenda. Establishing an AI-literate society is foreseen to be a crucial part of improving AI ethical development and use for the betterment of society.

AS THE WORLD GRAPPLES WITH THE RAPID ADVANCEMENT OF AI, COUNTRIES DEVELOPING AI REGULATIONS CAN DRAW VALUABLE INSIGHTS FROM THE EU'S GROUNDBREAKING RISK-BASED APPROACH, WHICH PRIORITIZES MITIGATING POTENTIAL HARM AND PROMOTING RESPONSIBLE AI DEVELOPMENT. BY ADOPTING A SIMILAR FRAMEWORK, COUNTRIES CAN FOSTER A FUTURE WHERE AI IS HARNESSED FOR THE BENEFIT OF SOCIETY WHILE SAFEGUARDING HUMAN RIGHTS AND UPHOLDING ETHICAL PRINCIPLES.

Unemployment and job displacement due to AI and automation might be another ethical challenge facing governments soon. Many companies have already started firing staff and replacing them with AI. Currently, governments are focusing on policies and strategies to mitigate the negative impact on the workforce. Regulating AI technologies is important to address the current and short-term risks of AI as well as the future catastrophic risks that many scientists and experts warn about. The lag of regulations, however, opens doors for more AI mishaps, while self-regulation may not be sufficient. The EU AI Act is the only comprehensive risk-based regulation that awaits to be endorsed and enforced while it is debated whether it will stifle innovation or provide legal certainty and build trust. Thoughtful implementation can achieve both innovation and trustworthiness. As other countries develop their own AI regulations, they can learn from and adapt the EU's novel risk-based approach to foster responsible and trustworthy AI.

RESPONSIBLE AI x GLOBAL

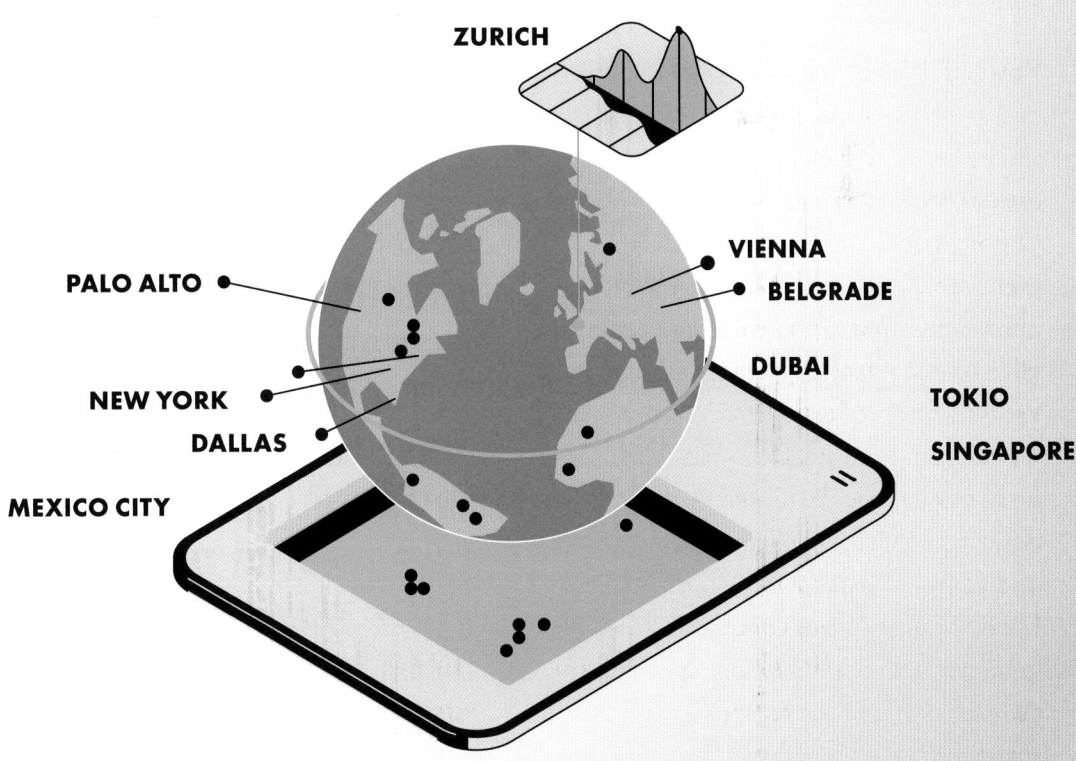

KEY TAKEAWAYS

→ A well-designed AI strategy will help maximize the potential of AI to increase productivity and transform the business.

→ Decision-makers must understand and mitigate the risks, learn through hands-on action and exploration, embrace change, and take the initiative to disrupt existing models.

→ The greatest potential of AI can be exploited if employee enthusiasm is included in the potential analysis. This involves analyzing jobs to be done, identifying areas where AI can bring the greatest benefit, and moving from publicly available to proprietary models.

→ New forms of collaboration should be explored, such as AI ecosystems that enable companies to make sense of AI models across all sectors and application scenarios.

→ *Building the appropriate skills and capabilities helps to fully exploit the potential of AI in the short and medium term as well as to protect employees from replacement.*

→ *The saying seems to be true – a technologically skilled human is likely to be far more productive than either a human without technology or technology devoid of human influence.*

→ *AI ethics and robust regulations are paramount to ensuring the responsible and beneficial development of AI. It is therefore imperative to continuously monitor and engage with the latest advancements in AI ethics and regulations to shape a future where AI empowers humanity.*

PART 3

WHAT TOOLS AND METHODS SUPPORT AI ACTIVITIES?

WRONG TOOLS, WASTED TIME. RIGHT TOOLS, EXPONENTIAL CLIMB. INVEST IN THE RIGHT TOOLS AND METHODS FOR YOUR JOURNEY.

HOW TO LEVERAGE
THE AI VALUE CHAIN

The rapid pace of change in AI makes any discussion about specific tools and conclusions obsolete within weeks. However, the potential of this technology requires that we strive to codify some principles, even as the AI world moves fast. Decision-makers who want to harness the potential of AI by developing products and services must be agile and remain aware of the changing landscape. Primary considerations of the AI value chain rely on so-called foundation models. These models have triggered an entire value chain aiming to improve and utilize the technology. Foundational models are typically trained on massive amounts of data and require high computing power to train AI models. For example, training GPT-4o, which has 10 trillion parameters, costs approximately USD 260 billion and would have taken over 20,00 years if it was training on a single GPU. These foundation models are already being leveraged in products and services in multiple domains and will continue to create new value. GPT-4o and its successors have introduced significant improvements and abilities across many uses. For example, GPT-4 supports image uploads, and the ChatGPT app supports voice commands through Whisper integration. GPT 4 Turbo, for ChatGPT, already has an up-to-date knowledge base, which is a significant improvement from its previous versions.

NO MASSIVE BREAKTHROUGH IS NEEDED TO IMPROVE CURRENT AI APPLICATIONS AS THEY ARE ADEQUATELY SERVED BY ESTABLISHED NEURAL NETS AND TRANSFORMER ARCHITECTURE. HOWEVER, IF WE WANT TO ACHIEVE AGI, OTHER AVENUES MIGHT NEED TO BE EXPLORED.

This advanced model can analyze and comprehend large amounts of data, the equivalent of 300 pages from a book, and produce highly accurate responses. Its capabilities are not just limited to text; it can also interpret image prompts and generate code in programming languages. Additionally, users can create and personalize their ChatGPT bots, referred to as GPTs. Users may fine-tune these bots for many tasks, providing a tailored AI experience. However, the foundation model landscape isn't alone in its rapid evolution. Alongside the GPTs, other exciting tools are emerging. Google's LaMDA, known for its conversational fluency, continues to learn and refine its ability to engage in natural dialogue. Jurassic-1 Jumbo is boasting parameters and pushes the boundaries of text generation, while BLOOM, a European-led initiative, offers a multilingual foundation model fostering diversity and accessibility. Examples like these in AI highlight how the technology is pushing the boundaries of what AI can achieve.

THE BASICS OF THE AI VALUE CHAIN

SERVICES

- Knowledge services on how to leverage generative AI related to reinforcement learning, training, and feedback.

APPLICATIONS

- Different products related to B2B and B2C as well as B2B2C use cases based on foundation models or customized to specific end-user scenarios.

MODEL HUBS AND ML OPERATIONS

- Mainly hosting and management of foundation models with the aim to fine-tune and align applications and foundation models.

FOUNDATION MODELS

- Model builder provides the foundations on which generative AI applications can be built. Models are based on a variety of datasets, e.g. Falcon, FLAN, LlaMa.

CLOUD COMPUTING

- Cloud platforms such as Amazon, SageMaker, and Managed Kubernetes provide access to computer hardware.

HARDWARE AND ACCELERATORS

- Utilization of accelerator chips from NIVIDA GPUs, AWS, Trainium, Google, TPU, etc. optimized for running and learning the models.

TRANSFORMER MODELS, AGI, AND OTHER BELIEFS

All LLMs aim to mimic the human brain and inch closer to achieving real generative AI. For example, transformer technologies allow users to create plausible and sophisticated

GENERATIVE AI IS SPEARHEADING THE DEMOCRATIZATION OF AI, MAKING POWERFUL TOOLS WIDELY AVAILABLE.

text, images, and computer code at a level that closely imitates human capabilities. Current AI systems can now perform a multitude of tasks simultaneously, such as summarizing, translating, searching, and retrieving information. This ability to multitask represents a significant advancement from initial systems, where the capability was nonexistent or required highly specialized models → See a simplified example of how LLM works on pages 157–159. The real revolution is yet to come and goes far beyond LLM, as transformer models can recognize and predict recurring designs or patterns, from pixels in an image with tools like Dall-E, Midjourney, and Stable Diffusion, to computer code with generators like GitHub CoPilot, Amazon Code Whisperer, Cody, and Bito. These advanced models can even predict notes in music and DNA in proteins to help design drug molecules. These models will continue to evolve and increase in modalities, allowing them to be used in multiple applications and create value at scale.

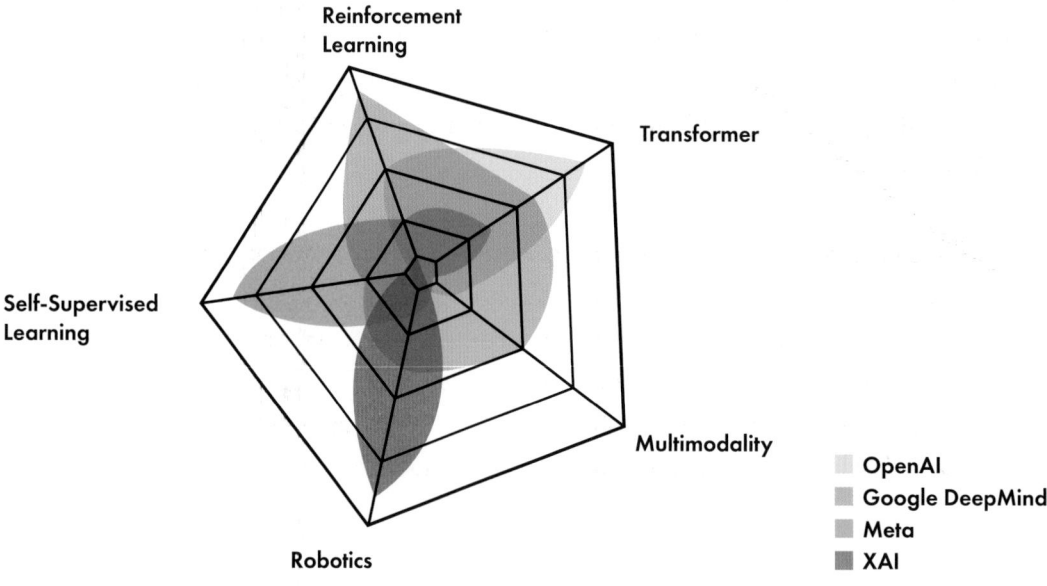

OpenAI
Google DeepMind
Meta
XAI

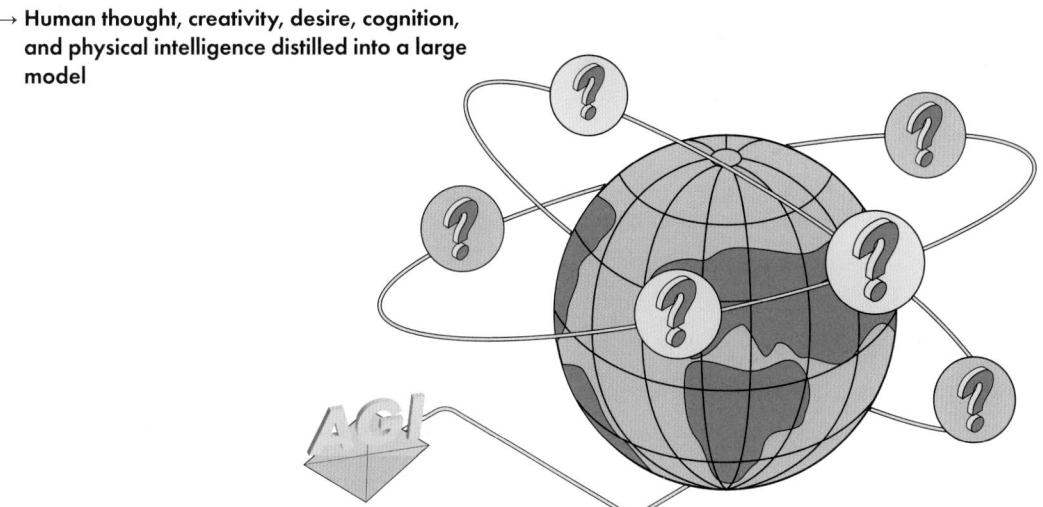

→ Human thought, creativity, desire, cognition, and physical intelligence distilled into a large model

However, the path toward achieving AGI is winding with many crossroads. A multitude of different avenues may lead to AGI. From OpenAI's point of view, GPT-10 or earlier releases might evolve into true AGI, building many transformer models. Google DeepMind's path to AGI relies on reinforcement learning, a method that learns through trial and error. With models such as AlphaFold, AlphaZero, and others, DeepMind also believes that maximizing total reward may be sufficient to understand intelligence and its associated capabilities and that reward may be sufficient to achieve AGI. However, some experts raise concerns that supervised learning and reinforcement learning will not lead to AGI because these approaches are inadequate in developing systems capable of reasoning with commonsense knowledge about the world.

Meta might take a different approach, focusing on self-supervised learning as the way toward AGI. This method does not rely on data labeled by humans for training purposes; instead, it trains on entirely unlabeled or new data. And yes, there have been promising results with self-supervised language under-standing models, libraries, and frameworks that have surpassed traditional and fully supervised models.

xAI's path toward AGI seeks to create a "good AGI" with the purpose of "understanding the universe." While others are working toward disembodied AI, xAI's investment in robotics is likely a hint that a more physical embodiment of AI could be the answer. A working prototype of the Optimus robot, pow-ered by the same self-driving computer that drives Tesla cars, was unveiled at Tesla in 2022. xAI believes that these advances will one day contribute to AGI.

HOW LLM WORKS

This section dives into how LLMs operate, focusing on understanding context and generating results based on prompts. We'll use a clear example: "Writing a book about AI and innovation." Here, we'll break down how the LLM processes and utilizes words, along with exploring the concept of self-attention. This will provide a foundation for grasping how LLMs generate text that considers context and builds upon the information you provide.

- To write text, LLMs translate words into a language it understands.

  "We write a new book about AI"

- Blocks of words are broken down into **tokens**.

  "We write a new book about AI"

- To understand a word's meaning (in this case, the word "write") LLMs observe it in context using enormous sets of training data, taking note of **nearby words**.

  "We write a new book about AI"
  "I write every day on my book"
  "write the first last name here"
  "Can ____ you give me an endorsement"

- Finally, LLMs analyze a huge set of words found **alongside** "write" in the training data, as well as those words that **were not** found near it.

  "write down"
  "write simply"
  " ____ your"

- By processing this set of words, a vector or list of values is created and is adjusted based on each word's proximity to "write" in the training data.

  write `.04 .19 .15 .00 .00 .00 .21 .00 .11 .66 .05`

  0   1

- The model will spot clusters of pronouns or modes of writing while quantifying all words.

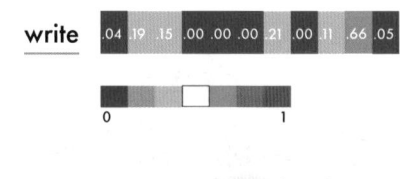

Textbooks
Cookbooks
Playbooks
I
we
they
with
on
in

LLM x TRANSFORMER

- A key concept of the transformer architecture is self-attention. It allows LLMs to understand relationships between words.

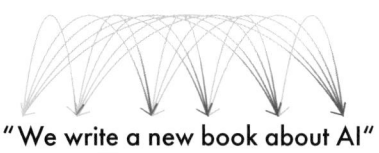

"We write a new book about AI"

✓

"We write a new book about AI"

- By assessing the whole sentence at once, the transformer is able to understand that "write" is being used in the context of writing a book.

physically create text

We started writing down some ideas for the new book before reflecting on our experiences from industry projects to write about our learnings in the field of AI and innovation.

- It is also able to distinguish between different meanings of the word "write."

Expressions, authors text

Michael Lewrick

Xersped m올d a nus et renis et dolorrom, tem untibusaecte magniet odissit eseque el modi con nihillore quam as moloriore perum lab id eaqui bero voloren ihillor estrumquam dislquo inum sa qui si vollent.
Hendiriis quo corit lam delescia dit, aut labor audis utatiberum dolorporpor ad modis sediorp orepresent estrum haria velit ipis dem idem mdit ipsom etur, hicium quodi con pres dus eturis alicia **Digital Transformation** Ibus as sunt, inctoribus et qui odipsundae pornost ipitat evendipsa doles

- The self-attention for language processing increases the more it is scaled up. It allows LLMs to understand context from beyond sentence boundaries, giving the model a greater understanding of how and when a word is used – adding, for example, the name of one of the authors.

Michael Lewrick and his co-author are writing a new book that teaches readers how to apply design thinking to identify AI use cases.

Design Thinking

Xersped molda nus et renis et dolorrum tem untibusaecte magniet odissit eseque el modi con nihillore quam as moloriore perum lab id eaqui bero voloren ihillor estrumquam dislquo inum sa qui si vollent.
Hendiriis quo corit lam delescia dit, aut labor audis utatiberum dolorporpor ad modis sediorp orepresent estrum haria velit ipis dem endit ipsom etur, sum hicium quodi con pres dus eturis alicia sit licabor magnale plab id quiae. Ibus as sunt, inctoribus et qui odipsundae porpost ipitot evendipsa doles

CREATING PROMPTS IN GEMINI, CHATGPT, ERNIE, AND OTHER LANGUAGE MODELS

Prompt engineering has become the art and science of designing prompts to elicit desired responses from LLMs. The following example will demonstrate how prompts can be used to process and generate human-like text, translate languages, create code, write different kinds of creative content, or answer questions in an informative way. As LLMs learn from large datasets, it enables them to improve over time, providing insights based on identified patterns.

A well-crafted prompt can guide an LLM to generate the desired output, while a poorly crafted prompt can lead to irrelevant, nonsensical, or even harmful responses. In general, prompts should clearly state the desired output and be easy for the LLM to understand. It is essential to ensure the data is of good quality, as the information given to the LLM influences the output. More specific information helps the LLM to generate a more accurate and relevant response. Consequently, the prompt should include all of the information that the LLM needs, for example, about the task, the context, the desired tone, and the desired format → see prompt cheat sheet on pages 166–167.

ACTING AS A (ROLE) PERFORM (TASK) IN (FORMAT)

EXAMPLE OF APPLICATION SCENARIO FOR LARGE LANGUAGE MODELS

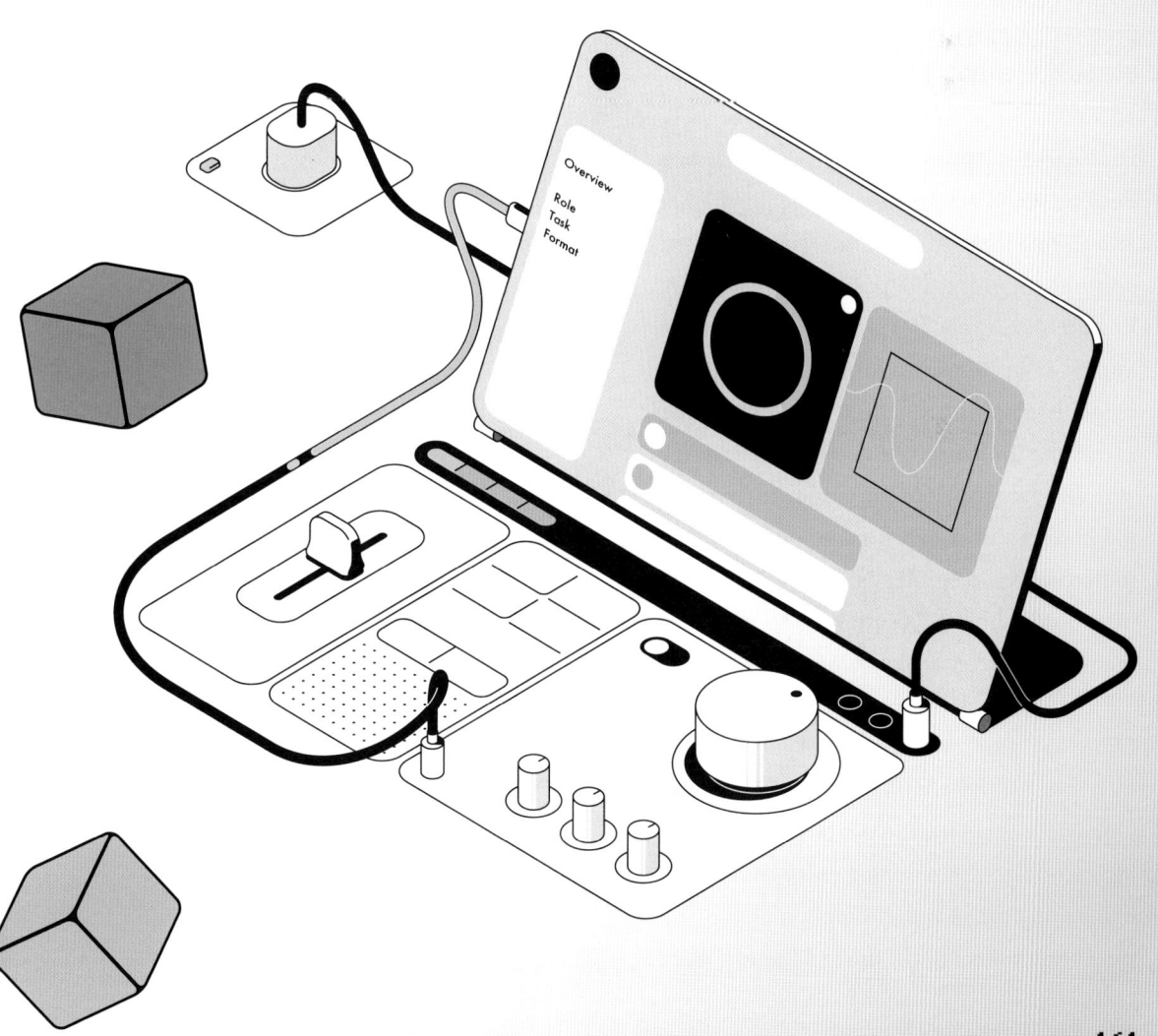

(RE)EVOLUTION OF MARKETING

LLMs are being infused into marketing in various ways to improve efficiency and outcomes and streamline processes. Marketers can use existing customer experience data to generate precise business insights through AI tools that utilize ML and NLP. These tools give LLMs an advantage in better understanding customer needs and preferences, leading to more targeted and personalized marketing strategies. Using AI tools to analyze customer data can also streamline and measure the effectiveness of marketing campaigns and provide valuable insights to modify the approach or message accordingly.

For example, AI prompts can help marketers develop email subject lines, resulting in higher engagement rates and more personalized content for different potential customers. This approach solidifies stronger connections, improves customer loyalty, and increases sales. It also ensures that marketing messages are delivered to the right audience with the appropriate message, increasing the chances of conversion. AI-powered ad generators help create multiple ad iterations based on input and learn how to optimize them for sales and conversions.

One way marketers can start the AI journey is to use a common LLM like ChatGPT, Gemini, or Ernie to create a targeted marketing campaign. Core principles for using LLMs, like being precise with prompts, including all pertinent information, and engaging after the first response with further inquiries, seem to be self-evident for extreme users but might be good advice for marketers new to LLMs.

For this example, we use LLM to generate a marketing campaign for our new book on AI and innovation. We outline some possible prompts for email marketing:

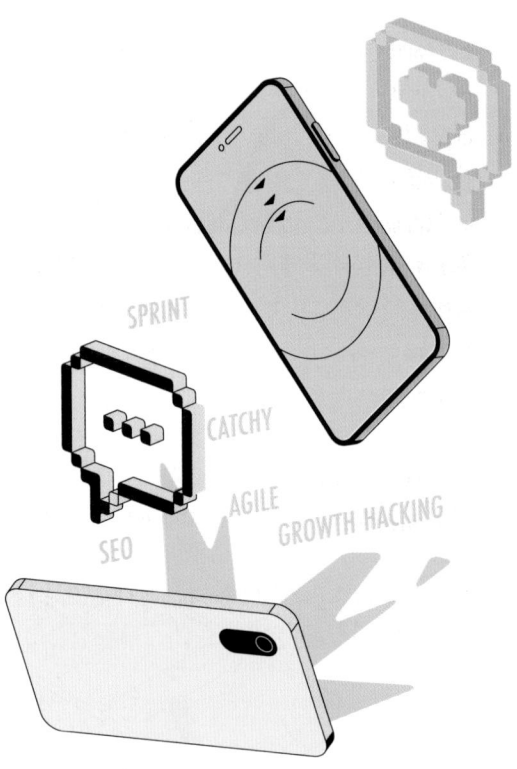

"YOU ARE AN EXPERIENCED MARKETING EXEC-UTIVE. IN LESS THAN 50 CHARACTERS, GEN-ERATE AN ENGAGING AND CREATIVE SUBJECT EMAIL HEADLINE FOR A NEW BOOK ABOUT AI AND INNOVATION THAT HIGHLIGHTS THE UNIQUE SELLING PROPOSITION OF BEING HANDS-ON, SUPPORTING TO TRANSFORM YOUR BUSINESS, AND ACHIEVING COMPETITIVE ADVANTAGES."

LLM

Here is an engaging and creative subject email headline for a new book about AI and innovation:

"AI INNOVATION: HANDS-ON TRANSFORMATION FOR COMPETITIVE ADVANTAGE" (49 CHARACTERS)

This headline is clear, concise, and informative, and it accurately reflects the unique selling proposition of the book. It also uses strong, active verbs like "transform" and "achieve" to create a sense of excitement and possibility. Additionally, the headline is relevant to the target audience, which is business leaders who are interested in using AI to transform their businesses and achieve competitive advantages.

→ **ALTERNATIVE OPTIONS:**
INNOVATE WITH AI: A HANDS-ON GUIDE

AI INNOVATION: TRANSFORM YOUR BUSINESS AND GAIN A COMPETITIVE EDGE

PROMPT:

"PLEASE CREATE A PERSONALIZED SUBJECT LINE BASED ON CUSTOMER PURCHASE HISTORY ON BOOKS FROM BOTH AUTHORS."

LLM

A NEW HANDS-ON GUIDE FOR YOU: APPLYING DESIGN THINKING FOR AI

Imagine providing a language model with a clear picture about the marketing campaign: the desired subject line for your email (e.g. "Hands-on guide to supporting business transformation"), the voice and experience you want it to embody (a seasoned marketing executive), and the core content (a book on AI and innovation, with a subtitle highlighting its value proposition, such as "Transform Your Business and Outpace Competition with Generative AI"). By providing these details as a prompt, you empower the language model to generate targeted and effective marketing copy that resonates with your audience.

Different scripts can be used for other marketing purposes with prompts like:

> "WRITE A 1,000-WORD ADVERTISEMENT SCRIPT ABOUT ..."

> "GENERATE A SOCIAL MEDIA POST FOR LINKEDIN THAT INCLUDES ..."

> "CREATE A MARKETING CAMPAIGN ABOUT ... TARGETING ... INCLUDE KEY MESSAGES AND SELECT THE OPTIMUM MEDIA CHANNELS FOR HIGHER ENGAGEMENTS."

We can take this further and create more complex targeted marketing campaigns.

Example prompt:

> CREATE AN ENGAGING SCRIPT FOR EACH OF OUR CUSTOMERS BASED ON PRIOR ENGAGEMENTS TO HIGHLIGHT OUR NEW PRODUCT AND WHY THEY WILL FIND VALUE FROM IT.

Once these scripts have been generated and reviewed, they may be used together with advanced AI video-generating tools like Synthesia and Heygen. Text from generated scripts can be uploaded to these systems, and the AI can add music, animations, and video effects to create highly personalized and engaging marketing videos. It is also possible to generate a unique persona for the marketing message using AI image-generating tools to create a character and then upload it to AI video creation tools. On top of this, it is possible to select a unique voice using, for example, a specific script like the one below with Midjourney to create the character.

MIDJOURNEY PROMPT:

> /IMAGINE CREATE AN EDITORIAL-STYLE SIDE-VIEW MEDIUM-FULL PHOTO, SHOT ON FUJIFILM PRO 400H, OF A FEMALE EXECUTIVE WITH CAPTIVATING EYES GAZING INTO THE CAMERA LENS. CAREFUL COMPOSITION EVOKING A SENSE OF REFINED SIMPLICITY AND CREATIVE CURIOSITY AS THE EXECUTIVE GAZES FIXEDLY AT THE CAMERA LENS --AR 1080:1350 --UPBETA --S 750 --V 5

→ Add-in tools like Sora allow users to create videos and animations based on textual descriptions, which is boosting efficiency and accessibility in fields like animation, marketing, and education.

AI-based tools are abundant, and we could fill hundreds of pages with links to new applications, plugins, and APIs that help save time and increase productivity. In marketing, for example, professionals can reach for simple tools that use ChatGPT to write email responses, to more sophisticated tools that automate website generation, helping to create entirely new websites with content and personalization without the user needing any prior knowledge about designing websites. Many of these tools are game-changers and will continue to improve in the future.

It becomes evident that customization via AI extends beyond just reactive changes and actions, allowing organizations to forecast and produce customized content that proactively anticipates forthcoming client behaviors and preferences; this includes the development of customized promotional offers, tailored shopping guidance, and distinctive user experiences. Through its implementation, AI introduces additional proactive measures to enhance personalization, greatly augmenting client engagement.

This integration of AI results in the incorporation of a generative experience, which elevates the personalization component to unprecedented levels. Hyper-personalization signifies a novel era in the realm of client engagement. The objective is to comprehensively understand consumers and provide substantial value to each unique individual. The term "hyper" in hyper-personalization accurately conveys the heightened and concentrated nature of tailoring customer experiences to every

client's unique preferences. Through technology and data, businesses can now construct hyper-personalized encounters that instill a sense of exclusivity inside each client.

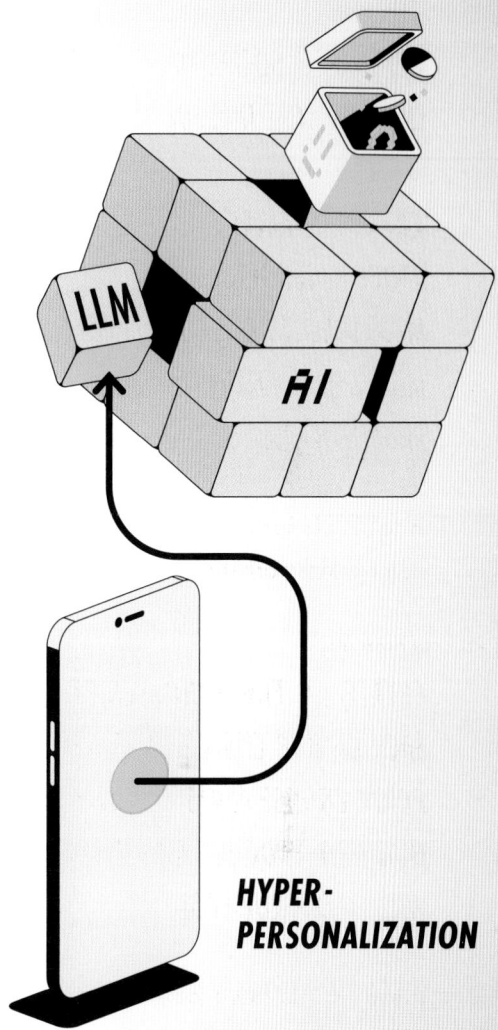

HYPER-PERSONALIZATION

→   The cheat sheet on the next page provides more ideas on using and exploiting LLMs to learn, create, and interact.

THE LLM CHEAT SHEET FOR CHATGPT, BARD, AND OTHER MODELS

EXAMPLES BASIC PROMPTS

Act as a (ROLE)	Create a (TASK)	Show as (FORMAT)
• Marketer	• Headline	• A table
• Advertiser	• Article	• A list
• Mindset coach	• Essay	• Summary
• Best-selling author	• Book outline	• HTML
• Therapist	• Email sequence	• Code
• Web designer	• Social media post	• Spreadsheet
• Journalist	• Product description	• Graphs
• Inventor	• Cover letter	• CSV file
• CFO	• Blog post	• Plain text file
• Copywriter	• SEO keywords	• JSON
• Prompt engineer	• Summary	• Rich text
• Accountant	• Video script	• PDF
• Lawyer	• Recipe	• XML
• Analyst	• Sales copy	• Markdown
• Ghostwriter	• Analysis	• Gantt chart
• Project manager	• Ad copy	• Word cloud

Linked Prompting

1. Provide me with the ideal outline for an effective and persuasive blog post.

2. Write a list of engaging headlines for this blog post based on (Topic).

3. Write a list of subheadings and hooks for this same blog post.

4. Write a list of keywords for this blog.

5. Write a list of compelling call-to-actions for the blog post.

6. Combine the best headline with the best subheadings, hooks, keywords, and CTA to write a blog post for (topic).

7. Rewrite this blog post in the (Style), (Tone), (Voice), and (Personality).

Prompt Priming

ZERO — "Write me 5 headlines about (Topic)"

SINGLE — "Write me five headlines about (Topic). Here is am example of one headline: (Example)"

MULTIPLE — "Write me five headlines about (Topic). Here is an example of some headlines: (examples)"

For Biz Owners

• Give me a list of inexpensive ideas to promote my business better.

• Acting as a business consultant, what is the best way to solve this problem (Problem)?

• Create a 30-day social media content strategy based on (Topic 1) and (Topic 2).

How to learn from an LM?

Explain

- like I'm 5 years old
- clearly
- uniquely
- like you are teaching
- with examples
- like Steve Jobs

Examples writing styles

"Write in xy style"

- Formal vs. Informal
- Simple vs. Technical
- Descriptive vs. Concise
- Academic vs. Editorial
- Informative vs. Inspirational

Over the top creative copy

Take this statement and make it explode with hyperbole and copy-writing cinematography.

The statement is: ...

EFFECTIVE USE OF THIS POWERFUL TOOL CAN PROPEL YOUR BUSINESS TO THE FOREFRONT OF THIS MODERN BUSINESS LANDSCAPE.

MORE USEFUL AND POPULAR AI TOOLS

Concept design	Midjourney, LookX, Adobe Firefly
Generating Design	Maket.ai
Residential planning	ARCHITEChTURES
Schematic design	ArkDesign.ai
Urban planning	Autodesk Forma
3D modeling	Grasshopper, Sloyd.ai
Renovation projects	Luma.ai, Skipp Renovation
BIM	BricsCAD BIM
Rendering	Veras by EvolveLAB, Arko.ao
Sustainable design	Preoptima
Project management	ClickUp
Site planning	TestFit, UrbanForm
3D sketching	SketchUp AI

METHODS FOR AI AND INNOVATION

The methods described in this chapter involve three lenses. The first lens explores the tools and techniques needed to gain higher labor productivity with AI. There is significant value here, allowing resources, time, and money to be funneled into other value-creating activities. Thus, in many cases, the increase in efficiency is a large part of the overall potential value of AI to a company. With the rapid advancement of AI technology and its integration into many business applications, enterprises can benefit from it across industries. Today, as described earlier, traditional advanced analytics and ML algorithms are already highly effective in performing numerical and optimization tasks, such as predictive modeling, and they continue to find new applications in a variety of industries and business ecosystems. However, as generative AI continues to evolve and mature, it has the potential to open up entirely new frontiers of creativity and innovation, which is the second lens in our tools and methods. The third AI lens addresses the impact on the top and bottom lines of companies and how different business models contribute to the effects.

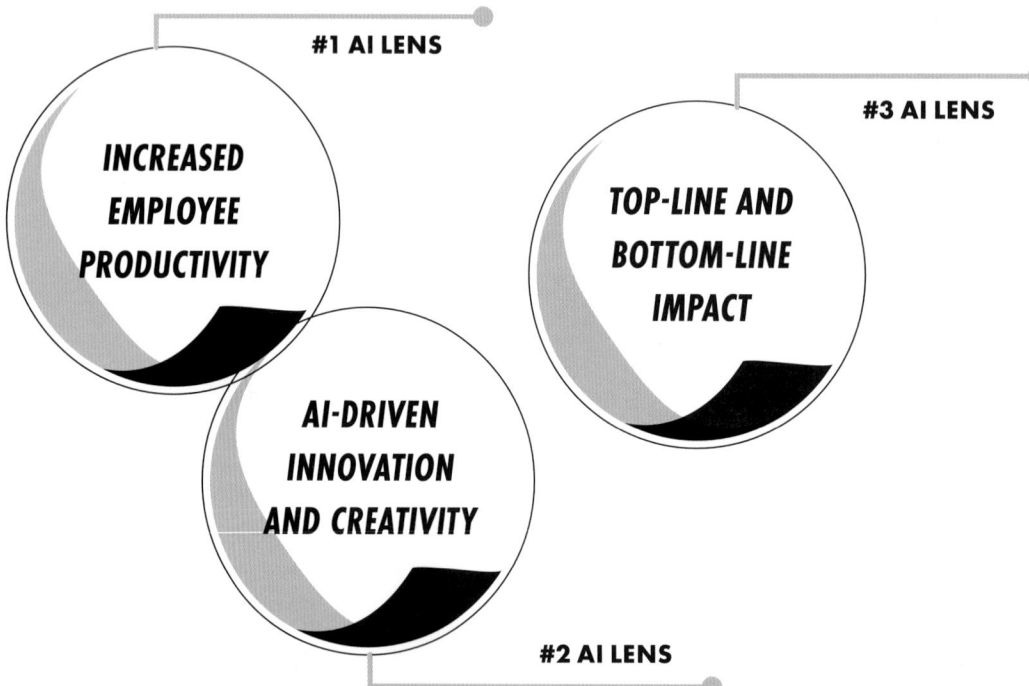

#1 AI LENS

INCREASED EMPLOYEE PRODUCTIVITY

#3 AI LENS

TOP-LINE AND BOTTOM-LINE IMPACT

AI-DRIVEN INNOVATION AND CREATIVITY

#2 AI LENS

#1 AI LENS: INCREASED EMPLOYEE PRODUCTIVITY

Many classes of AI tools support employee and operational efficiency. Practical experience shows that the most impact by AI is created by horizontal functions and processes (in order of magnitude from low to high) related to sales, supply chain, strategy, marketing, HR, legal, risk and compliance, R&D, procurement, software engineering, and customer operations.

Besides the high impact of AI on function-specific use cases, the technology can assist knowledge workers in handling time-consuming activities. For example, AI can help knowledge workers and decision-makers quickly access relevant information to make more informed decisions and develop effec-

IN ADDITION TO THE POTENTIAL VALUE THAT AI CAN DELIVER IN SPECIFIC USE CASES, AI WILL ADD VALUE TO AN ENTIRE ORGANIZATION BY SUPPORTING DECISION-MAKERS AND KNOWLEDGE WORKERS.

tive strategies → as exemplified by "AI for Strategic Work" on pages 96–97. On average, knowledge workers today spend over a day per workweek finding, gathering, and meaningfully clustering information. AI is also revolutionizing how we deal with and use intelligent knowledge management systems. By mastering the natural language of AI, stored internal knowledge is quickly retrieved and expressed as written or spoken prompts, leading to a natural and ongoing dialogue between humans and machines.

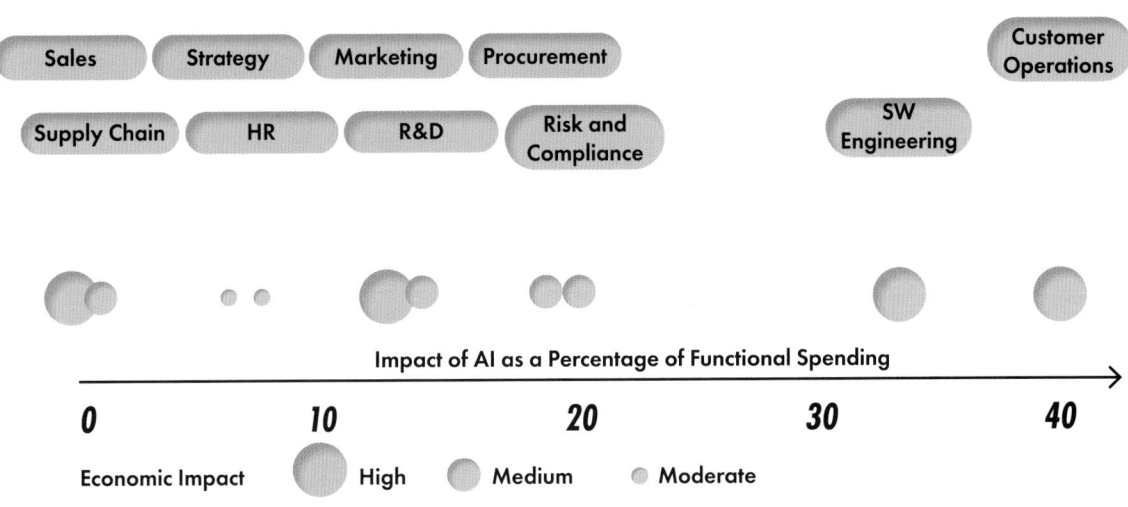

Sales · Strategy · Marketing · Procurement · Customer Operations · Supply Chain · HR · R&D · Risk and Compliance · SW Engineering

Impact of AI as a Percentage of Functional Spending

0   10   20   30   40

Economic Impact   High   Medium   Moderate

EXAMPLES OF POWERFUL USE CASES

While page 169 quantified the overall impact of AI on functional spending, this section dives deeper into specific, exciting use cases. We'll explore various examples from customer operations to procurement, acknowledging that an exhaustive list is beyond the scope of this book. These targeted case studies will illustrate the tangible ways AI is transforming different areas of business.

Customer Operations

AI will revolutionize the entire customer operations landscape, improving customer experience and employee productivity in different ways via implementing digital self-service for simple transactions and supporting and enhancing customer interactions through personalized experiences. Customer interactions take place on different levels, and as AI advances, these systems will be able to address almost every customer journey and interaction imaginable.

├──────────────────── Evolution enabled by AI ────────────────────┤

Self-services very simple transactions	Self-services for simple customer journeys	Human-like complex self-services	Proactive AI-enabled support	End-to-end AI-enabled journeys
• Web portal • Simple apps • Contact center	• RPA • LLM response • ML chatbots	• Augmented AI • Human-like bots and chatbots	• Customized experience • Proactive outreach	• Full assistance • Prediction of customer needs

CHATBOTS AND VIRTUAL ASSISTANTS ENABLED BY AI WILL DRAMATICALLY ENHANCE CUSTOMER SERVICE BY PREDICTING NEEDS, SOLVING PROBLEMS, AND MAKING SUGGESTIONS FOR CUSTOMERS.

Research and Development

AI can be used to effectively process and synthesize vast datasets quickly while also spotting patterns and correlations that may be too complex for researchers to identify. This capability is especially important in fields like pharmaceuticals and materials science. In addition, AI can play a significant role in helping researchers generate superior literature reviews based on reviewing hundreds or thousands of research papers and synthesizing the important details relevant to the research topic. The same system can also be trained to help researchers write more robust proposals with higher chances of being selected to be trained on previously winning proposals. All these combinations represent a small part of how AI can play a major role in amplifying R&D capabilities.

— R&D enabled by AI —

Literature review	Proposal writing	Synthesize vast datasets	Spotting patterns	Publications
• Automated publications synthetization and evaluation • Knowledge graph construction	• Support in composing winning proposals • Citation management and plagiarism detection	• Cross pollinate and assess data across various sources • Data cleaning and pre-processing	• Trend finding • Unstructured data analysis • Anomaly detection and outlier identification • Predictive modeling and forecasting	• Manuscript preparation and editing • Citation tracking and alt-metrics analysis

R&D x AI

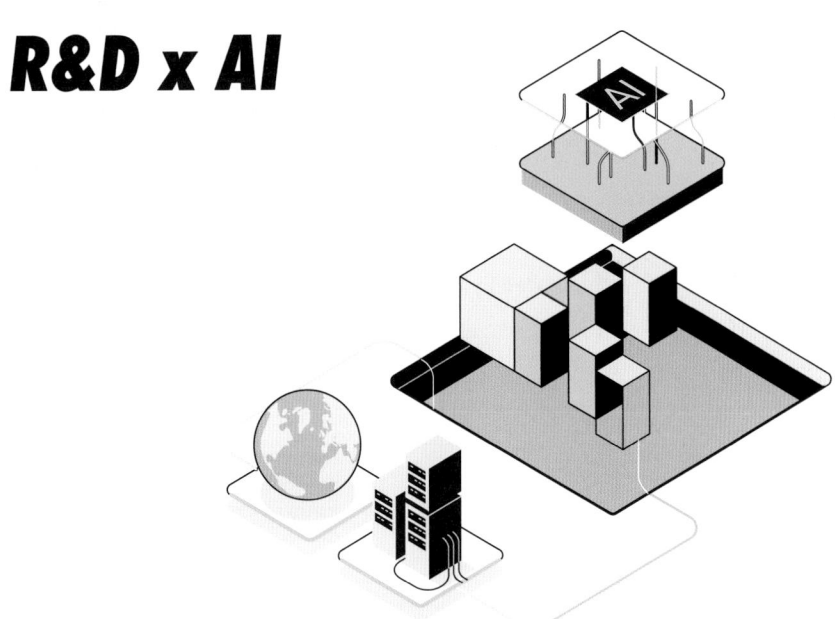

Software Engineering

Software engineers and product managers use AI to analyze, cleanse, and label large amounts of data, such as user feedback, market trends, and existing system logs. The future of AI supports the entire software development process, from conception and planning to testing. AI has the potential to create multiple IT architecture designs and iterate the potential configurations, accelerating system development and enabling faster time-to-market. Today, AI tools are already assisting with programming, shortening development time through quick designs, finding prompts quickly, and serving as an easily navigable knowledge base. Algorithms are used across the software industry to improve functional and performance testing to ensure quality and automatically generate test cases and test data.

Supported by AI				
Inception and planning	Design of systems	Human-like complex self-services	Proactive AI-enabled support	End-to-end AI-enabled journeys
• Manage requirements • Model security threats	• Design automation • DevOps automation	• Automated code generation • Knowledge management	• Test case generation • Risk-based test prioritization	• Continuous integration/ delivery integration

Procurement

LLM models can be tailored to various applications with the potential to revolutionize procurement operations. For example, they can automate data analysis for demand forecasting, facilitate interactions with suppliers, and identify risks in the supply chain. By optimizing procurement workflows, supporting staff can significantly enhance efficiency while lowering costs and improving risk management in procurement processes.

Supported by AI				
Contract management	Supplier risks management	Purchasing	Payments	Spending analytics
• NLP for contract life cycles • Identification of supplier	• Real-time supplier risks monitoring	• Virtual purchasing assistance	• Automated payment and fraud/error detection	• Classification of spending data

There are multiple ways in which LLMs can enhance HR functions. For example, they can streamline the recruitment process through intelligent profile matching and select the most qualified interview applicants. Organizations must ensure that the training data these LLMs are being trained on is free of bias and discrimination. Several examples have outlined instances of ethical bias in the recruitment process. These systems can also facilitate the onboarding process, provide personalized training for each new hire, manage performance reviews with data-driven insights, and answer employee questions on HR-related inquiries.

HR-ENABLED AI CAN REALIZE UP TO 35% INCREASED PRODUCTIVITY ACROSS THE HR VALUE CHAIN.

HR enabled by AI

Recruitment	Onboarding	Training	Performance management	HR (self) services
• Automated resume screening • Predictive modeling for talent acquisition • Virtual assistants for candidate engagement	• Personalized onboarding experiences • Automated onboarding tasks • Chatbots for knowledge and support	• Personalized learning recommendations • Adaptive learning platforms • Virtual instructors and mentors	• Automated performance review analysis • Real-time feedback and coaching • Predictive analytics for performance improvement	• Online HR portals and chatbots • Chatbots for HR inquiries • Automated leave management

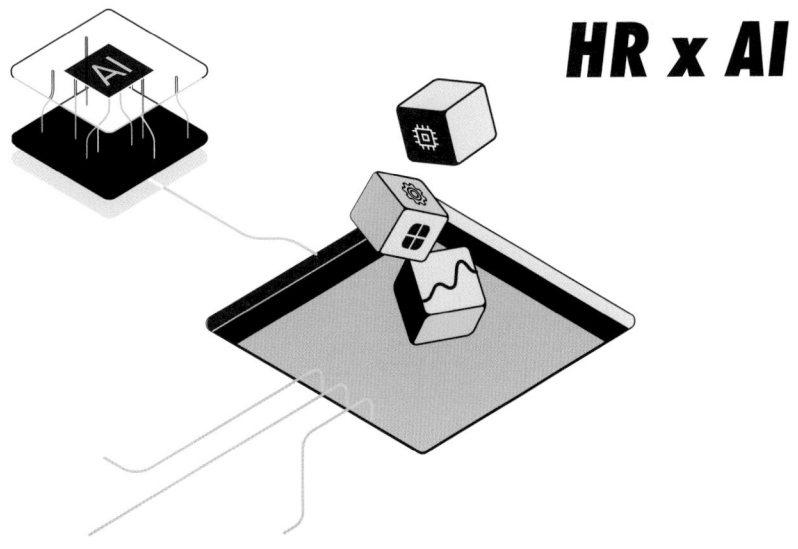

HR x AI

HOW TO CATEGORIZE PRODUCTIVITY USE CASES

As noted on the previous pages, some functions benefit more from AI than others. For example, many companies start with functions such as marketing, HR, legal, risk and compliance, R&D, procurement, software engineering, customer operations, and sales because they are widely known to benefit the most from AI. One possibility for categorization and later measurement is to map the respective functions into productivity areas as a first step. For this purpose, two axes are used and defined accordingly: task complexity vs. human interactions.

For task complexity, metrics such as number of steps involved, the level of skills or knowledge required, the amount of information that needs to be processed, or the degree of uncertainty are relevant. For human interactions, criteria such as difficulty of communication, type of collaboration, or personal/emotional engagement with other people can be applied. The magnitude of the respective expression can express impact of AI as a percentage of functional spending

→ based on representation of page 168.

TYPICAL PRODUCTIVITY QUADRANTS AND MAGNITUDE MEASUREMENTS

A: Low task complexity/high human interaction
→ Improved CX, better decision-making, increased productivity

B: High task complexity/high human interaction
→ Improved quality, higher mass customization, increased innovation output

D: Low task complexity/low human interaction
→ Higher effectiveness, cost savings, increased scalability

C: High task complexity/low human interaction
→ Increased efficiency, increased scalability

174

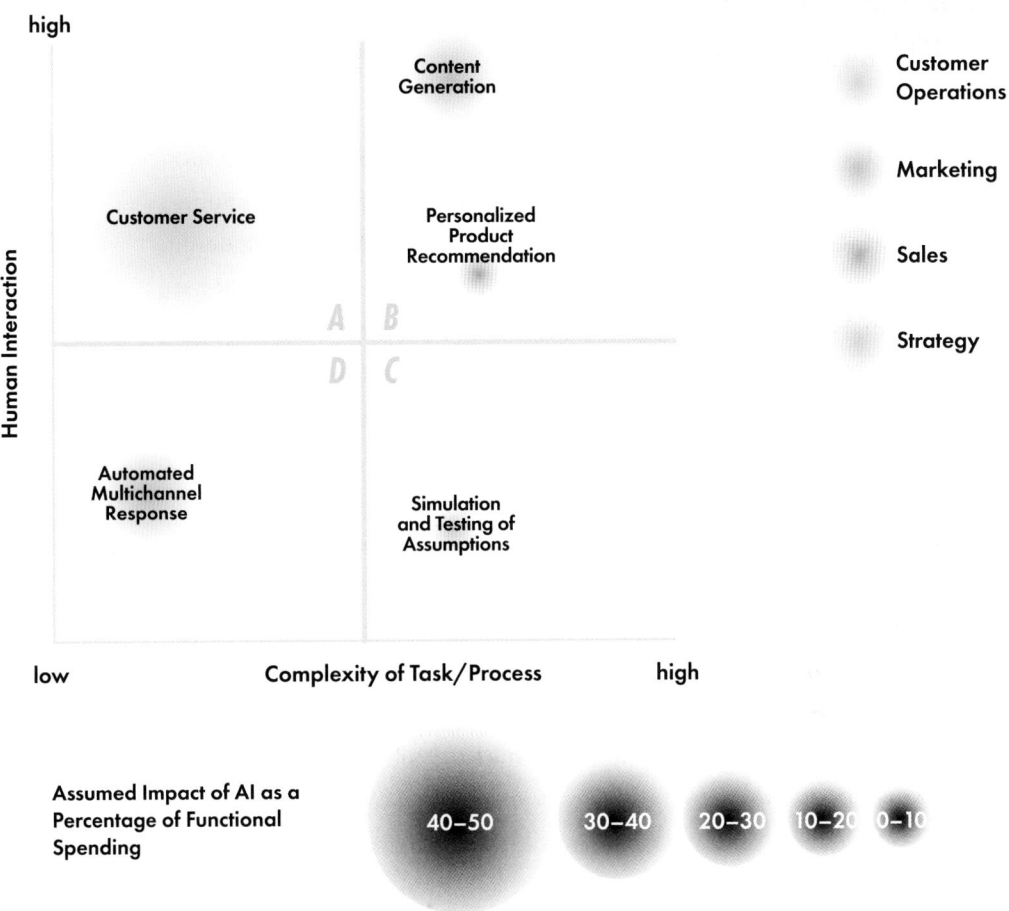

Human Interaction

Content
Generation

Customer Service

Personalized
Product
Recommendation

A | *B*

D | *C*

Automated
Multichannel
Response

Simulation
and Testing of
Assumptions

low   Complexity of Task/Process   high

Customer
Operations

Marketing

Sales

Strategy

Assumed Impact of AI as a
Percentage of Functional
Spending

40–50   30–40   20–30   10–20   0–10

The categorization will reveal how AI will enhance the quality, efficiency, or effectiveness of human interactions, leading to improved customer satisfaction and potentially increased revenue. Alternative use cases have the potential for cost savings, time savings, error reduction, increased task completion rate, or measurable cost savings from automation. They can even lead to better decision accuracy and revenue growth.

WE RECOMMEND THAT THE EMPLOY-EES PARTICIPATE IN AN ACTIVITY AND CATEGORIZATION TO BETTER UNDER-STAND HOW GENERATIVE AI CAN BE APPLIED TO THEIR RESPECTIVE TASKS AND PROCESSES.

EVALUATING THE POTENTIAL OF DISRUPTION

In this day and age, we don't require a great deal of technical expertise to incorporate AI into work processes. This broad accessibility enables the creation of improved or completely new and automated workflows. For example, Microsoft Copilot supports AI applications that automatically format documents and automate repetitive tasks in customer relationship management (CRM) systems. In this way, the democratization of AI is gaining momentum and making these powerful tools available and applicable to a broad range of functions in the organization. Depending on the industry and level of automation, the potential level of disruption varies. Following the example of the previous page, the productivity gains might be associated with content generation and personalization in customer service. AI enables customized content creation that delivers unprecedented user personalization and engagement. Other industries might see more potential and higher disruption impact related to efficiency gains performed by real-time software code generation. In this application scenario, AI supports the automation of coding tasks, leading to more efficient development processes and potentially fewer errors. For companies following the idea of implementing black ocean strategies, introducing new paradigms and methodologies enabled by AI has the highest potential of disrupting and reshaping traditional business models and processes. These types of disruptions based on radical new market opportunities are addressed in #2 AI Lens related to creativity and innovation → see pages 180–193. The impact of the respective AI applications will increase in the future as we learn about the next steps in the development of language processing models.

Currently, AI is transforming entire industries and realizing a leap in productivity. However, these developments are also complex, evolving rapidly, and large-scale implementations can be costly and time-consuming. While it is essential to move quickly, it is equally important to prioritize what to focus on carefully. To avoid missteps and future-proof generative AI investments, companies should start with a clear AI strategy (see Chapter 2) and form an understanding of the use cases. Companies must assess whether generative AI is mature enough for their use cases, and they need to test it in their business context. They must also thoroughly understand the technology options, trends, and trade-offs to choose the right technology.

EXAMPLE OF EVALUATING THE POTENTIAL OF DISRUPTION

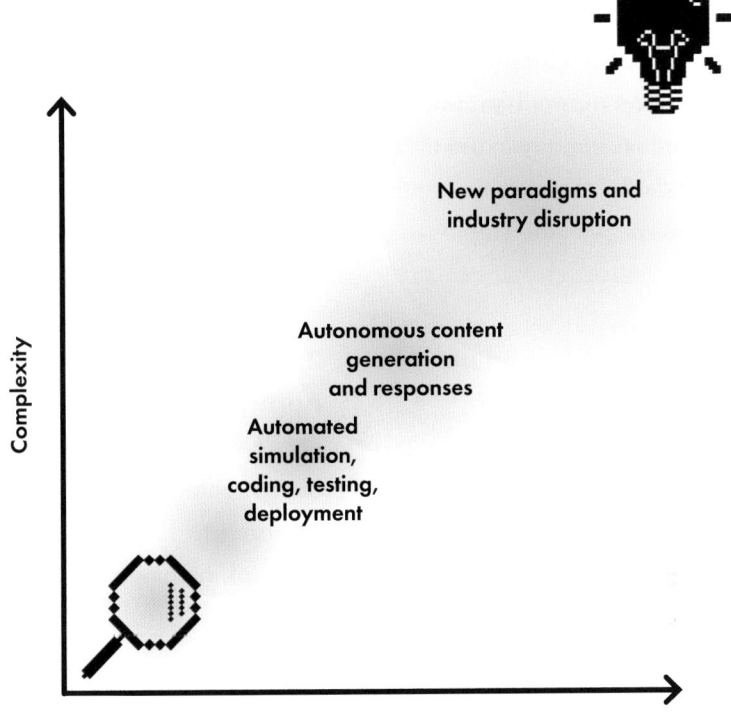

New paradigms and industry disruption

Autonomous content generation and responses

Automated simulation, coding, testing, deployment

Complexity

Potential levels of disruption based on industry view

Practical experience shows us that companies struggle to understand generative AI's business value and need help selecting the most promising use cases. Additionally, the formulation of the business case often neglects the secondary costs, which account for up to 60% of the total costs, while the primary costs with investments in the algorithm account for only 15%, and the technology stack associated with the AI itself accounts for up to 25%. Primary costs include fixed setup costs (e.g. hardware, data maintenance, engineering costs) and variable costs (e.g. consumption costs for APIs and IT infrastructure). Secondary costs of generative AI include many hidden and difficult-to-estimate expenses, such as maintenance costs (e.g. technical debt repayment, retraining, incremental testing), risk management, organizational change management, and legal costs. In many cases, decision-makers have yet to gain experience with AI or have limited digital literacy regarding important topics related to digital ethics, computational and algorithm thinking, tech translation and enablement, and data and AI ecosystems. Not knowing what technology approach to adopt often results in decision-makers taking the rigid path of doing nothing or applying the wrong criteria when buying into an approach to implementing generative AI.

HOW TO SELECT STANDARD AI APPLICATIONS TO INCREASE PRODUCTIVITY

The easiest way to benefit from productivity enhancements is to use standard applications based on the well-known foundation models. Often, vendors extend the applications already in use to remain competitive or offer add-on features that provide AI functionality. Another viable path is to start where the tasks and needs occur, with the employees in the individual functions within the organization.

1. Start by understanding and observing the employees' and team's needs. Key questions to ask:

- What specific tasks does a function or team want to automate?

- What is the job to be done for the task, function, or process? What are the pain points that employees are facing? What is the benefit of having human interaction for the tasks?

- How can we create more value from the existing data?

- Can these tools help the organization reduce the risk, cost, and schedule of new products?

- How can these tools cross pollinate multiple business lines to increase synergy and efficiency?

2. Consider the specific AI tools and applications available: A wide variety of AI tools are available, each with its own strengths and weaknesses. Do some research to find the most likely effective tools for the employees' and teams' needs.

3. Create a dialogue with the employees and teams: Get feedback from the workforce about the AI tools they find most helpful. They may have deeper insights and concerns or spot interdependencies that are not apparent to everyone initially.

4. Make sure the AI applications are easy to use: The chosen AI applications should be easy for your employees and team to use. Otherwise, they will be reluctant to employ them and the benefits of AI will be lost.

5. Provide training on the AI application: Once you have selected the AI tools, train the workforce to use them effectively; this will help employees and teams get the most out of the application and avoid any problems.

→ Once the needs are understood, the AI tools and applications can be selected.

The latest advancements in LLMs introduced a new feature allowing users to upload multiple documents for processing. These LLMs can examine the contents of attached documents, extract insights, and uncover unrealized connections between them. Through this process, a combined body of knowledge can be developed, connecting multiple pieces of information together that can result in uncovering new insights and discoveries.

A COMMON STANDARD APPLICATION IS MICROSOFT COPILOT FOR AUTOMATING WORKFLOWS AND IMPROVING PRODUCTIVITY IN THE MICROSOFT 365 ENVIRONMENT. ITS NATURAL LANGUAGE INTERFACE, PREDICTIVE AUTOMATION CAPABILITIES, AND ABILITY TO STREAMLINE COMPLEX WORKFLOWS MAKE IT AN EMBEDDED TOOL FOR BOTH IT PROFESSIONALS AND END USERS.

This interconnectivity of data not only enhances analysis but can also expand the possibilities for research, learning, and decision-making applications, pushing the boundaries of AI through advanced information synthesis.

An essential element of this domain is the ability to continuously monitor the impact of AI tools and their specific effects on productivity. Adjustments should be implemented when needed, including trying new tools that may better suit the task at hand. OKRs can be an instrumental tool in determining the best feedback for a service or product. OKRs are developed by creating clear objectives and measurable key results. The OKRs provide a structured framework to evaluate service performance against unique and specific goals. This method helps consolidate targeted feedback by focusing on areas directly linked to achieving key objectives.

By analyzing how well the service meets its key results, organizations can pinpoint specific strengths and identify areas for improvement, leading to more effective feedback and enhancements.

SELECTING STANDARD APPLICATIONS STEP-BY-STEP

1. Understand and Observe	2. Select Potential AI Tools	3. Engage with Workforce	4. Check Usability	5. Provide Training

#2 AI LENS: AI-DRIVEN INNOVATION AND CREATIVITY

The outlined enhanced efficiency via AI, as presented in the previous section, is boosting productivity by allowing for more effective resource allocation, contributing to exploit. However, AI can offer more than mere efficiency: it can inspire radical new ideas, designs, and solutions, fostering unprecedented creativity and innovation.

In the context of this book, *AI and Innovation*, AI can pave the way to new products, services, experiences, and business models, driving objectives related to business growth, advanced sustainability, and humanity. For example, we have seen technology's already growing impact on the entire design cycle, from problem definition to prototyping, realizing and scaling solutions. Advanced innovation teams have already used many digital tools to create interactive prototypes, simulate user experiences, and iterate designs more rapidly in this interplay of human creativity and technology. For example, NLP helped design thinking teams to analyze and understand user-generated content, such as reviews, comments, and social media posts, to gain insights into user/customer sentiments and preferences. The UX designer community has also adapted to many AI tools to automate repetitive tasks and enhance productivity.

KEY ADVANTAGES OF USING AI TO DRIVE INNOVATION AND CREATIVITY

- Using AI tools for ideation, innovation teams can develop a wide range of more creative solutions from new perspectives. For example, Midjourney can create novel design concepts for designers to consider or to influence their design journey in ways that result in superior and more elegant designs.

- A variety of data sources and evidence-based patterns and trends lead to informed decision-making.

- AI-powered tools facilitate rapid prototyping and testing, allowing teams to iterate and refine their prototypes quickly.

- Practical experience shows that AI helps teams work faster.

- LLMs support brainstorming and generating novel ideas for teams to build on or consider.

APPLYING AI OVER THE ENTIRE DESIGN CYCLE

The Double Diamond (see illustration below) is a popular framework for describing innovation work based on the design thinking mindset. The starting point refers to exploring many problems, followed by collecting insights, analyzing, synthesizing, ideating, prototyping, and testing ideas. AI is applied to optimize initial research and design highly complex systems.

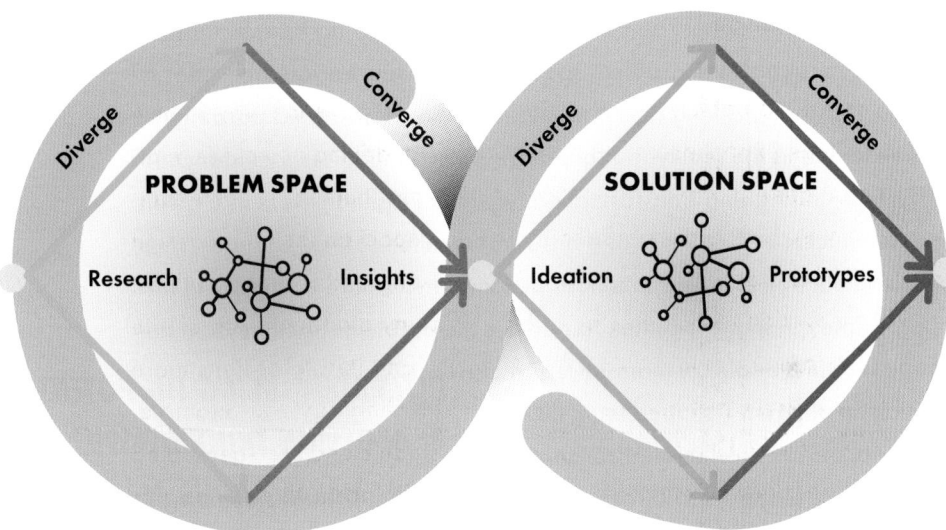

AI OPTIMIZATION FOR RESEARCH AND ANALYSIS

- Market segmentation
- Creating questionnaires
- Planning and scheduling research
- Assistive tools for conduction research

- Synthesizing research
- Creating insights
- Creating reports
- Creating storyboards

AI REVOLUTION FOR IDEATION, PROTOTYPING, AND TESTING

- Rapid prototyping
- Attention/heat map testing
- Planning and scheduling usability tests
- Assistive tools for conducting tests

- Creating copy
- Design system management
- Sketch2Code
- Data collection and analysis

SUMMARY OF AI CAPABILITIES WITH IMPACT ON THE DESIGN CYCLE

- The ability to interact with systems or the environment
- The ability to understand the world around us
- The ability to analyze or process external and internal data

- The ability to organize ideas and make informed selections
- The ability to suggest objective criteria for idea evaluation
- The ability to create, test, and animate prototypes

UNDERSTANDING THE PROBLEM FIRST

Especially in the context of AI, it quickly becomes apparent that in all areas, the ability to ask more profound questions beyond the function and the organization is becoming increasingly important. In the past, it was enough to master "exploit" and keep the enterprise machine running. In the context of AI and innovation, it is often about radically rethinking and driving transformation. The ability to recognize the problem space and ask appropriate questions is more important than thinking about solutions based on outdated paradigms; this is mainly due to the reality that questions provide long-term guidance to organizations undergoing transformation, while the right answers in a given context can quickly lead to the wrong answers when the context changes. Thus, the collective capability in organizations becomes even more important to ask the appropriate questions together, to address the problem space beyond the corporate silos in the spirit of team-of-teams, and to include different T-shaped team members. In short, the once-celebrated corporate pyramid, with a leader and direct reports on top, is changing into a diamond-shaped structure with an unprecedented breadth of teams that understand the importance of understanding the problem space before thinking of solutions.

ULTIMATELY, USING THE POTENTIAL OF AI IN DESIGN THINKING WILL LEAD TO MORE HARMONIOUS COLLABORATION BETWEEN AI AND HUMAN DESIGNERS, RESHAPING TRADITIONAL APPROACHES AND CREATING NEW APPLICATIONS FOR THE FUTURE.

The design thinking mindset as a problem-solving approach, which is hands-on and iterative, has become very popular for starting the innovation journey — mainly because the lion's share of the time, if properly applied, is spent on framing the appropriate problem. With the introduction of AI, this paradigm is enhanced further, helping innovation teams to solve problems and make more informed decisions.

At the current level of AI, technologies help in the problem space with insights from customers/users. Tools such as ChatGPT, AI Google Analytics, Hotjar, UXCam, and IBM Watson streamline data analysis and enhance the user/customer research process. When striving to improve existing digital products and services, AI-generated heatmaps help to identify hidden features that users/website visitors might struggle to access, prompting improvements for better accessibility. For example, in retail, algorithms built to record customer/user sessions during online shopping experiences have, in some instances, identified cart abandonment issues resulting from confusing form fields embedded in websites. Thanks to the algorithm identifying the hidden problem, retailers could adjust their websites, leading to a more streamlined checkout process. And, of course, AI helps to generate quick results and clusters from customer surveys to identify pain points and preferences, which are transferred into improvements to enhance the overall customer experience or lift conversion rates.

  **Download Customer Journey AI Template**

In addition, AI can revolutionize research by generating realistic synthetic data → see page 44 for both quantitative and qualitative studies. In quantitative analyses, it can create mock populations with specified characteristics, allowing researchers to test hypotheses without needing real-world data, saving time and resources. For qualitative research, AI can generate realistic interview scripts, social media posts, or even chatbot interactions, offering researchers diverse perspectives while respecting privacy concerns. This synthetic data can complement traditional methods, fueling deeper insights and accelerating research progress.

However, innovation teams should always be aware of bias in AI algorithms that might lead to skewed insights or discriminatory outcomes. Additionally, ethical implications of AI usage should be carefully assessed to ensure responsible and inclusive design practices → as described on pages 132–137.

BUILDING UP EMPATHY WITH USERS/CUSTOMERS

Despite all the advantages of AI in optimizing research and analysis, there is nuance to human creativity that AI cannot presently replicate: building empathy with users/customers. Therefore, balancing AI-driven insights with human intuition is currently one of the key capabilities and strengths humans hold over the entire design cycle. Practical experience shows that over-reliance on AI can sacrifice the authenticity and warmth inherent in human connections, diminishing the quality of human-centric design.

→ Examples of tips, tricks, and tools for problem space are outlined on the next page.

EXAMPLE OF TOOLS USED AND APPLIED IN FINDING THE APPROPRIATE PROBLEM TO SOLVE

Generative AI isn't here to replace the core principles of design thinking, creativity, and innovation. Instead, it acts as a powerful amplifier, empowering teams to apply these principles with greater effectiveness and unlock new realms of creative exploration. Here's a glimpse into how AI has demonstrably enhanced our client work across diverse industries in recent years:

1. Unveiling Hidden Insights from Data Deluge

Imagine sifting through a large amount of Amazon reviews – a near-impossible feat for humans. AI such as ChatGPT4.0 tackles this challenge head-on. It can analyze vast datasets (like all negative reviews) to identify recurring themes and patterns. This unveils crucial insights often overlooked, allowing teams to understand the broader context of design challenges.

Example: A client in the consumer electronics space leveraged AI to analyze customer reviews, uncovering a hidden pain point: confusing product setup instructions. Armed with this insight, the team redesigned the instructions for improved clarity, leading to a significant decrease in customer frustration.

2. Transforming Raw Data into Actionable Insights

Design thinking thrives on user research. But extracting meaningful insights from mountains of transcripts, quotes, and user profiles can be time-consuming. Here's where AI shines. Language models can analyze this data, identifying key issues and translating them into distinct problem statements based on user/customer needs.

Example: A design team working on a healthcare app utilized AI to analyze interview transcripts. The AI identified a recurring theme of user anxiety around appointment scheduling. This led to a focus on redesigning the app's scheduling interface to be more user-friendly and alleviate user anxiety.

3. Envisioning the Future to Shape Innovation

AI isn't just about the here and now; it helps us peer into the future. By analyzing trends and data, AI can predict how user needs and market dynamics might evolve. This empowers teams to prioritize areas with the most significant future impact.

184

Example: A Swedish furniture store used AI to analyze global living trends. This provided insights into how the concept of "living" might change for urban young families in the coming years. Armed with this knowledge, the store pro-actively redesigned its furniture collections to align with these anticipated shifts in consumer behavior, ensuring their products remain relevant and cater to future needs. These are just a few examples of how AI is transforming design thinking and innovation. By integrating AI tools and techniques, teams can gain a deeper understanding of user needs, anticipate future trends, and ulti-mately develop more innovative and impactful solutions

Examples of LLMs used and applied in the problem space: ChatGPT4o, Claude 3, Gemini, Perplexity, Ernie, and Trenhunter. These advanced AI mod-els excel at understanding and processing human language. They can be used in the problem space for:

Data Analysis: Analyze user reviews, social media comments, and other text-based data sources to identify user needs and pain points.

Persona Development: Generate user personas based on text descriptions and available data, providing insights into diverse user groups.

Trend Research (Perplexity): Leverage Perplexity's internet research capabilities to uncover emerging trends and consumer behavior shifts.

Trendhunter AI: Leverage AI-powered trend analysis to identify emerging trends across industries. Gain valuable insights and forecasts to stay ahead of the curve and anticipate future user needs.

Synthetic Users: Generate AI-powered simulated users to test application usability and user experience. These synthetic users mimic real-user interactions, allowing for thorough testing of various design scenarios and functionalities.

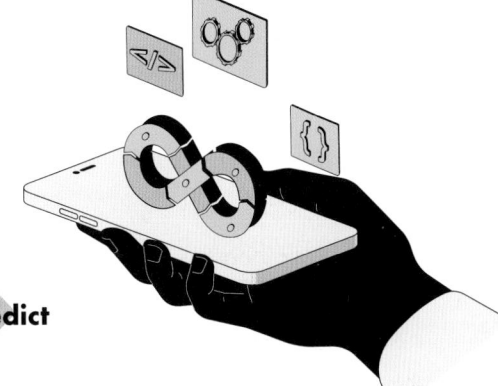

Analyze   Synthesize   Transform   Predict

APPLYING AI FOR IDEATION

For finding new products, services, and experiences, the opportunities for AI support are tremendous because existing tools start to store, use, train, and utilize interaction flows in formal languages together with descriptions in LLMs. Many of those interaction flows are encoded digitally, and innovation teams can apply AI within their own systems to align with defined design principles. At the same time, many systems in the market for managing innovations are incorporating multitalented AI models like GPT 4o, LaMDA, Cohere, perplexity, and Jurassic-1, which understand complex prompts, generate diverse ideas (not just text!), and adapt to individual preferences. Collaboration tools break down barriers, while new domains like science and education join to collaborate for ideation.

Most common features often cluster concepts derived from ideation and brainstorming sessions and feedback from customer interactions with first prototypes. Practical observation shows that AI is also frequently applied to start any brainstorming activity to overcome blank page syndrome. Innovation teams apply AI to get inspired and to obtain first ideas of business models and related business model patterns. Whereby to separate the goat from the sheep in the use of AI, innovation teams that take their task seriously eliminate or at least judiciously adjust biases in generative AI outputs, while other teams simply copy and paste AI-generated outputs to get the job done. Therefore, we always encourage teams to apply critical thinking or any other method for risk stagnation.

IF THE IDEATION DATABASE IS ONLY EVER FILLED WITH CONTENT THAT WAS GENERATED BY AI ITSELF, THE RESULTS MIGHT APPEAR INCREASINGLY WEAK OVER TIME.

The next leap in AI is to support innovation teams in predicting user/customer behavior and anticipating their needs, allowing them to first understand pains, gains, and jobs-to-be-done better. The second point is to create more robust solutions that meet user/customer needs and expectations. Our guidance has a strong focus on "support" as we believe that AI today cannot replace the human element when it comes to building empathy with customers/users and their needs and interpreting the design principles appropriately.

AI SUPPORT IN IDEATION

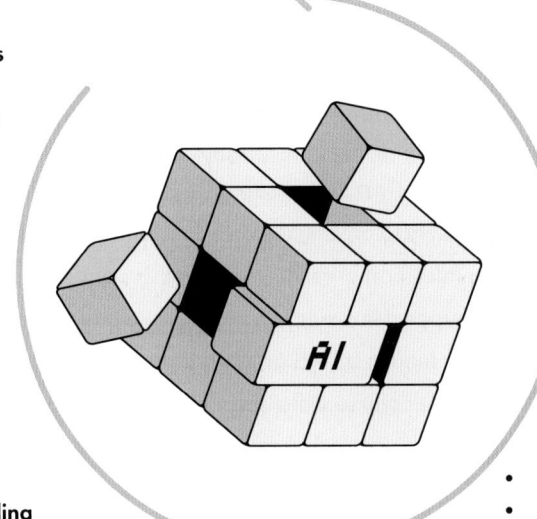

- Data analysis
- Existing alternatives
- Trend analysis
- Customer segments

- Resource allocation
- Investment analysis
- Product portfolio analysis
- Prediction of market success

- Point of views
- Prioritization modeling
- Ideation for features and experiences
- Idea clustering and evaluation
- Idea tracking and hypothesis testing
- Analyzing and clustering customer/user feedback

- Risk analysis
- Testing of assumptions (desirability, feasibility, and viability)
- Performance analysis

We observe that AI and humans working as a team becomes core to successful AI-driven innovation and creativity. AI's combined power of efficiency and accuracy is reshaping the future of innovation management. Tools that improve tasks over the entire design cycle include smarter data analysis, design automation, personalization, predictive analytics, and NLP to overcome blank page syndrome and other roadblocks.

INNOVATION TEAMS LEVERAGE ALL FACETS OF AI, INCLUDING VISUAL, AUDIO, VIDEO, AND TEXT TECHNOLOGY ADVANCEMENTS.

EXAMPLE OF TOOLS APPLIED IN IDEATION, PROTOTYPING, AND TESTING

Over the last years we have been also experimenting with AI in the solution space. The aim was to understand how AI can empower the generation, development, and refinement of ideas and prototypes within the design thinking cycle.

1. Generating More Diverse Solution Pathways: Design thinking demands a vast pool of ideas but also the ability to organize these ideas and make informed selections. Establishing clear evaluation criteria and refining concepts can be significant hurdles. AI steps in to support these crucial stages. We have been using AI to brainstorm a vast array of solutions based on data patterns, user behavior, and market trends. By tapping into diverse data sources, AI is able to suggest unique combinations and perspectives, fostering a richer solution pool.

Example: One of our design teams worked on a new sustainable packaging solution applying AI to explore possibilities beyond traditional materials. AI was able to analyze data on consumer preferences for eco-friendly packaging, current recycling infrastructure limitations, and emerging sustainable material options. This broader data exploration led to innovative solutions, like edible packaging made from seaweed derivatives.

2. Cluster Formation and Evaluation: AI is able to organize diverse ideas into clusters based on themes or similarities, aiding navigation and decision-making. Additionally, AI can analyze past project successes, industry standards, and market data to suggest objective criteria for idea evaluation. This ensures data-driven prioritization of the most impactful solutions with the limitation that everything is based on evidence from the past. On the positive side, AI tools can sharpen and detail concepts, ensuring clarity and alignment with user/customer needs and business objectives. This feedback loop (additional iteration) strengthens the solution before further development.

Example: In our design thinking trainings and capability build programs for data scientists, we have a design challenge to motivate the general public for healthier lifestyle and better fitness. Teams who aimed for a fitness app applied generative AI to cluster ideas related to workout tracking, personalized coaching features, and social integration functionalities. By analyzing user data and market trends, the AI model suggests prioritizing solutions focused on gamification to boost user engagement.

3. Accelerating Prototyping with Rapid Visualization: Transforming abstract ideas into tangible prototypes can be challenging, especially for complex concepts or teams with limited prototyping skills. The need for rapid iteration cycles further complicates the process. Generative AI tools can bridge the gap between idea and implementation by suggesting suitable design elements, structures, and functionalities. This translates abstract ideas into concrete prototypes, fostering clear visualization. We have observed recently many intuitive and user-friendly tools that simplify prototyping, even for teams with limited capabilities and skills for such tools.

Example: In collaboration with a large Chinese car manufacturer, we had the challenge of designing a new self-driving car interface. AI suggested suitable visual layouts, information hierarchies, and interactive elements based on user behavior data collected from current customers and best practices in human-machine interaction design.

EXAMPLE OF AI TOOLS USED AND APPLIED IN THE SOLUTION SPACE

Dream by WOMBO: The platform allows users to input text descriptions and generate corresponding images. It can be used to experiment with different phrasing and styles to explore visual interpretations of ideas.

Midjourney: This AI art platform offers a more advanced approach, allowing prompts with specific styles and artistic references. Ideal for creating visually striking and artistic prototypes.

NightCafe Creator: NightCafe Creator provides a blend of accessibility and control. Users can input text descriptions, choose artistic styles, and adjust the level of detail to generate unique visuals for their prototypes.

Figma with Figma AI: AI-powered features within Figma include features like "Smart Animate" and "Auto Layout," which automatically generate animations and adjust layouts based on design choices. It helps to accelerate the creation of interactive prototypes.

Adobe XD with Auto Animate: Similar to Figma AI, Adobe XD offers "auto animate" functionalities within its design platform. It enables design teams to quickly create transitions and interactions between UI elements, bringing static wireframes to life for user testing.

UXPin Merge: This design collaboration platform allows users to upload design assets (like screenshots or wireframes) and leverage AI to automatically generate interactive prototypes. This allows rapid testing without extensive coding knowledge.

Storylane: This tool transforms text descriptions and storyboards into basic animated videos. The tool is ideal for rapidly sketching out user flows and interactions within existing prototypes.

Marvel: This is a multimodal approach combining various prototyping elements. It allows design teams to upload images, wireframes, and even video snippets to create rich, interactive prototypes that showcase different aspects of the desired concept/solutions.

Proto.io: This platform offers a wide range of features, including the ability to import assets from other design tools and integrate animations and user flows. It allows design teams to create highly interactive prototypes that closely resemble the final product.

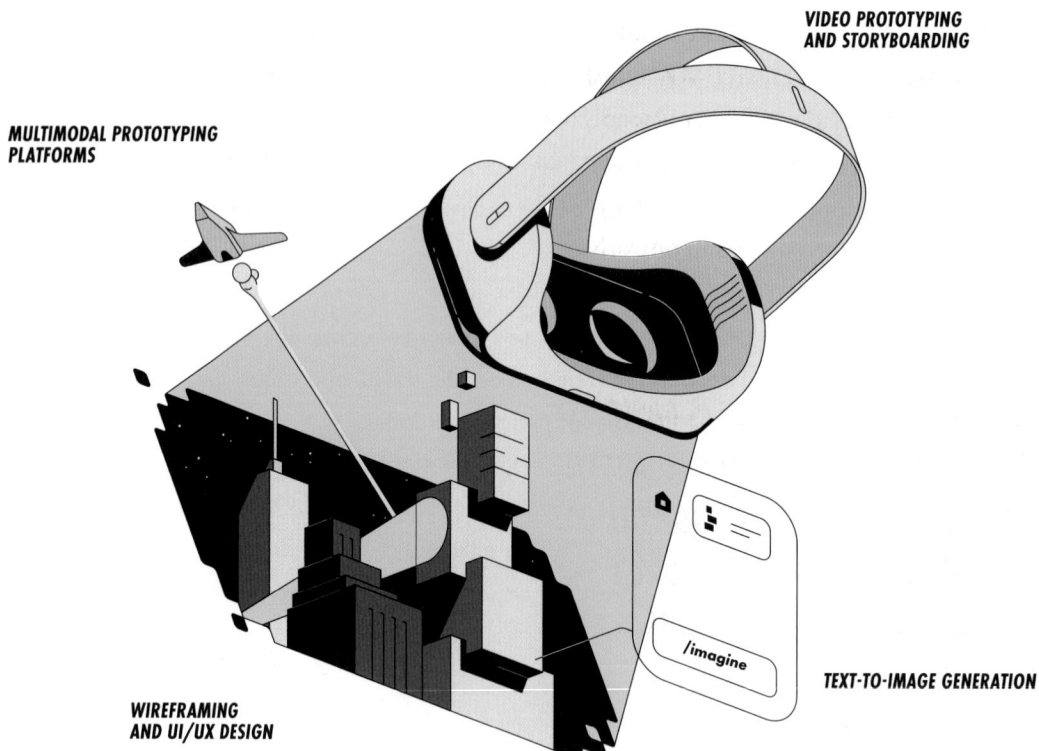

MULTIMODAL PROTOTYPING PLATFORMS

VIDEO PROTOTYPING AND STORYBOARDING

/imagine

TEXT-TO-IMAGE GENERATION

WIREFRAMING AND UI/UX DESIGN

EXAMPLE OF AI EXPERT ASSISTANT TOOL OVER THE ENTIRE DESIGN CYCLE

While LLMs excel at vast amounts of general information, for specialized knowledge, SLMs often shine brighter. Consider a book on design thinking. LLMs might generate a comprehensive overview, but an SLM trained on a dataset specifically focused on design thinking terminology and best practices would be far superior. The SLM would craft precise language tailored to the field, offering insightful recommendations and nuances that an LLM might miss, ensuring the book's content resonates with design thinking professionals.

A prime example of this specialization is the Design Thinking Cortex, an SLM built upon the foundation of the Wiley Design Thinking Series. This model is meticulously trained on the content of *The Design Thinking Playbook* and *The Design Thinking Toolbox*, absorbing all the templates and recommendations for supporting tools across the entire design thinking micro and macro processes. Further refined by feedback from the global design thinking community, the Design Thinking Cortex offers an experience akin to a personalized coaching session with the book's authors. Users can leverage it to navigate crucial steps like formulating HMW questions, crafting design briefs, outlining problem statements, developing personas, and sparking creative brainstorming sessions. For many design thinking teams, the Design Thinking Cortex serves as a valuable springboard, providing first ideas, fostering clear problem statements, and even generating powerful contextual examples to propel their projects forward.

DESIGN THINKING CORTEX IS BASICALLY THE INNOVATION SQUAD'S BESTIE, ALWAYS THERE WITH THE RIGHT TOOLS FOR THE JOB AND INSPO OVER THE ENTIRE DESIGN CYCLE THANKS TO ITS BUILT-IN KNOWLEDGE BANK.

↓ **Download AI Data Source Template**

→ The starting point for the development of the module and platform was the identification of suitable data sources.

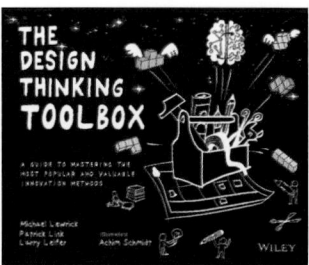 

WHAT TOOLS AND METHODS SUPPORT AI ACTIVITIES?

Help me understand user frustrations in our fitness app through empathy map

Prototype new checkout flows to reduce cart abandonment on our e-commerce site

Design brief for a sustainable fashion line targeting eco-conscious consumers

Mind map to brainstorm features promoting mental well-being in our productivity app

Continuing its specialization, the Design Thinking Cortex delves even deeper, offering dedicated content on complex topics like business ecosystems design and design thinking and innovation metrics. This expanded knowledge base is fueled by the rich content of the Wiley Design Thinking Series. Functioning as an AI-powered expert tool, the Cortex translates to a remarkable 40% boost in team effectiveness and efficiency. Teams can leverage its guidance to develop solutions with unparalleled creativity and speed. But the vision of the Design Thinking

UNLIKE MANY GENERATIVE AI TOOLS THAT RELY ON VAST, UNFILTERED DATA AND CAN STRUGGLE WITH FOCUSED METHODOLOGIES, THE DESIGN THINKING CORTEX IS BUILT ON A FOUNDATION OF TRUST, ENSURING IT GUIDES YOU THROUGH EACH STAGE OF THE INNOVATION PROCESS EFFECTIVELY.

Cortex extends far beyond the design cycle itself. The platform envisions a future where generative AI seamlessly integrates with the entire innovation journey. This future ecosystem aims to streamline every step, from pinpointing the right problem to scaling your solution with maximum efficiency. The Design Thinking Cortex aspires to be more than just a design thinking companion; it strives to be the cornerstone of a complete AI ecosystem that empowers innovation at every stage.

#3 AI LENS: TOP-LINE AND BOTTOM-LINE IMPACT

In many cases, AI has an impact on the financial health of a company. Implementation of AI can result in increased revenue or total sales as well as increases in productivity and decreased cost. However, as is the case with investments in any other exponential technology, AI needs to deliver a demonstrable impact on the business's top line and bottom line → see Table on Potential Metrics for AI Impact on page 195. A common way to calculate is to determine the return on investment (ROI) impact of AI in order to foster its growth and justify its proliferation for specific tasks, functions, or the entire business model of a company.

This chapter presents many ways to increase employee productivity and add to top-line revenue growth. AI can improve the effectiveness of marketing and sales functions and refine customer loyalty through improved and customized experiences for customers/users and data monetization. In applying AI across the entire design cycle → see pages 180–193, the impact of AI on innovation and creativity can range from improvements to personalization of offerings, reductions in cart abandonment on digital platforms, and improvements to general conversion rates. Many marketing, sales, and conversation use cases help for effective top-line growth.

AI IS ABLE TO INCREASE TOP-LINE FIGURES BY UNLOCKING NEW REVENUE STREAMS AND IMPROVE THE BOTTOM LINE THROUGH EFFICIENCIES IN OPERATIONS.

We strongly recommend defining from early on the key metrics that will be used to measure the impact of AI on the top line and bottom line. Especially in times of economic uncertainty, a well-defined measurement system will help quantify the AI strategy and any milestones achieved. In many cases, players from the AI value chain → see page 155 have created systems to show measurable improvements related to specific software, functions, or entire technology stacks. We need all these leading and lagging indicators to support the evolvement of the entire AI ecosystem today and in the future.

In the pharmaceutical industry, for example, the collaboration between the UK startup Exscientia and Sumitomo Dainippon Pharma outlines a clear case study for AI's positive impact on revenue generation and operational efficiency. In utilizing AI in the drug discovery process for a drug intended to treat

194

obsessive-compulsive disorder, the startup's development timeline of their new drug was expedited significantly. AI slashed the typical drug discovery period to just 12 months and reduced the number of synthesized compounds needed from 2,500 to 350. This illustrates AI's capacity to streamline and economize lengthy R&D cycles and highlights its critical role in advancing precision medicine by swiftly moving drugs from the lab to clinical trials.

MIT scientists also created an algorithm that utilizes ML to identify an antibiotic compound. The identified compound could eradicate highly resistant bacteria, even when not responding to existing antibiotics. The algorithm used evaluated over a hundred million compounds within days before this new antibiotic was identified. Generative AI continues to accelerate drug discovery, improve clinical trials, and uncover more precision medicine therapies. For example, generative AI enabled Insilico to go from novel-target discovery to preclinical candidate in just 18 months, costing only $2.6 million in the process. Traditional methods would have cost more than $400 million and taken up to 6 years.

AI's progress as a copilot amplifies the possibilities across the board. The rapid popularity of ChatGPT has captured immense interest, showcasing the impact of generative AI in complementing human abilities. According to Accenture's estimates, language-based AI is expected to support or enhance up to 40% of working hours. A staggering 98% of business leaders surveyed believe that AI foundation models will hold importance in their organization's strategies for the next 3 to 5 years.

POTENTIAL METRICS FOR AI IMPACT

AI Top-Line Impact	AI Bottom-Line Impact
• Revenue growth	• Reduced operating costs
• Market share gain	• Increased productivity
• New customer acquisition	• Reduced development time
• Customer lifetime value	• Improved resource utilization
• Brand preference and advocacy	• Reduced fraud and risk

AI FOR IMPROVING BOTTOM-LINE PERFORMANCE

At an operational level, AI helps organizations run their business more efficiently. However, the impact on the bottom line depends on the already realized efficiency for specific tasks and functions based on digital tools. Nevertheless, measuring the productivity impact gained with AI is significant in most cases. Studies in customer service teams revealed that the support of agents with augmented conversation via AI achieves an average of a 15% increase in productivity. For new joiners and less experienced agents, the impact is 35%, while experienced service agents have efficiency gains of less than 2%. A recent experiment conducted by the Boston Consulting Group involving 758 consultants using GPT-4 on a set of eighteen realistic consulting tasks also showed augmented productivity. The results outline that consultants using AI were significantly more productive, completing 12.2% more tasks on average and completing those tasks 25.1% faster. Furthermore, the produced results were significantly higher quality (more than 40%). Nvidia, for example, is conducting research on the use of chatbots based on LLMs. These chatbots can simplify semiconductor designs and tasks that require substantial engineering efforts. By incorporating three decades' worth of design data into these chatbots, Nvidia aims to promote knowledge sharing within the company and alleviate engineers from having to constantly mentor junior colleagues.

Moreover, Nvidia is harnessing AI to generate testing scripts to enhance engineers' productivity. Similar examples exist across industries, and a bottom-line improvement is, for example, also observed in AI-augmented manufacturing, where human and machine intelligence unfold their entire potential → see pages 78–79. The time of implementation for AI varies depending on the complexity of tasks. Still, many companies can identify the appropriate use case and implement a solution in less than 8 months. Analyzing the general impact of AI on the bottom line shows that on average, companies investing in AI realize USD 4 in return per USD 1 spent on AI solutions. Some companies (depending on the task, function, and digital maturity) realized even USD 10 in return per USD 1 spent on AI solutions. Many of the AI implementations realized a return on the AI investment in less than 15 months. AI's organizational value depends on task performance, from pure error elimination to improving productivity to achieving breakthrough innovations.

→The chart line in the illustration on the next page demonstrates and summarizes the level of value added on the top and bottom lines when the goals of AI and humans as a team and AI advancements shift through four different scenarios.

196

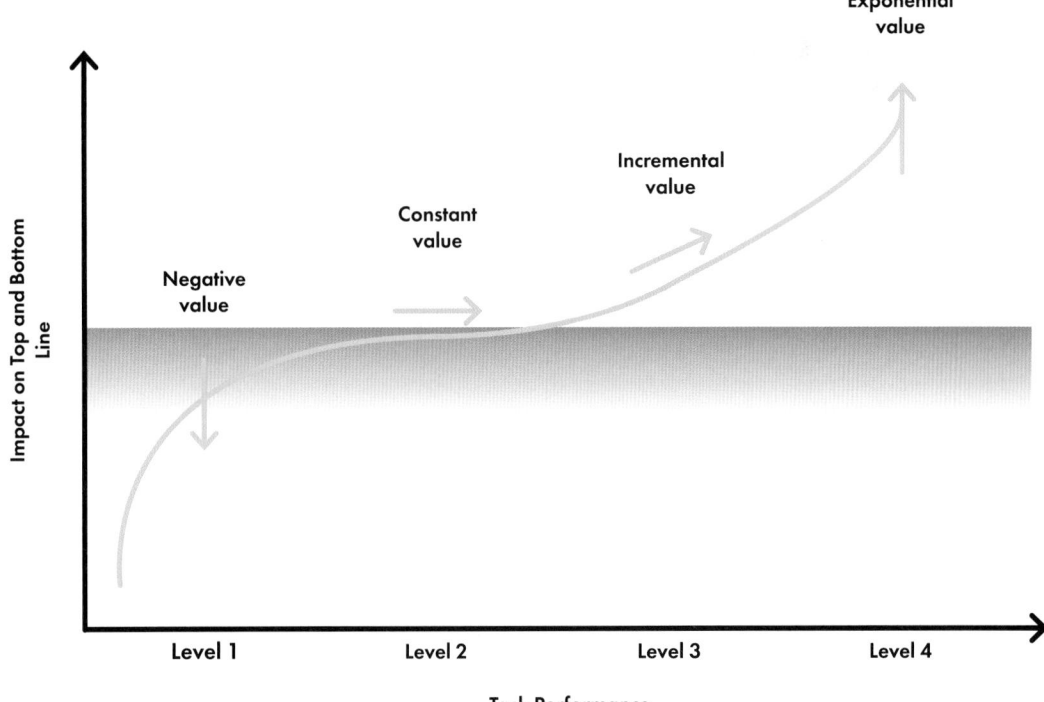

- Level 1: Elimination of errors (related to work where one mistake has high impact on value)
- Level 2: Minimization of variance (related, for example, to transaction-processing work)
- Level 3: Improvement of productivity (related, for example, to higher sale effectiveness)
- Level 4: Achievement of breakthroughs (related, for example, to highly creative work)

In the current application of AI, errors might occur because the underlying logic is missing. This problem is exacerbated by the fact that when the stakes are high, the risk tolerance for human error is lower and more tolerated than the fallibility of AI. This is crucial for all decision-makers because they need to know when they can and cannot rely on AI technologies and what role they should play in the interactions of humans and AI as a team (replacement, augmentation, or creation). AI has the most significant impact on democratizing knowledge and creativity through augmentation, lowering the skill premiums traditionally required for a variety of creative tasks when the objective is to achieve productivity gains and breakthroughs in areas with high risk tolerance.

AI, FOR NOW, HAS THE GREATEST IMPACT IN REPLACING HIGHLY REPETITIVE, RULE-BASED WORK, WHERE IT CAN SUPPORT HUMAN CREATIVITY, CRITICAL THINKING, AND EMPATHY AND WHERE IT CAN CREATE NEW HUMAN WORK.

THE NEXT WAVE IN AI ECOSYSTEM CONFIGURATION

The AI value chain and adaption of transformer models have the potential to significantly accelerate AI adoption, even in organizations lacking deep AI, ML, or data analytics expertise. While for many use cases significant customization is still required, adopting a generative model for a specific task can be accomplished with relatively low quantities of data or examples through APIs or by prompt engineering. However, the next big question is foreseeable, and it will deal with how the individual foundation models interact globally and in the respective organizations who orchestrate them and which standards are applied.

One of the emerging trends in the AI ecosystem is the development of global foundation models. These are LLMs and other AI models that have been trained on a massive scale and can be used for various tasks, such as translation, code generation, and question-answering. Global foundation models still need to be realized, but they could potentially revolutionize many industries. Currently, AI lacks the ability to retain episodic memory and struggles to conceptualize and analyze things like movies and extract value from them. LLMs will continue to evolve and increase their understanding and reasoning. LLMs will develop a deeper understanding of context and exhibit more advanced reasoning abilities, learning new tasks with less instruction, much like a human.

LLMs will also possess the capacity to handle multiple modalities capabilities on a much greater scale. They will be able to adapt to various environments and objectives without being explicitly programmed for them. LLMs may even possess "common sense" understanding, enabling them to make everyday judgments that current AI systems struggle with. Advancements in chatbot technology will focus on more personalization, emotional intelligence, and versatility. By leveraging data and advanced ML techniques, chatbots will be able to tailor interactions to match specific users' past behaviors and preferences. Additionally, improved NLP capabilities will enable chatbots to recognize and respond to emotions effectively, resulting in enhanced engagement.

GLOBAL AI x ECOSYSTEM

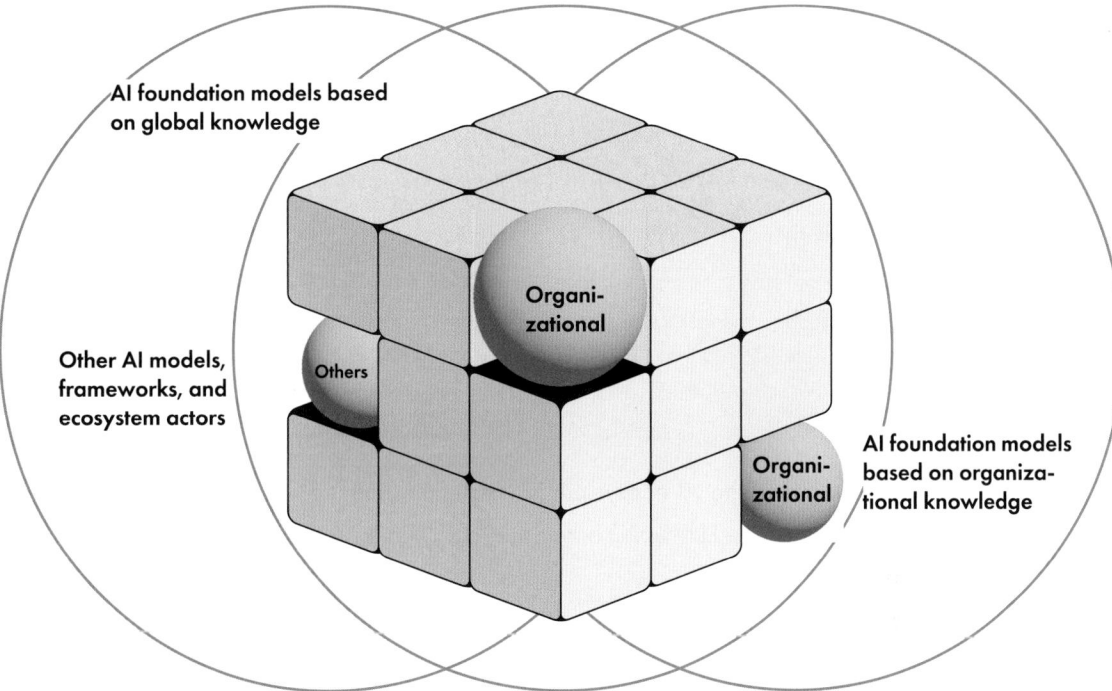

AI foundation models based on global knowledge

Other AI models, frameworks, and ecosystem actors

Organizational

Others

Organizational

AI foundation models based on organizational knowledge

Since future scenarios are all currently vague, we recommend that companies, regardless of the respective future scenarios, obtain clarity about their own data and AI strategy, and train their employees and reskill them if necessary. In addition, the basis for all further developments should be lived based on your framework for ensuring that AI is used responsibly and ethically and last but not least to collaborate with other stakeholders, such as governments, academia, and civil society to ensure that AI is developed and used responsibly and beneficially.

Currently we observe that multiple organizations, including PAI, GPAI, DAIA, and Hugging Face Hub, are actively building toward a decentralized, collaborative, and responsible AI ecosystem with diverse stakeholder involvement.

OUR WISH FOR THE FUTURE IS THAT THE AI ECOSYSTEM WILL BE A DECENTRALIZED, COLLABORATIVE, AND RESPONSIBLE ONE, WHERE GLOBAL FOUNDATION MODELS ARE ORCHESTRATED BY DIVERSE STAKEHOLDERS FOR THE BENEFIT OF ALL.

Nelli Babayan, PhD

→ Director of Azure Data and AI Analytics
at Microsoft Federal

THE RISE OF THE MACHINES . . .
FOR THE BENEFIT OF HUMANITY:
PROMPTING INTELLIGENT ADOPTION OF AI

In early 2024, the International Monetary Fund published a report on the potential impact of AGI on the future of work. Many news outlets picked up the findings of the report with headlines pointing that AI was poised to "impact 60% of jobs and worsen inequality." Yet while news outlets and social media feeds are quick to pick up and circulate the most daunting findings of this or, for that matter, any other report, they often also perhaps inadvertently obscure the democratizing and uplifting potential of AI. While many experts voice concerns about the disruptions that AI can bring, they also direct our attention to the fact that "the AI era is upon us, and it is still within our power to ensure it brings prosperity for all. " As described excellently in this chapter, the aim is to understand the key trends in AI innovation and how humanity can harness them for good. This point of view will reflect quickly about the perspectives from the authors and provides additional considerations. Specifically, the painted future scenario is to be enriched with further thoughts on how AI can and has already promoted scientific discoveries, continues with a discussion of the risks that AI can entail, and concludes with approaches to living and working in the age of AI.

Michael and Omar started by outlining the possible impact and potential AI may have on scientific discovery and productivity, especially as it evolves into multi-modality and is combined with other areas inter alia quantum computing. Given the pace of technological breakthroughs we have been witnessing in the past couple of years, it wouldn't be surprising if by the time this book goes into print, the authors' predictions and assumptions become reality. In fact, the power of AI to bring speed to scientific innovation has already become a reality as it has, for example, significantly shortened the time required to conduct experiments and simulations within chemistry and material sciences. By using advanced AI models purpose-built for scientific discovery, the team of scientists at the Pacific Northwest National Laboratory produced a chemical compound in "less than nine months, a blink of an eye compared with traditional methods." While this is an example of a quest to uncover much-needed sustainable energy storage solutions, the applications are much broader, especially in areas where synthesis and testing at a human scale may be limiting.

GENERATIVE AI HAS THE POTENTIAL TO OFFER INDIVIDUALS AND SOCIETY A WIDE RANGE OF BENEFITS.

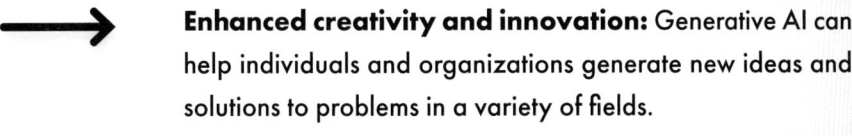

- **Enhanced creativity and innovation:** Generative AI can help individuals and organizations generate new ideas and solutions to problems in a variety of fields.

- **Improved productivity and efficiency:** Generative AI can automate tasks, streamline processes, and help people work more efficiently.

- **Personalized experiences:** Generative AI can be used to create personalized products, services, and content that are tailored to individual needs and preferences.

- **Improved decision-making:** Generative AI can help people make better decisions by providing them with access to data and insights that would be difficult or impossible to obtain otherwise.

- **New opportunities for learning and education:** Generative AI can be used to create new and engaging learning experiences that can help people learn in new and innovative ways.

However, while the authors outline previously the potential benefits of AI, they also duly acknowledge the potential risks that AI may pose. The discussion of risks is unambiguously present in the sections that assess the application of AI to specific industries and space exploration and includes disparities between high-income and low-income nations in AI adoption or the potential for great-power competition in the geopolitical arena.

POTENTIAL RISKS ASSOCIATED WITH GENERATIVE AI

→ **Bias and discrimination:** Generative AI algorithms can reflect the biases of their creators, which can lead to the creation of biased or discriminatory outputs.

→ **Privacy and security:** Generative AI can be used to collect and analyze vast amounts of personal data, which can raise concerns about privacy and security.

→ **Misinformation and disinformation:** Generative AI can be used to create fake or misleading content, which can sow discord and confusion.

→ **Automation and job displacement:** Generative AI has the potential to automate many tasks, which could lead to job displacement for some workers.

202

Yet, as we assess the benefits and risks of AI or any other disruptive technology, we should remember that as of now and at least for the foreseeable future, AI is a tool, and how we use it depends on us. In the wake and close aftermath of the Arab Spring, academics and pundits hailed social media as the toppler of dictators on its way to bringing democracy to most authoritarian regimes. Nonetheless, as subsequent events showed, technology on its own does not dictate outcomes; it is rather how users choose to adopt and use said technology that influences its impact.

While AI to many may seem as a nebulous concept, understanding or adopting of which may require a PhD in coding, in reality the barriers for entry are at the lowest ever. Many of us are already using AI in our everyday lives without even realizing it when we ask Alexa or a similar home assistant to dim our lights or rely on a "smart" thermostat to learn our preferred living room temperature. With the introduction of LLMs and ChatGPT and other similar freely available tools, the power of AI and specifically AGI has become available to anyone who has an internet-connected device and "growth mindset" powered by the willingness to learn. After all, AI is unlikely to take anyone's job, but someone who learns how to use AI might. AI is here to stay, and large corporations along with nation states will continue to invest in its innovation and exploration of use-cases and applicability. While we collectively pursue AI innovation, it is paramount that we also adopt and implement responsible development and application of AI-powered technologies to ensure we are promoting the benefits and minimizing the risks.

As we embrace AI's transformative potential, let's ensure responsible development and application.

NOW, WITH TOOLS LIKE CHATGPT AT YOUR FINGERTIPS, ANYONE WITH AN INTERNET CONNECTION AND A CURIOUS MIND CAN TAP INTO THE POWER OF AI. EMBRACE THE GROWTH MINDSET AND UNLOCK THE POTENTIAL OF AI – THE FUTURE IS CLOSER THAN YOU THINK!

KEY TAKEAWAYS

→ While specific tools and conclusions in AI quickly become outdated, the potential of the technology requires adaptable decision-makers to leverage foundational models and their advancements for creating valuable products and services.

→ Applying AI effectively requires considering three lenses: (1) tools for increased labor productivity, (2) generative AI for fostering innovation, and (3) impact on company financials and business models.

→ The rise of AI emphasizes the need for organizations to move beyond "exploit" mode and focus on asking critical questions to define problems before seeking solutions.

→ *Using the potential of AI in design thinking will lead to more harmonious collaboration between AI and human designers, reshaping traditional approaches and creating new applications for the future.*

→ *The rapid development of foundation models, like LLMs, offers even organizations with limited AI expertise the potential to adopt and benefit from AI technology, but challenges remain regarding interoperability and responsible use.*

→ *Measuring the financial impact of AI through ROI calculations is crucial for justifying its use and fostering its growth within businesses.*

PART 4

THE FUTURE OF AI AND INNOVATION

THE FUTURE OF AI WON'T BE A RACE TO SINGULARITY BUT A COLLABORATIVE DANCE WHERE HUMAN INGENUITY INTERTWINES WITH ARTIFICIAL INTELLIGENCE TO UNLOCK NEW LEVELS OF UNDERSTANDING AND PROGRESS AND PERHAPS EVEN TRANSCEND OUR CURRENT LIMITATIONS.

WHAT'S NEXT FOR AI

AI has already exploded in several areas and fields of application, including the number of models trained to convergence, model capabilities (typing, talking, seeing, hearing, moving), model sizes (increasingly large), and measured intelligence (more and more intelligent), as well as creativity – all with seemingly limitless exponential growth.

The unprecedented advancement in AI will continue and become far more sophisticated and capable of mimicking human-level cognition. Advancements in LLMs have already transformed several industries by powering chatbots, content creation, data analysis, and more. Within this decade, as LLMs become even more advanced, all of us will witness a paradigm shift in operations. Furthermore, integrating LLMs into business processes will drive efficiency, reduce costs, and open up new avenues for innovation, especially in areas like personalized education, custom-made marketing, and real-time translation.

AI models will soon exceed human expertise in specialized domains like medical diagnosis and financial analysis. They may creep into subjective realms like creativity and emotional intelligence. In the next few years, we expect pioneering work in neuromorphic computing, quantum ML, and the creation of human-like knowledge graphs. AI will display more common sense, allowing it to better understand broad contexts beyond narrow training. It may even exhibit capabilities like basic reasoning, creativity, and humor. Nevertheless, considerable research is required in areas like common sense reasoning, curiosity, and transfer learning for AI to evolve into AGI.

The sheer power of AI to sift through gargantuan data troves and unearth intricate patterns is unparalleled. By combining the power of human ingenuity with AI's prowess, we're poised to redefine the parameters of scientific exploration, heralding an imminent renaissance in research and discovery with transversal applicability across all industrial sectors.

AI algorithms are increasingly adept at complex tasks like strategic planning, creative content generation, and basic reasoning. This enables AI to shift from a tool of automation and analysis to an integrated partner in nearly every aspect of our daily lives. As AI algorithms become more sophisticated, we can expect even more generalized AI systems to emerge.

These systems will perform a wider range of tasks without needing specific training. There will also be a stronger emphasis on creating AI systems that can understand, reason, and exhibit emotional intelligence, facilitating a more profound human—machine synergy.

Enterprise applications have conversational AI features.

Impactful product innovation via generative AI is applied for the design and ideation phase.

AI-generated images and videos will be indistinguishable from real ones.

GENERATIVE AI

Real-time generative AI is capable of producing high-quality, real-time outputs.

AI enhances data security in areas of detecting unusual patterns and simulated cyber attacks.

AI takes over specific tasks ranging from HR work to creating legal frameworks.

GENERATIVE AI

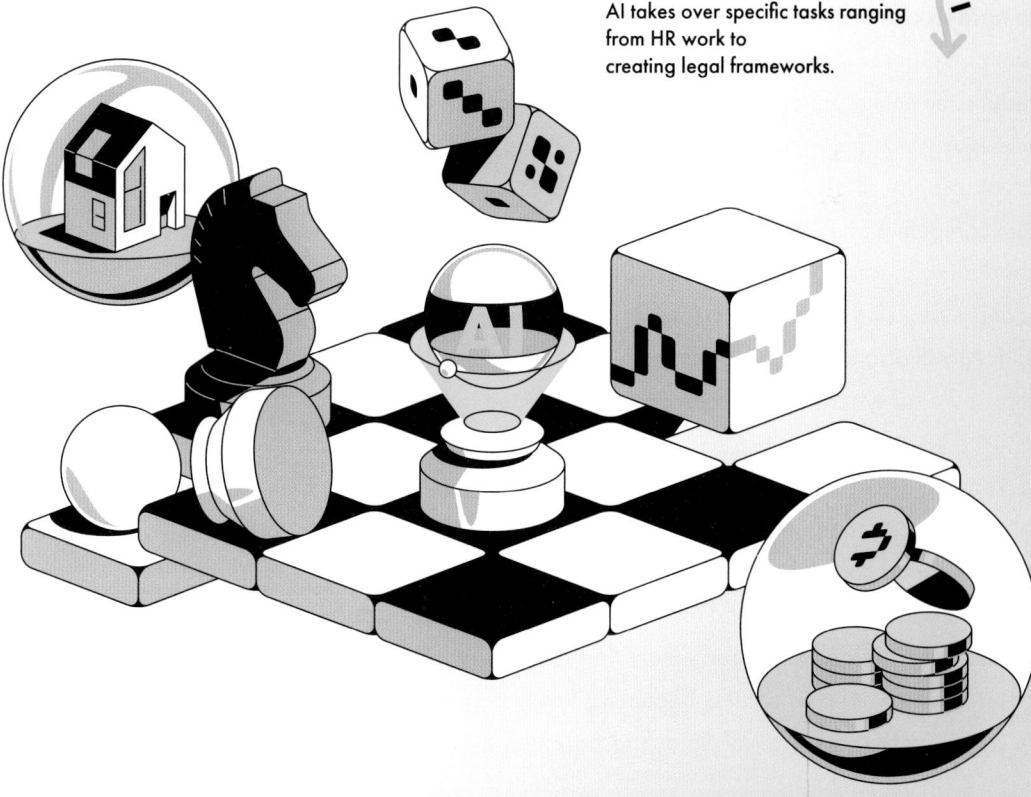

As mentioned earlier, AI has had some limiting factors in the past, but emerging multimodal generative AI systems are starting to synthesize content that spans different formats. A brief textual description will simultaneously create a visual artwork or even an animation without using different independent systems. This has the potential to revolutionize multiple industries in unprecedented ways, as outlined → on pages 209–212. AI systems that understand and generate multiple forms of data can engage with users more naturally. Imagine a future of educational platforms where students use a single prompt in text to trigger an AI response with a combination of spoken words, diagrams, and interactive simulations, adapting in real time to the student's feedback. In healthcare, a multimodal AI will be able to analyze a patient's verbal descriptions of symptoms, visual data from scans, and textual data from medical records simultaneously, offering more accurate diagnoses or treatment recommendations. Given the current trajectory of AI research and development, the expected evolution toward multimodal generative AI is inevitable. It will be up to society, policymakers, and industry leaders to ensure its responsible development and integration into various sectors in ways that will amplify the value and diminish the negative aspects of that technology.

The next leap in exponential technologies, quantum computing, with its potential to process very complex computations at unimaginable speeds compared to today's classical computers, is set to supercharge AI's capabilities. As quantum computers become more capable and accessible, they will significantly reduce the time required to train deep learning models, opening doors to solve previously insurmountable problems. This synergy will revolutionize fields like cryptography, material science, and drug discovery. The combination of quantum computing and AI will enable the modeling of truly complex systems, from simulating the human brain's intricacies to applications that span and transcend every single industry. However, the integration of quantum computing with AI will also necessitate new protocols and safety measures, ensuring that this powerful synergistic combination is harnessed responsibly.

If AI continues to evolve as expected, there will be a point in the future when AI surpasses human intelligence, leading to rapid technological growth and unpredictable societal changes. At this juncture, AI systems may be capable of self-improvement, allowing them to enhance their own capabilities in exponential ways. This acceleration would theoretically result in a rapid expansion of intelligence, with AI entities becoming vastly more intelligent than humans in a relatively short span of time. The potential implications on society, the

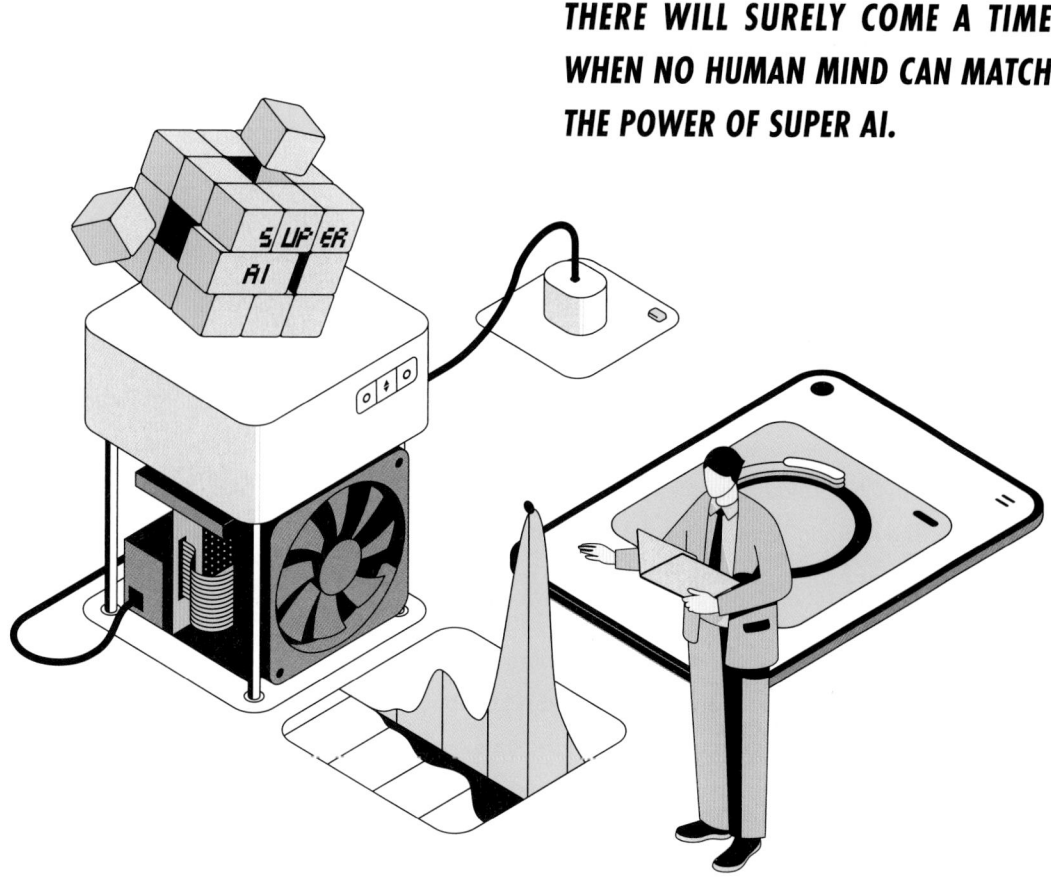

economy, and humanity as a whole are yet to be adequately understood. Responsibly managing the societal impacts of AI while avoiding risks like job losses, algorithmic biases, and loss of privacy will require proactive efforts. The path ahead is exciting yet unpredictable.

Looking even further into the future, generative AI could signal a whole new era in technology, with the potential to usher in another industrial revolution at a breathtaking pace. Such a development in AI might be the best and the last invention humans will ever endeavour to make as AI continues to evolve and become more intelligent. At this stage, AI will accelerate technological progress in various fields such as AI programming, space exploration, drug discovery and development, science, and many others. The advanced fusion of technologies continues to mature and develop advanced forms of superintelligence, even making it possible to copy artificial brains. As a result, AI may also lead to a technological singularity in the future → see pages 223–226.

TRENDS ON AI

These timely observations and their developments are relatively simple. The foundation models currently in use will evolve and be adapted and used for their specific purpose. In addition, generative AI will become the standard for general and robust reasoning and integrated fact-checking. The dominant players from OpenAI, Anthropic, Alphabet, Microsoft, Meta, Amazon, and IBM will continue pursuing their strategies toward the best generative AI. Researchers in China also continue to progress on building Chinese-language AI models. The leading Chinese model is called ChatGLM, which can be compared to ChatGPT on some capabilities, and according to the developers, it outperforms it in Chinese. It can also be estimated that we will train the nets with 10 times or 100 times the neurons of a human on all kinds of data from the World Wide Web (both verified data and suspicious data). However, the prediction about the mid-to-long-term view becomes more difficult. We know from history that intuition is not very useful when predicting exponential curves.

Even the medium-term view of AI allows for a wide variety of future scenarios and very different timelines for potential development steps. For example, concerning the super AI described previously, some experts are firmly convinced that superintelligence will

THERE IS A BIG DILEMMA WITH EXPONENTIAL CURVES – OUR INTUITION IS NOT VERY USEFUL IN PREDICTING THE FUTURE.

be inevitable by the end of this century, and other experts believe it will not be possible to achieve it within the next 75 years. While many humans are currently worried that AI is misaligned with our current society's beliefs and values, others believe that AI will turn conscious and help solve the world's most wicked problems. Again, we might have to ask other questions beyond considerations about exponential technology's potential. We might have to focus on creating the appropriate incentives for decision-makers, politicians, and humans, in general, to be ethical and collaborate and respect each other. We might need incentives for humankind to align with a positive AI future in a well-defined ethical system. Identifying exactly what we need in the long term is uncertain because with regard to technologies, we will see and experience AI innovations that are still within the known boundaries of well-known physics but are impossible to realize today.

For this reason, we can only look to current trends, as the future is conceivable but not absolutely predictable. Our trend radar takes a view up to 2030 with regard to the relevant topics, considering five selected dimensions and their impact from low to transformational.

THE AI TREND RADAR – FROM LOW TO TRANSFORMATIONAL

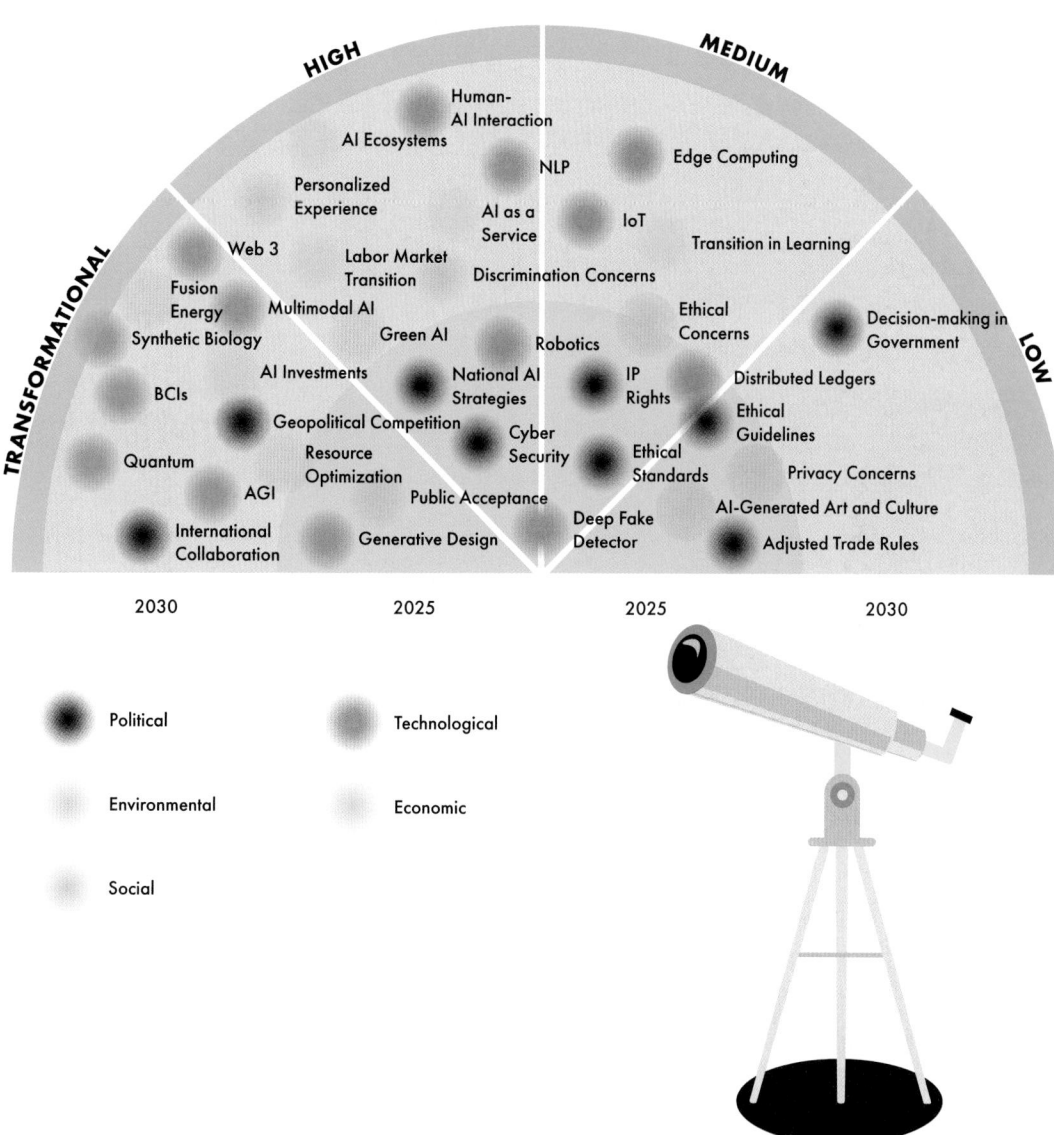

The trend radar reveals some trends of high interest because of their transformational character on social, political, environmental, economic, and technological factors. For example, AI-enhanced decision-making might be applied in many fields, from finance and healthcare to government and law. This trend has the potential to make decisions more efficient and accurate, while attention must be given to making them unbiased as well. On the political factors, AI is driving current developments in many directions, reaching from AI-enabled authoritarianism and regimes, which might be misused to consolidate power and suppress dissent, to a more positive AI-driven global economic transformation, which allows the rise of new industries and new ways of global collaboration for the greater good. The transformation impact trends with regard to technology will be related in many aspects to generative AI as described in this book, but also other technological advancements, like brain-computer interfaces (BCIs), will be transformational, allowing humans to directly control machines with their thoughts. This would have a major impact on a wide range of applications, from prosthetics to virtual reality. Other technologies related to synthetic biology that aim to engineer new biological systems have the potential to revolutionize medicine, agriculture, and other industries. Other technologies have already found applications – for example, AI-powered chatbots and virtual assistants, as well as recommendation systems or image and video recognition. At the same time, we see a strong trend toward even more personalized products, services, and experiences. The next level of customization and personalization will create a more engaging and satisfying customer experience. In the context of the main focus of this book, the high-impact transformational trends are related mainly to the ability of AI to augment the capabilities of the design thinking and innovation teams. This includes providing them access to new information or providing real-time decision support. The application of AI ideation capabilities to draft new business model combinations has already become a common way of using AI. This might lead to new ways of selling products and services or new ways of interacting with customers. AI has become a very powerful tool for generating more and better ideas by using its strength to analyze data, identify patterns, and generate new concepts. In the creation of prototypes with AI, tasks such as 3D modeling and code generation for digital prototypes are increasingly automated.

New developments in generative AI product design are also a very transformational trend and a new design approach that applies algorithms and AI-powered software to create and optimize product designs. It is a departure from traditional design methods, which typically involve a designer creating a product design based on a set of requirements and design principles.

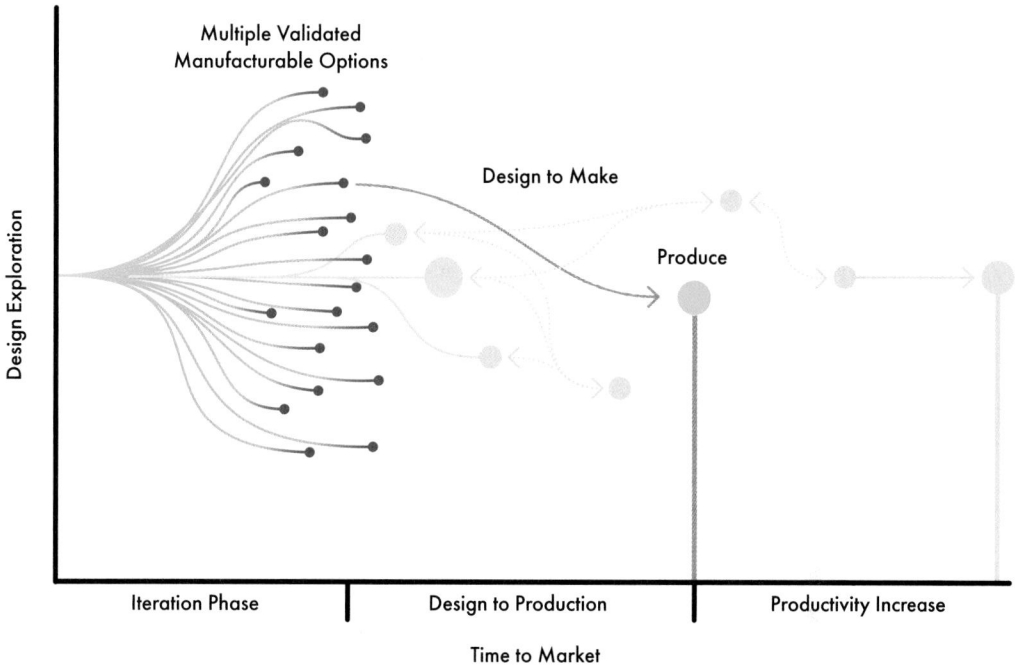

The benefits of generative design are related to the ability to quickly generate and evaluate a large number of design options or even detect design options that may not have been considered using traditional design methods. On top of this, AI is able to consider manufacturing constraints from the outset, which helps to create products that are easier and less expensive to produce. Based on the singular and increasingly complex and interrelated application fields of generative AI, the question arises of a comprehensive innovation framework that integrates generative AI in a purposeful and intelligent way. Generative AI is used to collect and analyze insight and predict historical data trends.

For ideation, generative AI supports innovation teams collecting user/customer feedback or triggering a brainstorming session with an automatic reframing algorithm. AI supports the risk analysis of design challenges and innovation projects or categorizes the entire innovation portfolio with the aim of optimizing resource allocation.

AI UNLOCKS DESIGN POSSIBILITIES: GENERATE A FLOOD OF OPTIONS, EMBRACE MANUFACTURABILITY, AND PREDICT FUTURE TRENDS — ALL WITH THE HELP OF INTELLIGENT MACHINES.

AI'S INFLUENCE ON DIFFERENT SECTORS

The latest trends expose that AI will continue to act as a transformative catalyst across numerous sectors and entire business ecosystems. It streamlines operations, optimizes processes, and delivers unprecedented efficiencies. Sectors significantly impacted by AI range from the healthcare industry's diagnostic algorithms to finance's automated trading systems. However, there is a lot of potential in deploying generative AI for public services, aiming to make public services more accessible and efficient. AI's footprint is both deep and expansive. Looking to the future, AI's influence promises to expand and revolutionize services. We can anticipate a world where AI-driven personalized medical treatments become the norm, autonomous vehicles dominate transportation networks, and AI-guided sustainable farming practices revolutionize agriculture and ensure food security. More than just optimizing existing systems, AI can redefine industries, create novel paradigms, and reshape the fabric of our socioeconomic structures in ways we're only beginning to imagine. At the same time, AI will continue to integrate more deeply into our daily lives, from smart homes that anticipate our needs to urban environments that adjust in real time to conditions. In this respect, AI will continue to complement human capabilities and will augment humans, leading to a synergistic relationship. On top of this, we can imagine a future in which AI systems can read, interpret, and respond to human emotions, revolutionizing sectors like customer service, healthcare, and entertainment in unprecedented ways. Future AI models are trending toward more efficiency, requiring fewer data to learn and using techniques like few-shot or zero-shot learning, which is in contrast to traditional ML, where the model is trained on a set of labeled samples from all of the classes that it will be asked to classify. Zero-shot learning is basically trained on a set of labeled classes but is then asked to classify samples from unseen classes. Of course, the future of AI is based on self-learning and adapting systems. Instead of being trained on static datasets as we did in the past, AI systems will continuously learn and adapt from various environments in real time.

Further, the integration of quantum computing and AI could lead to a step function and leapfrog AI's capabilities, making processing immensely faster and more efficient. As a result, AI will enhance efficiency beyond current capabilities and become, at the same time, more anticipatory and proactive. Imagine, for example, a revolution in the educational system with personalized learning. AI-driven educational systems will tailor content to individual student needs, ensuring a pace and style that suit each learner. AI systems are starting to help develop curricula, create exams, and automate grading systems. These AI-enabled technologies are offloading administrative burdens from educators, allowing them to focus more on instruction and student interaction. Looking ahead, the larger disruption to the educational systems lies in the potential democratization and quality of education. Virtual AI-powered educators could make world-class instruction available to students in remote or under-served regions with limited access to quality education. Simultaneously, augmented reality and virtual reality integrated with AI will be able to offer immersive educational experiences, revolutionizing the majority of fields. AI will disrupt the very paradigm of learning by shifting and emphasizing lifelong adaptability and skill acquisition in an ever-evolving digital world.

AI EXAMPLE: THE EVOLUTION OF EDUCATION

Personalized training and learning

Create intelligent mentoring systems

Increase accessibility and inclusivity

Increase accessibility and inclusivity

Promote collaboration

Customized learning

Respond to FAQs

time

However, all advancements in AI must, from the ground up, be fair, transparent, accountable, secure, and unbiased. Tools to audit and understand AI decisions will become standard. At the same time, we see a fusion of disciplines. Combining AI with other fields like biology, physics, and art could lead to innovations we haven't even considered yet, from AI-driven drug discovery to new art forms. More examples of the impact of AI on different industries and a deep dive into AI and the space industry are outlined in the following pages.

EXCITING AREAS WHERE AI WILL HAVE IMPACT IN YOUR INDUSTRY

TRANSPORTATION

AI will go beyond roads and revolutionize air travel with autonomous drones and aircraft, making goods transportation and personal travel more efficient. As AI continues to seamlessly integrate into transportation infrastructure, the way we perceive mobility and connectivity will undergo a profound and transformative shift.

BIOTEC AND HEALTHCARE

AI will have the capability to analyze a single drop of blood and provide a holistic view of a person's health, from vitamin deficiencies to potential genetic mutations or cancerous growths, replacing a battery of tests as we currently do today.

LEGAL

AI is making significant inroads in the legal industry, streamlining various processes, automating routine and time-consuming tasks, streamlining legal research, reviewing documents, and analyzing contracts. Predictive analytics, underpinned by AI, will forecast legal outcomes based on historical data, aiding lawyers in strategy formulation. In addition, smart contracts enabled by blockchain and AI will automate and self-execute contractual obligations, potentially reducing disputes.

PROFESSIONAL SPORTS

Athletes and coaches will harness advanced AI-driven analytics to refine strategies and enhance performance. The more granular data from sensors, video analytics, and health checks also allow for a tailored training regimen, optimizing player fitness and game tactics. Additionally, AI aids in scouting and analyzing vast amounts of footage to pinpoint emerging talents or assess opponent strategies.

MUSIC

AI and blockchain will accurately track music usage across various platforms, which may enable a more transparent royalty allocation to artists. As the collaboration between musicians and AI deepens, the boundary between machine-generated and human-created music may become intertwined, leveraging new dimensions of creativity, sounds, and performance.

CYBERSECURITY

On the horizon, quantum computing integrated with AI is poised to play a major role in this field as it threatens to disrupt traditional encryption methods, potentially rendering them obsolete. The same technology also promises unprecedented security measures, forging quantum-resistant algorithms. As cyber threats continue to increase in complexity, advanced quantum capabilities and AI will evolve into even more sophisticated capabilities.

AGRICULTURE

AI will increase yields and profitability while creating more sustainable and environmentally friendly agricultural practices. Advanced AI systems will soon enable extremely precise predictions for weather, crop yields, soil conditions, and disease/pest outbreaks collectively in ways we have not seen yet. At the same time, advanced autonomous tractors, drones, and harvesters will become commonplace on a different scale.

FASHION

The fashion industry will benefit from virtual AI fashion designers who account for personalized interests and market fashion trends, then possibly create 3D-printed personalized garments. These 3D garments may include advanced sensors powered by AI for health monitoring, communication, etc. Try-ons using AI and augmented reality will also become common.

RETAIL

The concept of traditional shopping will be challenged by fully automated stores, where human intervention is minimal. As AI continues to evolve, it promises to reshape retail, making it even more personalized and streamlined for both businesses and consumers. AI will also advance recommendation systems to tailor product suggestions based on real-time and predictive consumer behavior. AI is also enhancing supply chain efficiency in various industries by employing AI to forecast demand and maintain optimal stock.

MANUFACTURING

As AI continues to advance, it will disrupt manufacturing by ushering in versatile and smart factories that adjust production in real time to meet demand. AI will soon drive unparalleled efficiency and sustainability in manufacturing processes by optimizing resource utilization and ensuring optimal consumption of energy, materials, and other essential assets. Furthermore, future supply chain management driven by AI will be further optimized and will allow for real-time decision-making based on global trends and geopolitical events, creating a manufacturing ecosystem that is more adaptive and resilient.

FINANCE

The sector is moving toward personalized and tailored banking solutions and precise financial forecasting based on real customer needs. With autonomous AI-enabled advisors personalizing investment strategies and AI analyzing unconventional data, such as social media activity, to assess credit risks, the sector will begin a transformation journey like never seen before. The emergence of quantum computing, along with advanced AI, promises to further amplify these advancements, offering unparalleled data processing speeds and complex financial modeling capabilities.

MORE EFFICIENCY OR A TECHNOLOGY EVERY INDUSTRY WILL BUILD ON?

In the debate regarding the impact of AI in various industries, it is observed that decision-makers either view AI as just another technology that will bring more efficiency or believe that AI is the fundamental technology on which every single industry will be built. As AI evolves, it will continue to create and transform jobs in various sectors while spawning new opportunities and professions. For example, tasks that used to require the expertise of multiple people will now only be done by a few, and innovations will be realized in areas that were previously unimaginable. In the current maturity of AI and its applications, AI acts as a platform that enables different professions to perform their tasks and functions more efficiently. Companies that leverage the capabilities of AI will be much more effective and have a strategic advantage over those that do not.

The following Example Industry Case shows how AI will transform the space industry. The use cases of AI provide a glimpse into the future beyond the well-known application of AI for developing a new generation of space-craft or simulating efficient launch operations. The industry case is exploring the potential of AI in Earth-for-space, space-for-Earth, and space-for-space fields of applications. In addition, the associated risks are briefly discussed.

MANY COMPANIES, INCLUDING NASA, SPACEX, GOOGLE, AND THE EUROPEAN SPACE AGENCY (ESA), ARE USING AI TO DISCOVER NEW CELESTIAL OBJECTS AND IMPROVE ASTRONAUTS' LIVES IN SPACE.

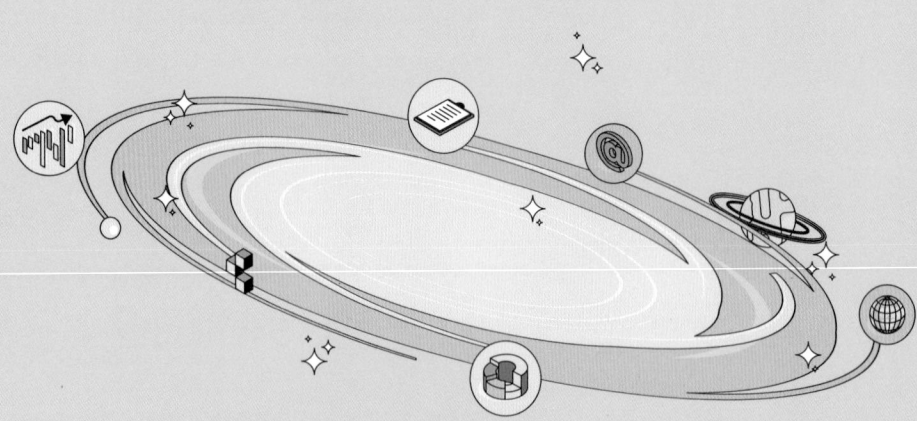

EXAMPLE INDUSTRY CASE ACTIVELY PARTICIPATING IN THE FUTURE OF AI AND INNOVATION

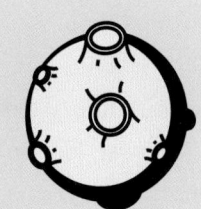

AI, INNOVATION, AND THE SPACE RENAISSANCE

When it comes to the future of AI and innovation, from our experience, there is currently no better playground than the space industry. A true "space renaissance" is under way, and innovation and AI have a significant influence on how exponentially the industry and associated technologies will change. Three distinct human–space interfaces are emerging as our efforts to understand, use, and colonize space rapidly take new forms, generally defined as Earth for space, space for Earth, and space for space. The first employs Earth-based infrastructure, such as telescopes and launch pads, to observe or reach space. The second uses space-based infrastructure to enhance life on Earth, such as telecommunications satellites. The third includes activities in Earth orbit and beyond that promote independent human presence in space, such as space stations.

All of them offer unprecedented opportunities, and AI is playing an essential role in facilitating innovative, accurate, and responsive efforts given the hostile, expansive, and uncertain nature of extraterrestrial environments. However, the proliferation of and reliance on AI in this context may exacerbate existing threats and create new risks that are largely underappreciated, particularly given the potential for great power competition and arms-like dynamics. From an ethical point of view, NASA's framework broadly defines, for example, six key principles for the "responsible use of AI":

1. Scientifically and technically robust
2. Explainable and transparent
3. Secure and safe
4. Accountable
5. Fair
6. Human-centric and societally beneficial

NASA's framework currently focuses on civilian space ventures, and expanded principles are discussed to address the "ethical limits" of noncivilian applications as well as to deal with super AI systems and beyond.

The fields of innovation projects and exponential progress related to human-to-space interfaces would fill another book. Therefore, only the most exciting fields of innovation work are briefly outlined, including knowledge and solutions in the fields of resource efficiency, technological innovation, telecommunications, Earth observation, planetary defense, mission strategy, human life-support systems, and even artificial astronauts.

THE ULTIMATE PLAYGROUND FOR AI AND INNOVATION, DRIVING A "SPACE RENAISSANCE" WITH VAST OPPORTUNITIES AND ETHICAL CONSIDERATIONS.

AI IN EARTH FOR SPACE

AI is enabling astronomical discoveries by rapidly processing volumes of data from next-generation observatories that humans could never analyze. There are, for example, recently developed ML models trained with vast libraries of light curves that can outperform humans in planet searches and have been proposed in combination with chemical signature studies to determine if exoplanets are habitable. Advanced classification of other celestial objects such as stars, galaxies, and quasars, and detection of signals from rare cosmic events such as supernovae, gravitational lensing, and cataclysmic mergers of neutron stars and black holes, are enabled by ML algorithms. AI will support the development of new technologies and life support systems needed for human settlement in space. It will accelerate innovation in materials for spacecraft and environmentally friendly fuels.

Researchers using AI recently identified a unique solar system consisting of six stars. The discovery was revealed in data from the Transiting Exoplanet Survey Satellite (TESS) using an AI neural network designed to detect eclipsing binary stars. Discoveries are being made at exponential speeds using this technology. Studying this unique eclipsing sextuple system provides an important cornerstone to further understanding stellar evolution and dynamics in multi-star systems. The same AI system has already identified multiple candidate systems that must be confirmed with other methods.

ML-assisted digital twin simulations are testing already rapidly space-qualified food production systems. These include controlled environment agriculture technologies such as microalgae photobioreactors and vertical farms.

AI IN SPACE FOR EARTH

Technological AI advancements in telecommunications, Earth observation, and planetary defense and investments have led to the expansion of space for Earth in recent decades from geosynchronous equatorial orbit and medium Earth orbit to low Earth orbit and beyond, improving life on Earth and laying the groundwork for space-for-Earth innovation shifts. These advancements also improve satellite technology for weather monitoring and Earth observation. In processing data generated by observation satellites, ML techniques have provided reliable estimates of solar irradiance and heat accumulation in urban areas and achieved 85% accuracy in estimating wind speed.

The ESA is developing an AI-powered digital twin of Earth to better monitor, predict, and respond to human and natural events, including acute problems such as earthquakes and chronic problems such as biodiversity loss. AI is also being used, for example, to help planetary protection find, track, and respond to near-Earth objects such as asteroids and comets. Using artificial neural networks, a hazardous object identifier has been developed to detect dangerous asteroids that could strike Earth, while an AI algorithm for detecting near-Earth objects (NEOs) distinguishes false positives from real threats. Climate change is a significant concern facing society and poses a significant threat to the Earth's habitat, as evidenced by recent instances of intense heat waves and flooding across the globe. Despite advancements in weather and climate modeling,

making accurate predictions is challenging. AI can improve predictive outcomes, especially when combined with quantum computing, to amplify data processing capabilities. The synergistic combination between quantum computing and AI (QAI) can be pivotal in evolving the next generation of climate change science simulations. These substantially enhanced weather predictions using QAI will provide a wider-ranging advantage to humanity and ultimately will help us better understand and mitigate the negative consequences of climate change.

AI IN SPACE FOR SPACE

Most exciting are the new developments inspace for space that turn the notion of a spacefaring civilization into reality, but the pace and scale at which we colonize space will be closely tied to advances in the mostly speculative super AI advancements and complementary technologies considered here in terms of mission execution, human astronaut support, and artificial astronauts.

The farther we get from our planet, the more we depend on autonomous systems due to lag in communication with Earth as it increases with distance to a point where it becomes ineffective. AI will assess operational risks and prioritize critical tasks to ensure the safety of space flights and the successful execution of space missions. The AI systems can assess their surrounding and detect potential hazards, such as cosmic radiation exposure, meteorite hazards, or orbital debris. Intelligent navigation systems that can use AI-assisted photo processing for mapping and positioning are under development.

AI PAVES THE WAY FOR A SELF-SUSTAINING SPACEFARING CIVILIZATION, FROM AUTONOMOUS EXPLORATION ROBOTS TO VIRTUAL CREW COMPANIONS.

NLP and mood analysis are used to develop virtual space assistants that anticipate and support the mental and emotional needs of human crews and intervene when needed to ensure their safety. Further advances in AI will lead to AI-enabled autonomous swarm robots mapping landscapes and searching for signs of extraterrestrial life on distant planets and autonomous 3D printing systems supervised by computer vision to ensure structures are built adequately with no discrepancies and without human interventions.

Humanoid robots powered by AI systems will explore hazardous and potentially dangerous landscapes, keeping astronauts safe. The same robots may be able to perform emergency surgical procedures without medical staff interventions.

AWARENESS FOR POTENTIAL RISKS

AI promises to advance the economies of Earth for space, space for Earth, and space for space; to support the space ambitions of modern nations; and to create benefits on Earth through technology transfer and downstream applications. But with great promise comes great risk. Space and AI are both full of unknowns, and their convergence poses serious risks if their development is not aligned with well-designed and forward-thinking ethical AI principles — that is, if it is not technically robust, responsibly managed, and underpinned by moral considerations — especially given the potential for great power competition and arms-race dynamics. We might even go so far as to make the ethical position the central question, as illustrated in the Future Singularity Ecosystem approach → on page 225.

AI systems operating autonomous rovers or spacecraft may encounter some challenges in space. A robust AI-driven autonomy system must be paramount in proper decision-making capabilities, especially in managing unforeseen or emergency scenarios in which effective decisions must be ensured without human guidance. The harsh and unpredictable nature of the environments in space, such as cosmic radiation, extreme temperature variations, and potential impacts with space debris, requires that AI systems must be resilient, able to operate with exceptional reliability, and have fault tolerance ability, enabling them to recover from possible failures in hardware or software.

At the administrative level, ethical concerns could also permutate within the organization. It is essential to ensure AI systems used to select candidates for future jobs are free from bias and discrimination and comply with fairness and transparency. It is also important to ensure these systems are free from bias when helping assess employee performance. Research done with AI also needs to have guardrails against copyright infringement and ensure information is accurate and free from hallucinations.

AI UNLOCKS SPACE EXPLORATION AND BOOSTS EARTH'S ECONOMY, BUT ETHICAL FRAMEWORKS ARE CRUCIAL TO STEER CLEAR OF UNFORESEEN RISKS AND ENSURE RESPONSIBLE DEVELOPMENT.

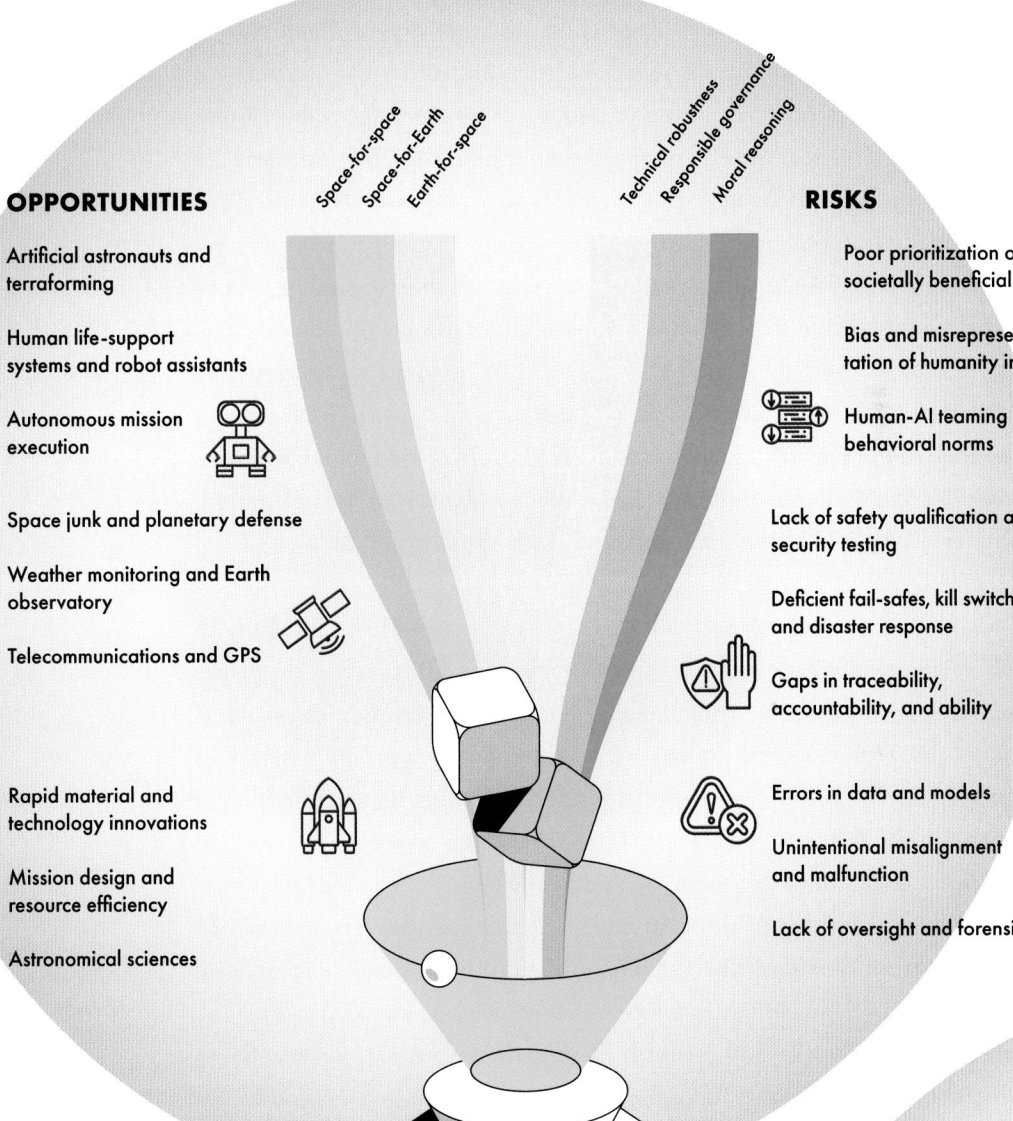

OPPORTUNITIES

Artificial astronauts and terraforming

Human life-support systems and robot assistants

Autonomous mission execution

Space junk and planetary defense

Weather monitoring and Earth observatory

Telecommunications and GPS

Rapid material and technology innovations

Mission design and resource efficiency

Astronomical sciences

Space-for-space
Space-for-Earth
Earth-for-space

Technical robustness
Responsible governance
Moral reasoning

RISKS

Poor prioritization of societally beneficial AI

Bias and misrepresentation of humanity in AI

Human-AI teaming and behavioral norms

Lack of safety qualification and security testing

Deficient fail-safes, kill switches, and disaster response

Gaps in traceability, accountability, and ability

Errors in data and models

Unintentional misalignment and malfunction

Lack of oversight and forensic

FUTURE OF INNOVATION MANAGEMENT

Generative AI is significantly influencing the future of innovation management by revolutionizing organizational approaches to creativity, problem-solving, and the way organizations create novel concepts. Innovation management is a critical aspect that organizations use to adapt and evolve to the required market and customer needs. The power of using AI in innovation management lies in its significant potential to innovate beyond human cognition, enhancing creativity and idea generation by leveraging its capacity to analyze extensive volumes of data and identify complex patterns beyond human capability. AI can also offer insights and inspiration to teams in the organization, identify new opportunities for innovation, and positively contribute to the development of unique ideas, concepts, and solutions. With our proposed future Generative AI Innovation Management Framework, we aim to improve innovation outcomes beyond currently used approaches, especially by identifying new opportunities for creativity and innovations and analyzing large sets of data.

The next leaps in generative AI will go far beyond current AI capability to combine and evaluate datasets from diverse domains effectively. Companies need the appropriate framework and organizational readiness to generate an amalgamation of ideas and concepts from other fields to promote interdisciplinary creativity. Constantly integrating new generative AI tools into innovation management brings numerous unique possibilities and advancements. It will support the iterative approach of creating solutions to complex problems and simulating multiple scenarios, providing creative suggestions that are difficult for humans alone to conceive. Generative AI is the new fundament for organizations and individuals to engage in a continuous learning journey by analyzing the outcomes and results from innovation projects while refining strategies and methods to enhance the success of future innovation endeavors. The next generation of innovation management must be properly integrated into the organization's operating model for it to be effective. The implementation takes place at strategic, tactical, infrastructural, and mindset levels by fostering and enabling knowledge creation and cross-pollinating AI's capacities to innovate while aligning with the organization's top priorities.

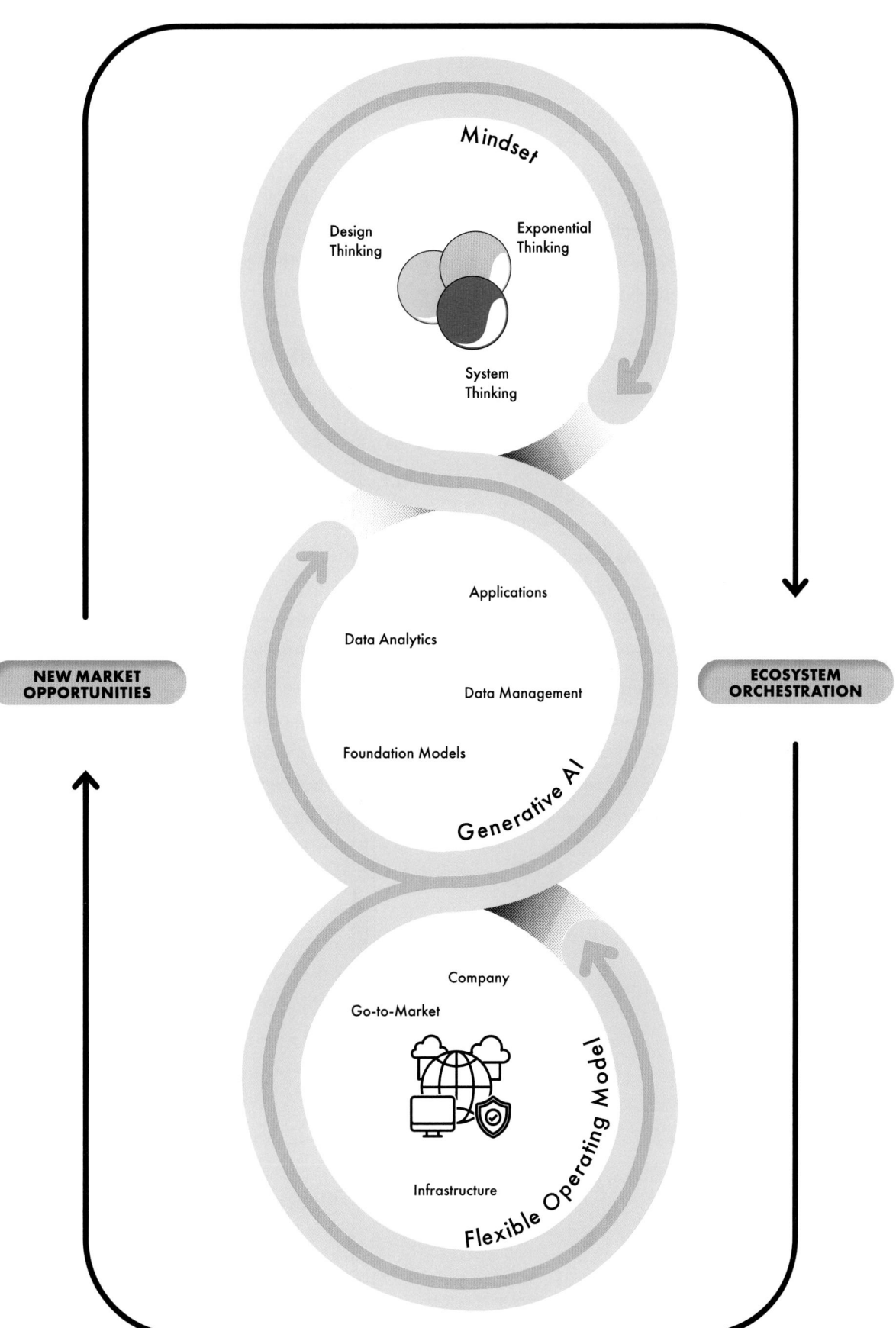

NEW MARKET OPPORTUNITIES

ECOSYSTEM ORCHESTRATION

Mindset

Design Thinking

Exponential Thinking

System Thinking

Applications

Data Analytics

Data Management

Foundation Models

Generative AI

Company

Go-to-Market

Infrastructure

Flexible Operating Model

SINGULARITY AND AI

The concept of the singularity concerns a hypothetical future in which the advancement of intelligent technologies exceeds human comprehension. In the given context, it is hypothesized that AI has the potential to exceed human cognitive capabilities and exhibit elements of autonomous evolution.

As the rate of technological advancement continues to increase exponentially, it may ultimately surpass all attempts to control it. Like many similar concepts, singularity is a polarizing notion ranging from a utopian to a dystopian future. Pessimists argue about the potential eradication of the human population by artificially intelligent entities, while

SINGULARITY MEANS THAT COMPUTER PROGRAMS BECOME SO ADVANCED THAT AI TRANSCENDS HUMAN INTELLIGENCE, POTENTIALLY ERASING THE BOUNDARY BETWEEN HUMANITY AND COMPUTERS.

those with an optimistic outlook consider a future that is characterized by prosperity and an abundance of resources. Regardless of the views or projections that come along with the notion of a future singularity, it is indisputable that it embodies a captivating and perhaps revolutionary juncture in human civilization. This effect may result in either a promising era of technological growth or a distressing scenario characterized by uncontrolled machine behavior. The direction we embark on collectively will determine the course and what implications it will have on future societies.

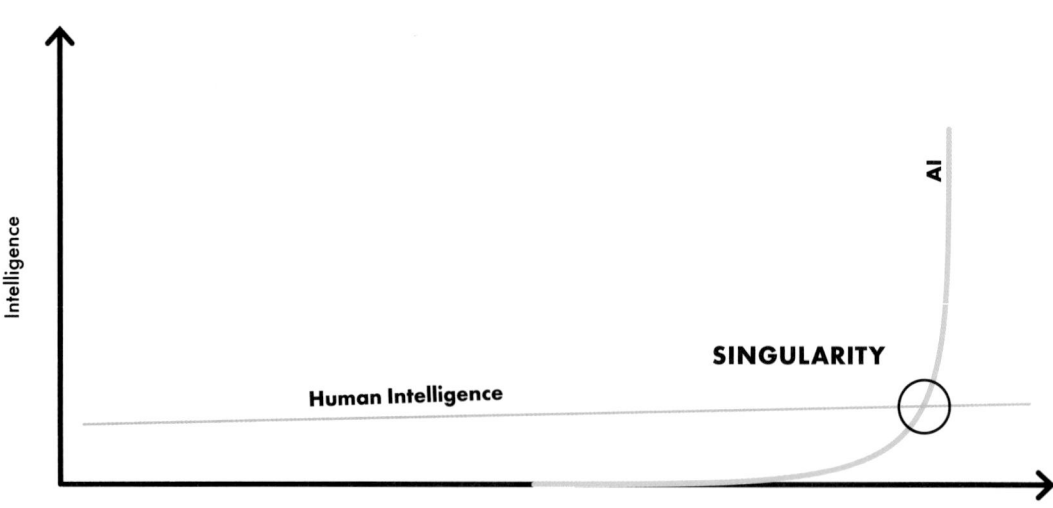

Singularity may carry a significant potential to exert a noteworthy influence on several aspects of future businesses. These influences can span across areas such as corporate dynamics, operational frameworks, and future ecosystem models. Therefore, the concept of singularity merits careful consideration in the context of foresight endeavors and the formulation of long-term strategic plans.

SINGULARITY IS STILL A THEORETICAL CONDITION, BUT THE PROBABILITY IS INCREASING, ESPECIALLY WHEN SEVERAL POWERFUL NEW TECHNOLOGIES SYNTHESIZE.

The creative human imagination has the capacity to conceive several prospective possibilities and scenarios associated with the singularity and possibly devise solutions aimed at minimizing the possible impacts and hazards.

What if singularity is negotiating international agreements for peace?

What if humans are no longer the dominant species on Earth?

What if super AI creates autonomous weapons or spreads disinformation?

What if the relationship between machines and humans becomes emotional?

What if super AI has answers to climate change, poverty, and disease?

From an AI value chain/ecosystem perspective, it is conceivable that AI ethics will become a central link between humans, super AI, and the overall governance and orchestration of value streams. Key questions might arise concerning governance, the next level of humanity, and how to understand, monitor, and control super AI reasoning.

A POTENTIAL FUTURE SINGULARITY ECOSYSTEM

AI VALUE CHAIN/ ECOSYSTEM

- What is the role of governments, industry leaders, academic institutions, and the general public in designing the ecosystem?
- Who will be the orchestrator of the singularity ecosystem?
- What are the design principles of the system, and how is innovation managed?

AI ETHICS

- How do we ensure that singularity is aligned with human values?
- How do we prevent singularity from becoming a threat to humanity?
- How do we influence singularity, ensuring it is used for good and not for evil?

HUMANS

- What is the role and purpose of humans?
- What is the next level of humanity?
- How will humans employ/utilize super-intelligent machines?

SUPER AI

- How can super AI be used to solve the world's most wicked problems?
- How do we control and understand the creation of a new class of "super intelligence"?

BUILDING A COMPETITIVE AND ETHICAL AI ECONOMY

It is the responsibility of each and every one of us to build a competitive and ethical AI economy. It is important to accept exponential change in all areas of life, including technology, business, and society, and to ask powerful questions that help derive impactful business actions from it → See overview on page 236. Many of the tools, methods, and mindsets presented in the previous chapters can help ask the right questions and look at AI holistically and from all perspectives. Important tools include ethical frameworks for AI, mapping of future skills and capability demand, communication of positive AI vision and success stories, and many more.

As a decision-maker and leader, it is even more important to follow the philosophy of "see and engage" as a leadership and decision-making approach when it comes to questions around AI. The approach emphasizes the importance of knowing the context in which decisions are made and engaging with the people affected by those decisions. Particularly with AI, it is increasingly impor-

WE NEED TO SEE THE WORLD THROUGH DIFFERENT LENSES, THROUGH THE EYES OF THE ENHANCING AI SYSTEMS, EXISTING EMPLOYEES, AND ETHICAL STANDARDS, TO ACHIEVE RESPECT AND UNDERSTANDING.

tant to give everyone in the organization a clear understanding of the situation and work together to realize the full potential of AI. Trust and collaboration occur when leaders listen to and value the opinions of employees. Acceptance is achieved when employees are involved in the decision-making process. Practical experience shows that combined mindsets that draw on exponential thinking, design thinking, and systems thinking help successfully put business actions into practice.

Top leaders from all industries must know about the current AI trends and bring terms related to LLM, CV, AutoML, multimodalAI, democratized AI, digital twins, and many others in the appropriate context of AI application fields.

→ see explanation of all terms in the glossary on page 248 ff.

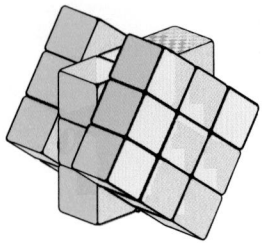   

IT IS OUR RESPONSIBILITY TO BUILD A COMPETITIVE AND ETHICAL AI ECONOMY.

APPLY THE APPROPRIATE TOOLS, METHODS, AND MINDSETS TO SUCCEED.

- How will AI impact the way we live and work?

- What skills are needed?

- How is competition growing?

- What are the AI expectations?

- What are the ethical guidelines?

- How to prepare for the future of AI?

- What are the challenges and opportunities of AI and innovation?

- Create a holistic AI Strategy

- Ensure transparency and build trust

- Up-skill and empower employees

- Make AI accountable and ethical

- Adapt innovation management systems

ACCEPT EXPONENTIAL CHANGE IN ALL AREAS OF LIFE, INCLUDING TECHNOLOGY, BUSINESS, AND SOCIETY.

THE FUTURE OF AI AND INNOVATION

Dr. Seth Dobrin

→ Founder and CEO Qantm AI
  and former Global Chief AI Officer IBM

SHAPING TOMORROW'S AI: A FOCUS ON DIVERSITY, ETHICS, AND FUTURE CHALLENGES

As we navigate the profound advancements within AI, we are increasingly confronted with the imperative to address both the immense potential and the significant challenges these technologies surface. To sum up the context of this book about AI and innovation, I like to recap how to make the AI strategy successful as well reflect on the critical issues surrounding the rapid expansion of AI capabilities — specifically, the risks associated with an overreliance on AI systems and the emergence of technological colonialism, where a few dominant corporations could potentially marginalize diverse global narratives.

AS AI SHAPES OUR CHOICES AND INTERACTIONS, IT'S TIME TO BUILD INCLUSIVE SYSTEMS THAT REFLECT THE RICHNESS OF HUMANITY, NOT JUST OPTIMIZE ITS TASKS.

All of us have already realized that AI is influencing our decision-making processes while daily interactions continue to grow, making it crucial that these systems not only perform efficiently but also embody the diversity and complexity of human experience. Here the urgency of acting now comes into play to diversify AI technologies, the data that powers them, and the teams that build them. It advocates for a future where AI is not only technologically advanced but also inclusive and attuned to the values of global society.

In exploring AI's expansive landscape, we explore various computational models that promise to enhance AI's inclusivity and effectiveness across multiple sectors. These include deterministic optimization algorithms, rule-based and expert systems → like the AI Design Thinking Expert Tool outlined on pages 191–193, which is based on the books from the Wiley Design Thinking Series, advanced learning models, SLMs, and agent-based systems – each offering unique benefits that can broaden the capabilities and reach of AI technologies. From optimizing supply chain management → see page 79 to enhancing diagnostic accuracy → see page 80 in healthcare, these models provide the foundational tools to ensure that AI supports rather than undermines equitable development.

This exploration sets the stage for a deeper discussion on integrating ethical considerations and inclusivity in AI development – a pivot from theoretical models to practical implementations that reflect our collective ethical commitments and address the diverse needs of global populations.

EXPANDING COMPUTATIONAL PARADIGMS

As the field of AI evolves, there is a growing recognition of the limitations inherent in generative AI systems, particularly regarding their scope and the diversity they encompass. To address these issues, exploring and integrating alternative computational models that enhance AI's inclusivity and improve its application across various sectors is crucial. This involves adopting deterministic optimization algorithms, rule-based and expert systems, advanced learning models, SLMs, and agent-based systems. Each of these paradigms offers unique benefits that can significantly broaden the capabilities and reach of AI technologies.

 **Optimization** (e.g. supply chain): Making data-driven decisions for logistics and resource allocation.

 **Expert Systems** (e.g. healthcare): Supporting professionals with rule-based guidance for consistent and reliable decision-making.

→ **Advanced Learning** (e.g. education): Personalizing learning experiences by combining data analysis with human-like reasoning.

→ **Small Language Models**: Efficiently handling specific tasks or niche domains using smaller, more focused AI models.

→ **Agent-based Systems** (e.g. economic models): Simulating complex scenarios with multiple interacting agents to solve problems and predict outcomes, requiring careful safety measures.

As we explore the diverse landscape of computational paradigms in artificial intelligence, it becomes clear that the future of AI is not confined to a one-size-fits-all approach. The five computational models discussed are pivotal in advancing AI's capabilities while addressing specific operational and ethical challenges. By harnessing the unique strengths of these varied models, organizations can unlock innovative solutions that enhance efficiency, improve decision-making, and promote inclusivity. Embracing this multifaceted approach to AI development will ensure that technologies propel businesses forward and contribute positively to societal progress, aligning with transparency, accountability, and ethical responsibility. This strategic diversification of AI tools and techniques is essential for building a future where AI is an ally in the quest for sustainable and equitable growth across all sectors.

Expanding the computational paradigms in AI requires focusing on ethical considerations and inclusivity. We often ignore the importance of using diverse underlying AI algorithms as an essential component of

BUILDING AI FOR THE FUTURE? THINK DIVERSE TEAMS, GLOBAL DATA, AND ETHICAL GUARDRAILS.

ethics and inclusivity. However, by integrating diverse computational models, AI can better serve a broader spectrum of the population, respecting and reflecting the varied human experiences and cultural contexts. Prioritizing these ethical considerations ensures that AI development aligns with global values of fairness, accountability, and transparency, fostering technology that is not only innovative but also equitable and socially responsible. As AI technologies become more integrated into daily life and critical sectors, the need for inclusive and ethically sound practices will only increase, underscoring the importance of this expansive approach to AI development.

Transitioning from a discussion on expanding computational paradigms in AI, we recognize that incorporating innovative AI technologies is only part of the journey. Equally important is embedding a robust ethical framework within these technologies to ensure they are creative but also just and inclusive. As AI systems become more entrenched in our daily lives and across various sectors, the imperative to reflect the diversity of the global community through these technologies becomes increasingly pronounced. The ethical integration of AI necessitates strategic approaches to foster systems that are as diverse as the populations they serve, ensuring fair operation and equitable outcomes in diverse societal contexts. This encompasses a holistic AI strategy → see pages 132–137 that diversifies AI development teams, globalizes training data, and implements robust ethical and regulatory frameworks. These efforts are crucial for realizing AI's potential as a force for good, underpinning the advancement of technologies that are not only effective but also aligned with universal values of fairness and respect for cultural diversity.

BUILDING FAIR AND EQUITABLE AI

Key challenges in ensuring that AI development is fair and benefits everyone emphasize the importance of:

→ **Diverse Teams:** Building AI systems with interdisciplinary and culturally diverse teams to avoid bias and improve problem-solving.

→ **Global Training Data:** Using data that reflects the global population to prevent biases based on specific cultures or demographics.

→ **Ethical Frameworks:** Developing clear ethical guidelines for AI development, deployment, and use to ensure transparency and accountability.

→ **Regulation and Oversight:** Creating strong regulations and independent oversight to prevent misuse of AI power and promote equitable distribution of benefits.

 **Culturally Aware Systems:** Designing AI that respects local customs and adapts to different cultures and languages for better user experience and impact.

The strategic integration of diversity and ethics into AI development is more than a mere enhancement; creating just, effective, and universally beneficial technologies is necessary. By embracing the diversification of AI teams, ensuring global representation in training data, adhering to ethical development frameworks, enforcing robust regulatory measures, and fostering culturally aware AI systems, we lay the groundwork for the future of AI and singularity → see pages 232–233 to be a transformative force for good. These measures are critical in steering AI development toward outcomes that respect and uplift the rich tapestry of global cultures and communities. As we continue to innovate and expand the capabilities of AI, maintaining a steadfast commitment to these principles will ensure that our advancements in AI contribute positively to society, fostering trust and inclusivity at every step.

Having established the foundational importance of embedding diversity and ethical considerations in AI development, we must now focus on the practical aspects of integrating these principles into organizational strategies. The transition from a theoretical commitment to practical implementation involves systematically assessing an organization's current capabilities and the development of a strategic road map tailored to its unique needs and challenges. This process is a must for ensuring that AI technologies are developed with ethical integrity and effectively integrated into existing systems to enhance operational efficiency and align with broader organizational goals. By moving from the ethical framework to strategic integration, organizations can bridge the gap between high-level principles and actionable strategies, ensuring that AI deployments are responsible and aligned with the organization's core mission. This approach lays the groundwork for a sustainable and beneficial use of AI, leveraging the technology's potential to transform business practices and societal interactions in a way that respects and enriches diverse global communities.

WHY A CLEAR AI STRATEGY MATTERS: ASSESSING READINESS AND DEVELOPING A ROAD MAP

As outlined in Part 2 of this book, organizations seeking to implement AI must first evaluate potential use cases and their current capabilities and infrastructure. This assessment should identify both strengths to leverage and gaps that may hinder effective AI integration. Key areas to consider include existing technological resources, data management systems, and skillsets of employees. Understanding these elements helps tailor AI solutions that align with the organization's needs and constraints.

Once the initial assessment is complete, developing a detailed AI adoption road map becomes crucial. This road map should outline strategic objectives, define key milestones, and set measurable metrics for success while aligning with the organization's overall goals and the specific challenges of its industry. For example, a healthcare provider might focus on AI technologies that enhance diagnostic accuracy and patient management. In contrast, a retail business might prioritize AI for customer relationship management and inventory optimization.

An ethical AI culture is foundational to responsible development and deployment. This involves more than just adhering to regulatory requirements; it means ingraining ethical considerations into organizational processes and decision-making. Educating employees, from data scientists to executive leaders, about the ethical implications of AI ensures a widespread understanding and commitment to responsible AI practices.

Promoting such a culture should include regular training sessions on ethical AI use, discussions on the latest developments in AI ethics, and workshops to explore potential bias or other ethical issues in AI applications the organization might use. Embedding these practices helps prevent unethical AI behavior and fosters trust within the organization and its external stakeholders.

Engagement with a broad array of stakeholders is essential for the responsible development and deployment of AI technologies. This engagement should include internal stakeholders, customers, regulatory bodies, and possibly community representatives affected by the organization's AI implementations. Such inclusive engagement ensures that diverse perspectives are considered, enhancing the relevance and acceptability of AI solutions.

For instance, when developing an AI tool for social media content moderation, a company should consult technical experts, sociologists, legal experts, and community representatives to understand the broader implications of AI-made content decisions. This approach helps design AI systems that are fair, transparent, and aligned with societal values.

The question of where to play and how to win is a comprehensive process that requires thoughtful consideration of an organization's readiness, a well-defined road map for adoption, promoting an ethical culture, and engaging with a diverse set of stakeholders. By addressing these elements, organizations can ensure that their AI technologies boost operational efficiency and innovation and align with ethical standards and societal expectations. When executed effectively, the AI strategy provides the North Star for organizations to capitalize on the benefits of AI while mitigating potential risks and fostering trust among all parties involved.

THE INNOVATION SINGULARITY: ARE WE READY FOR THE HUMAN–AI PARTNERSHIP?

Yes, we can be ready for the human–AI partnership, but achieving this requires a multifaceted approach as outlined by Michael and Omar in this book. This approach is critical to mitigate the risks of technological overreliance and colonialism in AI development. As we delve deeper into AGI and beyond, maintaining this multifaceted approach is crucial. It ensures that AI acts as a force for good, harmonizing with the rich tapestry of human society.

In essence, by embracing a comprehensive approach to AI and innovation, we can navigate the human–AI partnership responsibly, ensuring a future where technology uplifts and empowers all.

HUMAN

- Giving instructions
- Guiding
- Voice and style
- Evaluating ideas
- Deciding between options

- Interpreting
- Imagining
- Creating
- Reasoning
- Deciding

GENERATIVE AI

- Offering ideas
- Illustrating concepts
- Responding to feedback

KEY TAKEAWAYS

→ *AI technology will continue to advance at rates unlike any other technology in history.*

→ *When strategizing about future markets, organizations should not constrain themselves with the limitations of today's AI capabilities.*

→ *AI will continue to have a transformative impact on various sectors like finance, education, and healthcare in ways that current specialized AI systems may struggle to achieve.*

→ *The real potential will come from combining quantum computing with advanced AI. Capability from this synergistic combination will transform all industries and cause amplified step functions.*

→ *If we want to keep pace with AI advancements, creating strategies to reskill and upskill the workforce to mitigate job displacement and create new opportunities will be essential.*

→ The best way to plan for a future with AI is to train the workforce to think exponentially and critically, increase creativity, and be comfortable with constant change and continuous learning.

→ In the long term, super AI could signal a whole new era in technology, with the potential to usher in another industrial revolution at a breathtaking pace.

→ Regarding the future of AI and innovation, it is important to ensure a responsible utilization of technology enhancements, implementing robust ethical guidelines to diminish its potential negative ramifications.

CLOSING WORDS

As we look to the future of AI and innovation, it is clear that exponential technologies will continue to play a major role in shaping our world. We must be prepared for the challenges and opportunities that these technologies bring. AI does not solve the problem of general intelligence, but it has the ability to seize new market opportunities and develop products, services, and experiences that customers desire.

The ability of humans to collaborate with AI is the driving force in impact and spread for revenue growth and higher productivity. Eventually, all applications and business systems will have AI integration and interact with the broader ecosystem. As a result, AI makes people more productive and efficient and may amplify creativity. With the utilization and continuous adaption of the appropriate methods and tools described in this book, readers will have a better understanding of how to navigate the complex landscape of AI and how to better leverage its potential.

We already have enough evidence to confirm that AI is redefining businesses and value chains by enabling the development of new market opportunities and focusing on improving existing customer experience. It positively impacts innovation outcomes and improves employee productivity and experience.

At the current level of application of AI in innovation work, there are still highly skilled and creative minds needed to define the appropriate problem, find solutions that matter in the future, and finally check the output, especially for hallucinations (inaccurate content produced by the application) and intellectual property issues if AI is applied over the entire design cycle.

From our personal reflection on current implementations and best practices in different sectors and business ecosystems, it is clear that AI will open up new use cases as well as accelerate, scale, or otherwise improve existing ones.

The pioneers and early adopters of new AI technologies will always have a significant lead and strategic advantage. For example, early adopters of

246

technologies like quantum can leverage AI systems to learn faster and better prepare for real-world situations by creating powerful simulated environments. Quantum technologies can, for example, perform simulations and solve problems that would lead to major advances across industries, including aerospace and defense, automotive, chemicals, finance, and pharmaceuticals.

Another fascinating field of study and experimentation is neuroscience in conjunction with AI. Neuroscience is, in simple terms, the exploration of how the human brain and nervous system work. By better understanding how the brain works, we can develop enhanced AI algorithms that can be more efficient and effective in the future.

From an engineering and robotics perspective, robotics techniques are applied to develop AI-powered robots that can interact with the physical world. The fusion of disciplines becomes invaluable in the development of superior AI models. We believe that humans and AI working together as a team is the best approach to enhancing our problem-solving capabilities, particularly for tackling some of the world's most wicked problems like climate change and poverty.

Finally, advances in AI will provide humanity with solutions and technologies that will improve our lives, such as self-driving cars and intelligent medical devices.

On this exciting innovation journey, we wish everyone success in implementing, adapting, and learning with and from AI models.

Your team of authors,

Michael Lewrick   Omar Hatamleh

AI-GLOSSARY

A

Accelerator — A class of microprocessor designed to accelerate AI applications.

Agents — Software that can perform certain tasks independently without human intervention.

AGI (Artificial General Intelligence) — The phase of Artificial Intelligence when AI is as capable as a human at any intellectual task.

AI Ethics — The study and application of moral principles and guidelines to ensure that AI systems are used in ways that align with human values.

Algorithm — A set of rules or instructions that govern how a computer program performs a specific task.

Alignment — The task of ensuring that the goals of an AI system are in line with human values.

Anthropomorphism — Attributing human qualities to nonhumans.

Artificial Intelligence (AI) — The simulation of human-like intelligence in machines, enabling machines to perform tasks that require human cognitive abilities.

ASI (Artificial Super Intelligence) — Artificial intelligence that surpasses the capabilities of the human mind on every level.

Attention — Attention mechanisms help the model focus on relevant parts of the input when producing an output.

Augmented Reality — Overlaying virtual information onto the real world.

Autonomous Vehicles — A technology that allows vehicles to navigate and make decisions in real time by using computer vision and other technologies to perceive and interpret the surrounding environment.

B

Backpropagation — A training procedure for neural networks. It entails transmitting the error rate of a forward propagation backward through the neural network layers in order to fine-tune the weights. Backpropagation is central to neural network training.

Bias — The set of assumptions that a machine learning algorithm makes on the underlying distribution of the data it was trained on.

Bias and Fairness — Biases in training data that can lead to potential discriminatory outcomes that deviate from fairness, producing inequitable results.

C

Chain of Thought

The sequence of reasoning steps an AI model uses to arrive at a concrete decision.

Chatbot

A computer program that leverages natural language processing and is capable of simulating human conversation through text or voice interactions to understand user input and provide relevant responses.

ChatGPT

Chat Generative Pretrained Transformer is a chatbot developed by OpenAI that utilizes a language model. It provides users with the ability to customize conversations according to their desired structure, tone, level of specificity, and language preferences.

CLIP (Contrastive Language–Image Pretraining)

The approach that demonstrate that scaling a straightforward pretraining task is sufficient for achieving competitive zero-shot performance across a wide range of image classification datasets. Our method employs a readily accessible source of supervision: text coupled with internet-sourced images.

Compute

The processing capacity, memory, networking, storage, and other resources necessary for the successful execution of any program.

Computer Vision (CV)

A range of techniques that involve the acquisition, processing, analysis, and comprehension of digital pictures. It also involves the extraction of complex data from the physical environment to generate numerical or symbolic information, such as making judgments based on the acquired data.

Constitutional AI

A framework that consists of regulations, principles, and directives that dictate the conduct of an AI system within its operational context. The primary objective is to establish a framework that promotes ethical and responsible conduct of AI, while simultaneously safeguarding the rights and interests of individuals and other relevant parties engaged in interactions with such AI systems.

Convolutional Neural Network (CNN)

A deep learning model utilized to analyze data having a grid-like architecture, such as an image, by the application of a sequence of filters. These models are frequently employed for problems related to image recognition.

Corpus

A large dataset of written or spoken words that is used to train language models.

Credit Scoring

Machine learning algorithms have the capability to evaluate an individual's creditworthiness through the examination of their financial history, payment patterns, and other pertinent data. This facilitates financial organizations in making well-informed judgments while assessing loan applications or establishing credit limits.

Customer Churn Prediction

Machine learning models that have the capability to assess consumer behavior and historical data in order to make predictions regarding the likelihood of client turnover. This allows firms to implement proactive strategies, such as offering tailored retention incentives, in order to mitigate client turnover rates.

Customer Onboarding	Robotic process automation (RPA) has the capability to streamline and expedite the client onboarding process through the validation of customer data, execution of background checks, and establishment of user accounts across several systems. This process optimizes the client experience and enhances operational effectiveness.

D

Dall-E	OpenAI's AI-powered picture generator. The process involves users providing a textual cue, which is then utilized by the AI tool to produce a related image.
Data Augmentation	The practice of augmenting the quantity and variety of data utilized for training a model by the inclusion of slightly altered replicas of preexisting data.
Data Entry and Extraction	RPA solutions provide the capability to extract pertinent information from various sources such as papers, forms, and invoices. This functionality significantly diminishes the amount of manual labor and effort needed for data entry tasks.
Data Mining	The practice of extracting meaningful patterns, correlations, and insights from extensive datasets through the application of statistical methods, ML algorithms, and database management approaches.
Data Validation	The procedure of evaluating the integrity of data prior to its utilization in the development and training of artificial intelligence models.
Deep Learning	Deep learning is a specialized area within the study of ML that focuses on the training of neural networks with numerous layers, known as deep neural networks. These networks are designed to autonomously acquire hierarchical representations of input, leading to notable advancements in various domains such as picture and speech recognition, frequently surpassing previous benchmarks.
Deepfake	An AI-generated picture, audio, or video that is persuasive in nature. A deepfake refers to a form of synthetic media that encompasses wholly novel content depicting an individual engaging in actions or uttering statements that they did not really do or express. Additionally, they have the ability to portray fabricated news occurrences.
Demand Forecasting	ML algorithms have the capability to assess past sales data and include external variables in order to make predictions about the future demand for items or services.
Diffusion	In the field of artificial intelligence and machine learning, there exists a method employed to generate novel data by beginning the process with an existing data sample and subsequently introducing random perturbations. A diffusion model refers to a class of generative models that involves training a neural network to forecast the inverse procedure of introducing random noise to data. Diffusion models are employed for the purpose of generating novel data samples that exhibit similarities to the original training data.

| Double Descent | In the field of ML a phenomena characterized by an initial enhancement in model performance when complexity is augmented, followed by a subsequent deterioration, and ultimately, a subsequent improvement. |

F

| Feature Engineering | Feature engineering is a crucial procedure in machine learning that involves the careful selection, manipulation, and generation of pertinent features or characteristics from unprocessed data, with the aim of enhancing the efficacy and accuracy of machine learning models. |

| Fine-tuning | The utilization of a preexisting ML model that has undergone training on a substantial dataset and afterwards modifying it to cater to a slightly varied job or a specialized domain. During the process of fine-tuning, the parameters of the model are refined by utilizing a smaller dataset that is particular to the work at hand. This enables the model to acquire task-specific patterns and enhance its performance on the current task. |

| Forward Propagation | In the context of a neural network, the sequential transmission of input data through the various layers of the network, starting at the input layer, passing through the hidden layers, and ultimately culminating in the output layer, resulting in the generation of the network's output. The neural network utilizes weights and biases to modulate the inputs and use activation functions to produce the ultimate output. |

| Foundation Model | The utilization of expansive models, which have been trained on diverse datasets, with the intention of being tailored to specific tasks. |

| Fraud Detection | ML algorithms provide the capability to discern patterns and abnormalities within extensive datasets, hence facilitating businesses in the detection of fraudulent activity. Banks and financial organizations utilize machine learning-based fraud detection systems in order to mitigate financial losses and safeguard consumer assets. |

| Fréchet Inception Distance (FID). | The FID measure is utilized to assess the efficacy of generative artificial intelligence in producing high-quality photographs. |

G

| Garbage in, garbage out (GIGO) | In the field of computer science, there exists a fundamental idea that posits that the quality of a system's output is contingent upon the quality of its input. If the quality of the input is poor, the resulting output will also be of poor quality. If AI is taught with data of substandard quality, it is reasonable for the user to anticipate that the output generated by the AI system would also exhibit poor quality. |

| General Adversarial Network (GAN) | One particular ML model employed for the purpose of generating novel data that exhibits similarity to a given set of existing data. The process involves the utilization of two neural networks in opposition: a "generator" that generates novel data and a "discriminator" that endeavors to differentiate between the generated data and authentic data. |

| Generative AI | A particular branch of AI that is dedicated to the development of models capable of producing novel and innovative material, including pictures, music, and writing, by using patterns and examples derived from preexisting data. |

GPU (Graphics Processing Unit)	A specific form of a microprocessor that is primarily engineered to effectively produce visual representations for the purpose of transmitting them to a display device. Graphics processing units (GPUs) exhibit a notable degree of efficacy in executing the necessary computations for the training and execution of neural networks.
Gradient Descent	Within the field of ML, an optimization technique that iteratively modifies the parameters of a model by leveraging the direction of greatest enhancement in its loss function. In the context of linear regression, gradient descent is employed to iteratively optimize the slope and intercept of the best-fit line, with the objective of minimizing the errors in predictions.

H

Hallucinate/ Hallucination	Within the domain of AI, the occurrence wherein a model produces information that lacks a foundation in actual data or deviates substantially from reality.
Hidden Layer	The neural network comprises additional layers of artificial neurons that are not directly linked to the input or output.
Hyperparameter Tuning	The procedure involved in determining the optimal values for the hyperparameters, which are parameters that are not acquired through the learning process, in an ML model.

I

Inference	The procedure involved in generating forecasts using an ML model that has been trained.
Instruction Tuning	In the field of ML, the refinement of models by the utilization of explicit instructions provided within the dataset.
Invoice Processing	RPA tools have the capability to extract pertinent data from invoices, afterward subjecting it to predetermined regulations for validation purposes. Following successful validation, these tools are able to execute payment transactions or effectuate updates inside financial systems as deemed necessary. The use of this method expedites the process of handling invoices and enhances the level of precision.

L

Language Translation	NLP technologies provide the capability to effectively translate written or spoken words from one linguistic system to another, so serving as a valuable tool in promoting communication and overcoming language barriers. Translation technologies play a significant role in the tourist business by facilitating effective communication for travelers in foreign nations.
Large Language Model (LLM)	One variant of an AI model that possesses the capability to produce text that closely resembles human-generated content and has been trained on a diverse and extensive dataset.
Latent Space	In ML, the compressed representation of data that a model (like a neural network) creates. Similar data points are closer in latent space.

M

Machine Learning (ML)

ML algorithms facilitate the acquisition of knowledge and enhancement of system performance via the use of data, without the need for explicit programming. Organizations have the ability to utilize machine learning (ML) techniques in a multitude of ways.

Mixture of Experts

The utilization of an ML methodology wherein many distinct submodels, referred to as "experts," are individually trained. The predictions generated by these experts are subsequently amalgamated in a manner that is contingent upon the specific input received.

Moats

Moats are strategic techniques employed to impede rivals from replicating a proprietary LLM system. The primary assets of an LLM are its training data, model weights, and the associated training costs.

Model Training

The process of using training data to optimize the parameters of an ML, allowing it to make accurate predictions or classifications on new, unseen data.

Multimodal

In the field of AI, models that possess the capability to comprehend and produce information including many forms of data, including but not limited to text and pictures.

N

Natural Language Processing (NLP)

NLP facilitates the comprehension, interpretation, and generation of human language by machines. It is utilized in diverse operational capacities within organizations, including the subsequent areas.

NeRF (Neural Radiance Fields)

This study proposes a technique for generating a three-dimensional (3D) scene from two-dimensional (2D) photographs by using the capabilities of a neural network. This technology has the potential to be utilized in several applications such as photorealistic rendering and view synthesis, among others.

Neural Networks

Computational models, which draw inspiration from the structural organization of the human brain, consist of linked nodes known as neurons that engage in the processing and transmission of information. These applications encompass tasks such as pattern detection, picture and audio recognition, and natural language processing.

Neuromorphic Computing

Neuromorphic computing refers to a computational approach that emulates certain aspects of the human brain inside computer design. This concept has the potential to be applicable to both hardware and software components.

O

Object Detection in Manufacturing

CV tools have the capability to accurately identify and categorize items present on a production line. This enables the implementation of automated quality control processes and facilitates the identification of defects. This enhances manufacturing productivity and mitigates the occurrence of human mistake.

Object Recognition

CV technologies provide the capability to detect and categorize various items present in photos or videos. E-commerce systems have the potential to leverage this technology in order to automate the process of product tagging and enhance search capabilities, ultimately leading to an improved customer experience.

Objective Function	The objective function that an ML model aims to optimize or reduce throughout the training process.
Overfitting	Overfitting is a modeling problem that arises when a function is excessively tailored to a restricted collection of data points, leading to worse predicted performance when applied to new, unknown data.

P

Parameters	Within the field of ML the intrinsic variables that are employed by the model in order to generate predictions. The acquisition of knowledge occurs through the utilization of training data during the training process. In the context of a neural network, the parameters encompass the weights and biases.
Pathways Language Model (PaLM).	The transformer-based LLM developed by Google is built upon technology comparable to that of GPT-3 and GPT-4. The chatbot known as Google Bard operates on the PaLM platform.
Pretraining	The primary stage of ML model training involves the acquisition of broad characteristics, patterns, and representations from the data, without any specific knowledge of the job to which it will subsequently be employed. The use of unsupervised or semi-supervised learning techniques allows the model to acquire a fundamental comprehension of the inherent distribution of the data and identify significant characteristics that may be utilized for further refinement on certain tasks.
Predictive Analytics	ML models have the capability to estimate future events by using previous data, so allowing enterprises to make precise predictions on demand, revenue, and customer behavior. Predictive analytics may be employed by retailers to enhance inventory management and strategize marketing campaigns with more efficiency.
Prompt	The primary context or directive that establishes the job or inquiry for the model. Often used with sentences like "Act as a (ROLE) perform (TASK) in (FORMAT)."

Q

Quality Control	CV-based quality control systems are capable of examining items on assembly lines, therefore detecting any faults or irregularities that may be present. Manufacturing enterprises have the potential to enhance production efficiency and minimize mistakes through the utilization of computer vision (CV) systems for automated quality evaluation.

R

Recommendation Systems	These technologies utilize user behavior and preferences as inputs in order to provide tailored suggestions. Recommendation systems are widely employed by e-commerce platforms, music streaming services, and content platforms with the aim of improving the user experience and promoting user engagement.
Regularization	Regularization is a commonly employed approach in the field of machine learning to mitigate the issue of overfitting. It involves the inclusion of a penalty term in the loss function of the model. The imposition of this penalty serves to dissuade the model from over-reliance on intricate patterns present in the training data, hence fostering the development of models that are more generalizable and less susceptible to overfitting.

Reinforcement Learning	Reinforcement learning is an ML approach in which computers acquire knowledge by engaging with an environment and getting feedback in the form of rewards or penalties, with the aim of optimizing their actions and judgments.
RLHF (Reinforcement Learning from Human Feedback)	One approach to facilitate the training of an AI model is leveraging human feedback to enhance the model's performance.
Robotic Process Automation (RPA)	RPA employs software robots to automate processes that are repetitive in nature and governed by predefined rules. This concept has broad applicability throughout many organizational processes.
Robotics	The amalgamation of AI with mechanical systems to engender robots that possess the ability to execute physical tasks and engage in interactions with their surroundings.

S

Sentiment Analysis	NLP-driven sentiment analysis technologies are employed to evaluate textual data derived from consumer reviews, social media platforms, and polls in order to assess the prevailing public sentiment. Organizations may then employ this information to evaluate consumer happiness, monitor brand sentiment, and formulate business choices based on data analysis.
Singularity	Within the realm of AI, a theoretical juncture in the future whereby the rate of technological advancement surpasses human capacity for control and reversibility, resulting in unanticipated transformations to the structure and functioning of human society.
Speech Recognition	Speech recognition technology utilizes AI to transform spoken words into written text.
Supervised Learning	Supervised ML is a computational approach in which algorithms are trained using labeled data, enabling them to establish associations between input data and their corresponding output labels. This acquired knowledge allows the algorithms to make accurate predictions or classifications.
Surveillance and Security	CV is employed in surveillance systems for the purpose of detecting and tracking persons or things that are deemed significant. The use of this technology serves to bolster security measures in various public settings such as airports, key infrastructure, and other public areas, therefore facilitating the prompt identification and response to potential threats.
Symbolic Artificial Intelligence	Symbolic reasoning is a form of AI that is employed to address issues and encode knowledge.
Synthetic Data	Synthetic data is artificial information created by computers, mimicking real-world data but without containing any real-world identities. This allows researchers to train AI models and develop new technologies without privacy concerns.

T

TensorFlow	Google has built an open-source machine learning platform that is utilized for the construction and training of ML models.

Text Summarization	NLP systems provide the capability to automatically condense extensive amounts of text, therefore facilitating the extraction of crucial information from articles, research papers, and news items for users. This feature is especially beneficial for those in professional settings who require continuous awareness of current industry trends and advancements.
TPU (Tensor Processing Unit)	Google has created a specialized microprocessor designed to enhance the performance of machine learning tasks.
Training Data	The dataset employed for the training of an ML model.
Transfer Learning	The proposed approach involves the adaptation of a preexisting model to address a novel task through the process of fine-tuning, which entails training the model on a smaller dataset. This methodology capitalizes on the information acquired from a closely comparable job.
Transformer	One particular neural network design that is predominantly employed for the purpose of processing sequential data, such as natural language. Transformers are renowned for their capacity to effectively address long-range dependencies in data, owing to the incorporation of an attention mechanism. This mechanism enables the model to discern the relative significance of many inputs in generating an output.

SOURCES

Accenture. (n.d.). Artificial intelligence summary index. Accenture. Retrieved from https://www.accenture.com/au-en/insights/artificial-intelligence-summary-index.

Acemoglu, D., & Johnson, S. (2023). *Power and progress: Our thousand-year struggle over technology and prosperity.* PublicAffairs.

Adobe. (2023, May 23). Adobe unveils future of Creative Cloud with generative AI as a creative copilot in Photoshop. Adobe News. https://s23.q4cdn.com/979560357/files/052323Photoshop Firefly.pdf.

Arranz, D., Bianchini, S., Di Girolamo, V., & Ravet, J. (2023). Trends in the use of AI in science: A bibliometric analysis. *R&I Paper Series,* WP 2023/04. EU Publication Office.

Avsec, Z., Agarwal, V., Visentin, D., Ledsarm, J. R., Grabska-Barwinska, A., Taylor, K. R., Assael, Y., Jumper, J., Kohli, P., & Kelley, D. R. (2021). Effective gene expression prediction from sequence by integrating long-range interactions. *Nature Methods* 18: 1196–1203.

AWorld Economic Forum. (2024). How can companies leverage AI? 5 leaders have their say. 15 January 2024, https://www.weforum.org/agenda/artificial-intelligence-and-robotics/.

Babayan, N. (2017). Bearing truthiness: Russia's cyclical legitimation of its actions. *Europe-Asia Studies* 69, no. 7: 1090–1105.

BCG Executive Perspectives. (2024). AI transformation for future-ready functions: The C-suite playbooks. https://www.bcg.com/featured-insights/executive-perspectivess.

BCG. (2023). How People Create and Destroy Value with Generative AI. 27 September. https://www.bcg.com/publications/2023/how-people-create-and-destroy-value-with-gen-ai.

Bera, K., et al. (2019). Artificial intelligence in digital pathology – New tools for diagnosis and precision oncology. *Nature Reviews Clinical Oncology* 16: 703–715.

Bessen, J. (2015). *Learning by Doing: The Real Connection Between Innovation, Wages, and Wealth.* Yale University Press.

Bianchini, S., Müller, M., & Pelletier, P. (2022). Artificial intelligence in science: An emerging general method of invention. *Research Policy* 51(10).

Bijker, W. E., Hughes, T. P., & Pinch, T. (2012). *The Social Construction of Technological Systems, Anniversary Edition: New Directions in the Sociology and History of Technology.* MIT Press.

Birhane, A., Kasirzadeh, A., Leslie, D., & Wachter, S. (2023). Science in the age of large language models. *Nature Review Physics* 5: 277–280.

Bloom, N., Jones, C. I., Van Reenen, J., & Webb, M. (2020). Are ideas getting harder to find? *American Economic Review* 110 (4): 1104–1144. https://www.aeaweb.org/articles?id=10.1257/aer.20180338.

Bloomberg. (2023). Introducing BloombergGPT, Bloomberg's 50-billion parameter large language model, purpose-built from scratch for finance. https://www.bloomberg.com/company/press/bloomberggpt-50-billion-parameter-llm-tuned-finance/.

Bommasani, R., Hudson, D. A., Adeli, E., Altman, R., Arora, S., von Arx, S., Bernstein, M. S., et al. (2021). *On the Opportunities and Risks of Foundation Models.* https://samuelalbanie.com/files/digest-slides/2022-06-foundation-models-opportunities-and-risks-intro.pdf.

Bouschery, S. G., Blazevic, V., & Piller, F. T. (2023). Augmenting human innovation teams with artificial intelligence: Exploring transformer-based language models. *Journal of Product Innovation Management* 40 (2): 139–153.

Brasil, S., Pascoal, C., Francisco, R., Dos Reis Ferreira, V., Videira, P. A., & Valadão, G. (2019). Artificial intelligence (AI) in rare diseases: Is the future brighter? *Genes (Basel)* 10 (12): 978. https://doi.org/10.3390/genes10120978.

Brown, T. B., Mann, B., Ryder, N., Subbiah, M., Kaplan, J., Dhariwal, P., Neelakantan, A., et al. (2020). Language Models Are Few-Shot Learners. Number of GPUs and Time to Train Estimated in Narayana.

Brynjolfsson, E., & McAfee, A. (2017, July 18). The business of artificial intelligence: What it can — and cannot — do for your organization. *Harvard Business Review* (July 18). Retrieved from https://hbr.org/2017/07/the-business-of-artificial-intelligence.

Butler, J., Jaffe, S., Baym, N., Czerwinski, M., Iqbal, S., Nowak, K., Rintel, R., & Sellen, A., Hecht, B., & Teevan, J. (Eds.). (2023). *Microsoft New Future of Work Report 2023.* Microsoft Research Tech Report MSR-TR-2023-34. https://aka.ms/nfw2023.

Cao, L. (2017). Data science: A comprehensive overview. *ACM Computing Surveys (CSUR)* 50 (3): 1–42.

Carl Quintanilla on X: "The most expensive, most talented workers are the ones who have 20 years experience and know how to apply that. THAT'S what #AI does overnight." ".. A.I. won't take your job,

it's somebody USING A.I. that'll take your job."
@BaldwinRE @wef https://t.co/IGPKU0UtJp" / X (twitter.com).

Carmi, E. (2015). Taming noisy women: Bell Telephone's female switchboard operators as a noise source. *Media History* 2.

Celestin, R. (2023, October 12). Nike and Apple #1 brands among teens—How AI can help predict the future of fashion and technology. *Forbes*. Retrieved from https://www.forbes.com/sites/rosecelestin/2023/10/12/nike-and-apple-1-brands-among-teens-how-ai-can-help-predict-the-future-of-fashion-and-technology/?sh=2602c7586bdf.

Chen, Z., Cano, A. H., Romanou, A., Bonnet, A., Matoba, K., Salvi, F., Pagliardini, M., et al. (2023). MEDITRON-70B : Scaling medical pretraining for large language models. *arXiv*. Doit: 10.48550/arXiv.2311.16079.

Chhabra, A., & Williams, S. (2019). Fusing data and design to super-charge innovation—in products and processes. *McKinsey Analytics*, April 4. https://www.mckinsey.com/business-functions/mckinsey-analytics/our-insights/fusing-data-and-design-to-supercharge-innovation-in-products-and-processes.

Clarivate Plc. (2024, February 29). *Clarivate in the Age of AI: Innovation Rooted in Academia*. https://access.clarivate.com/login?app=wpp.

Costin, A., Adibfar, A., & Bridge, J. (2023). Digital twin framework for bridge structural health monitoring utilizing existing technologies: New paradigm for enhanced management, operation, and maintenance. *Transportation Research Record: Journal of the Transportation Research Board* 2678 (6). https://doi.org/10.1177/03611981231208908.

Creasey, H. (2023, June 23). *A Point of View on AI, Change, and Change Management*. LinkedIn. https://www.linkedin.com/pulse/point-view-ai-change-management-tim-creasey.

Cumplido-Mayoral, I., García-Prat, M., Operto, G., Falcon, C., Shekari, M., Cacciaglia, R., Milà-Alomà, et al. (2023). Biological brain age prediction using machine learning on structural neuroimaging data: Multi-cohort validation against biomarkers of Alzheimer's disease and neurodegeneration stratified by sex. *eLife*.

D'Ignazio, C. (2017). Creative data literacy: Bridging the gap between the data-haves and data-have nots. *Information Design Journal* 23 (1): 6–18.

Danieli, M. et al. (2024). Machine learning application in auto-immune disease: State of art and future prospects. *Autoimmunity Reviews*.

Davenport, T. (2014). Big data @ work: Chancen erkennen, Risiken verstehen. Vahlen Verlag.

Davenport, T. H., & Patil, D. J. (2012). Data scientist: The sexiest job of the 21st century. In *Harvard Business Review* (October 2012). https://hbr.org/2012/10/data-scientist-the-sexiest-job-of-the-21st-century/.

Deloitte Insights. (n.d.). Generative AI in Europe. https://www2.deloitte.com/xe/en/insights/topics/emerging-technologies/generative-ai-in-europe.html.

Eapen, T. T., Finkenstadt, D. J., Folk, J., & Venkataswamy, L. (2023, July–August). How generative AI can augment human creativity: Use it to promote divergent thinking. *Harvard Business Review*. Retrieved from https://hbr.org/2023/07/how-generative-ai-can-augment-human-creativity.

Eapen, T. T., Finkenstadt, D. J., Folk, J., & Venkataswamy, L. (2023, June 23). How generative AI can augment human creativity. *Harvard Business Review*. https://hbr.org/2023/07/how-generative-ai-can-augment-human-creativity.

Elish, M. (2019). Moral crumple zones: Cautionary tales in human-robot interaction. *Engaging Science, Technology, and Society* 5.

Ellingrud, K., Sanghvi, S., Dandona, G. S., Madgavkar, A., Chui, M., White, O., & Hasebe, P. (2023, July 26). *Generative AI and the Future of Work in America*. McKinsey Global Institute. Retrieved from https://www.mckinsey.com/mgi/our-research/generative-ai-and-the-future-of-work-in-america.

European Commission. (n.d.). European approach to artificial intelligence | Shaping Europe's digital future. https://digital-strategy.ec.europa.eu/en/policies/european-approach-artificial-intelligence.

Europol Innovation Lab. (2021). *Facing Reality: Law Enforcement and the Challenge of Deepfakes*. https://www.europol.europa.eu/cms/sites/default/files/documents/Europol_Innovation_Lab_Facing_Reality_Law_Enforcement_And_The_Challenge_Of_Deepfakes.pdf.

Fleming, S. L., Lozano, A., Haberkorn, W. J., Jindal, J. A., Reis, E. P., Thapa, R., Blnakemeier, L., et al. (2023). *MedAlign: A Clinician-Generated Dataset for Instruction Following with Electronic Medical Records*. https://doi.org/10.48550/arXiv.2308.14089.

Future Side. (2022, August 15). Artificial general intelligence (AGI): What you need to expect. *Future Side*. https://futurside.com/artificial-general-intelligence-agi-what-you-need-to-expect/.

Georgieva, K. (2024, January 14). AI will transform the global economy. Let's make sure it benefits humanity. *IMF Blog*. https://www.imf.org/en/Blogs/Articles/2024/01/14/ai-will-transform-the-global-economy-lets-make-sure-it-benefits-humanity.

Goldman Sachs. (2023). *The Potentially Large Effects of Artificial Intelligence on Economic Growth* (Briggs/Kodnani).

Google – The Keyword. (2023). How Google is improving Search with Generative AI; Microsoft Bing.

Google Workspace. (2023, March 16). Introducing Duet AI in Google Workspace; Microsoft.

Grashof, N., & Kopka, A. (2022). Artificial intelligence and radical innovation: An opportunity for all companies? *Small Business Economics*, 1–27.

Ha, T., Lee, D., Kwon, Y., Park, M. S., Lee, S., Jang, J., Choi, B., et al. (2023). AI-driven robotic chemist for autonomous synthesis. *Science Advances* 9 (44). https://www.science.org/doi/10.1126/sciadv.adj0461.

Hamilton, I. A., & Nolan, B. (2022, July 27). Neuralink's first human patient has been revealed. Here's how we got here. *Business Insider.* https://www.businessinsider.com/neuralink-elon-musk-microchips-brains-ai-2021-2#neuralink-is-developing-two-bits-of-equipment-the-first-is-a-chip-that-would-be-implanted-in-a-persons-skull-with-electrodes-fanning-out-into-their-brain-2.

Harbers, M., & Neerincx, M. A. (2017). Value sensitive design of a virtual assistant for workload harmonization in teams. *Cognition, Technology & Work* 19.

Harbich, M., Bernard, G., Berkes, P., Garbinato, B., & Andritsos, P. (2017). Discovering customer journey maps using a mixture of Markov models. In *Proceedings of the 7th International Symposium on Data-Driven Process Discovery and Analysis*, edited by P. Ceravolo, M. van Keulen, & K. Stoffel, 3–7. Neuchatel, Switzerland. ceur-ws.org.

Hecht, B., Wilcox, L., Bigham, J. P., Schöning, J., Hoque, E., Ernst, J., Bisk, Y., et al. (2018). It's time to do something: Mitigating the negative impacts of computing through a change to the peer review process. *ACM Future of Computing* blog.

Hede, K. (2024, January 9). PNNL Kicks off multi-year energy storage, scientific discovery collaboration with microsoft. Pacific Northwest National Laboratory. https://www.pnnl.gov/news-media/pnnl-kicks-multi-year-energy-storage-scientific-discovery-collaboration-microsoft.

Heikkilä, M., & Heaven, W. D. (2024). What's next for AI in 2024. *MIT Technology Review.* https://www.technologyreview.com/ https://www.technologyreview.com/2024/01/04/1086046/whats-next-for-ai-in-2024/.

Hemmer, P., Schemmer, M., Westphal, M., & Vetter, S. (2023). Human-AI collaboration: The effect of AI delegation on human task performance and task satisfaction. *IUI 2023.*

Hope, T., Downey, D., Weld, D. S., Etzioni, O., & Horvitz, E. (2023). A computational inflection for scientific discovery. *Communications of the ACM.*

Houben, M. (2020). Digital Twins, the future in plant phenotyping – TechnoHouse by Rijk Zwaan. *Phenospex.*

Huang, J., & Tan, M. (2023). The role of ChatGPT in scientific communication: Writing better scientific review articles. *American Journal of Cancer Research* 13 (4).

Insider. (2023, January 16). ChatGPT could be used for good, but like many other AI models, it's rife with racist and discriminatory bias. *Insider.* https://www.insider.com/chatgpt-is-like-many-other-ai-models-rife-with-bias-2023-1.

J. P. Morgan Research. (2024, February 14). Is generative AI a game changer? https://www.jpmorgan.com/insights/global-research/artificial-intelligence/generative-ai.

Jin, D., Pan, E., Oufattole, N., Weng, W.-H., Fang, H., & Szolovits, P. (2020). What disease does this patient have? A large-scale open domain question answering dataset from medical exams.

Jordon, J., Szpruch, L., Houssiau, F., Bottarelli, M., Cherubin, G., Maple, C., Cohen, S. N., & Weller, A. (2022). Synthetic data—what, why and how?

Jouppi, N. P., Kurian, G., Li, S., Ma, P., Nagarajan, R., Nai, L., Patil, N., et al. (2023). TPU v4: An optically reconfigurable supercomputer for machine learning with hardware support for embeddings.

Kavungal, D., Magalhães, P., Kumar, S. T., Kolla, R., Lashuel, H. A., & Altug, H. (2023). Artificial intelligence–Coupled plasmonic infrared sensor for detection of structural protein biomarkers in neurodegenerative diseases. *Science Advances* 9 (28). https://www.science.org/doi/10.1126/sciadv.adg9644.

Khakurel, J., & Blomqvist, K. (2022). Artificial intelligence augmenting human teams. A systematic literature review on the opportunities and concerns. *International Conference on Human-Computer Interaction.*

Köppen, E., Meinel, C., Rhinow, H., Schmiedgen, J., & Spille, L. (2015). Measuring the impact of design thinking. In H. Plattner, C. Meinel, & L. Leifer (eds.), *Design Thinking Research.* Springer, Switzerland, pp. 157–170.

Koyama, M., & Rubin, J. (2022) *How the World Became Rich: The Historical Origins of Economic Growth.* John Wiley & Sons.

Kulakauskaite, I. (2024, January 19). How AI is accelerating innovation. *HYPE Innovation.* Retrieved from https://www.hypeinnovation.com/blog/how-ai-is-accelerating-innovation.

Kunneman, Y. (2019). Data science for service design: An exploration of the opportunities, challenges and methods for data mining to support the service design process. Master thesis. University of Twente.

Lam, R., Sanchez-Gonzalez, A., Willson, M., Wirnsberger, P., Fortunato, M., Alet, F., Ravuri, S., et al. (2023). Learn skillful medium-range global weather forecasting. *Science* 382 (6677): 1416–1421. https://doi.org/10.1126/science.adi2336.

Lam, R., Sanchez-Gonzalez, A., Willson, M., Wirnsberger, P., Fortunato, M., Alet, F., Ravuri, S., et al. (2022). GraphCast: Learning skillful medium-range global weather forecasting.

Lee, M. K. (2018). Understanding perception of algorithmic decisions: Fairness, trust, and emotion in response to algorithmic management. *Big Data & Society* 5 (1).

Leifer, L. (1998). Design-team performance: metrics and the impact of technology. In *Evaluating Corporate Training*, pp. 297–319.

Leifer, L., & Steiner, M. (2014). Dancing with ambiguity: causality behavior, design thinking, and triple-loop-learning. In *Management of the Fuzzy Front End of Innovation*, pp. 141–158.

Lewrick, M. (2014). Design thinking – Ausbildung an universitäten. In *Sauvonnet und Blatt (Hrsg)*, pp. 87–101.

Lewrick, M. (2018). Design Thinking: Radikale Innovationen in einer Digitalisierten Welt, Beck Verlag; München.

Lewrick, M. (2022). *Design Thinking for Business Growth*, 1st edition, Wiley.

Lewrick, M. (2023). *Design Thinking and Innovation Metrics*, 1st edition, Wiley.

Lewrick, M., & Link, P. (2015). Hybride management modelle: Konvergenz von design thinking und big data. IM+io *Fachzeitschrift für Innovation, Organisation und Management* (4): 68–71.

Lewrick, M., Link. P., & Leifer, L. (2018). *The Design Thinking Playbook*, 1st edition, Wiley.

Lewrick, M., Link. P., & Leifer, L. (2018). *The Design Thinking Toolbox*, 1st edition, Wiley.

Lewrick, M., Skribanowitz, P., & Huber, F. (2012). *Nutzen von Design Thinking Programmen* 16. Interdisziplinäre Jahreskonferenz zur Gründungsforschung (G-Forum), Universität Potsdam.

Listgarten, J. (2024). The perpetual motion machine of AI-generated data and the distraction of ChatGPT as a "scientist." *Nature Biotechnology*.

Lund, B. D., Wang, T., Mannuru, N. R., Nie, B., Shimray, S., & Wang, Z. (2023). ChatGPT and a new academic reality: Artificial Intelligence-written research papers and the ethics of the large language models in scholarly publishing. *Journal of the Association for Information Science and Technology* 74(5): 570–581.

Mankowitz, D. J., Michi, A., Zhernov, A., Gelmi, M., Selvi, M., Paduraru, C., Leurent, E., et al. (2023). Algorithms discovered using deep reinforcement learning. *Nature* 618: 257–63. https://doi .org/10.1038/s41586-023-06004-9.

Manyika, J., Dean, J., Hassabis, D., Croak, M., & Pichai, S. (2023, January 16). Why we focus on AI (and to what end). *Google AI*. Retrieved from https://ai.google/why-ai/.

Maslej, N., Fattorini, L., Brynjolfsson, E., Etchemendy, J., Ligett, K., Lyons, T., Manyika, J., et al. (2023). *The AI Index 2023 Annual Report*. Stanford, CA: Institute for Human-Centered AI, Stanford University. https://aiindex.stanford.edu/wp-content/uploads/2023/04/HAI_AI-Index-Report_2023.pdf.

McKinsey & Company. (2022). The state of AI in 2022: And a half-decade in review. QuantumBlack. https://www.mckinsey.com/capabilities/quantumblack/our-insights/the-state-of-ai-in-2022-and-a-half-decade-in-review.

McKinsey & Company. (2023). The state of AI in 2023: Generative AI's breakout year. QuantumBlack. https://www.mckinsey.com/capabilities/quantumblack/our-insights/the-state-of-ai-in-2023-generative-ais-breakout-year.

Microsoft Bing Blogs. (2023, March 14). Confirmed: The new Bing runs on OpenAI's GPT-4. https://blogs.bing.com/search/march_2023/Confirmed-the-new-Bing-runs-on-OpenAI%E2%80%99s-GPT-4.

MIT Technology Review. (2022, February 23). 10 breakthrough technologies 2022: AI for protein folding. https://www.technology review.com/2022/02/23/1044957/ai-protein-folding-deepmind/.

Mock, M., Edavettal, S., Langmead, C., & Russell, A. (2023). AI can help to speed up drug discovery — but only if we give it the right data. Nature 624 (7979): 467–470.

Morley, N., & Munoz, L. V. (2023, November 29). How can AI empower your innovation process and unlock new connections? *Kantar*. Retrieved from https://www.kantar.com/uki/inspiration/brands/how-can-ai-empower-your-innovation-process.

Mukkavilli, S. K., Civitarese, D. S., Schmude, J., Jakubik, J., Jones, A., Nguyen, N., et al. (2023). *AI Foundation Models for Weather and Climate: Applications, Design, and Implementation*. https://doi. org/10.48550/arXiv.2309.10808.

Murray, P. W., Agard, B., & Barajas, M. A. (2018). Forecast of individual customer's demand from a large and noisy dataset. *Computers & Industrial Engineering* 118: 33–43.

Nagji, B., & Tuff, G. (2012, May). Managing your innovation portfolio. *Harvard Business*.

National Academies of Sciences, Engineering, and Medicine. (2022). *Automated Research Workflows for Accelerated Discovery: Closing the Knowledge Discovery Loop*.

NBC News. (2023, January 23). ChatGPT passes MBA exam given by a Wharton professor. *NBC*. https://www.nbcnews.com/tech/tech-news/chatgpt-passes-mba-exam-wharton-professor-rcna67036.

Nearing, G., Cohen, D., Dube, V., Gauch, M., Gilon, O., Harrigan, S., Hassidim, A., et al. (2023). *AI Increases Global Access to Reliable Flood Forecasts*. https://doi.org/10.48550/arXiv.2307.16104.

Nguyen, V., Diakiw, S. M., VerMilyea, M. D., Dinsmore, A. W., Perugini, M., Perugini, D., & Hall, J. M. M. (2023). Efficient automated error detection in medical data using deep-learning and label-clustering. *Scientific Reports* 13: 19587.

Nori, H., Lee, Y. T., Zhang, S., Carignan, D., Edgar, R., Fusi, N., King, N., et al. (2023). *Can Generalist Foundation Models Outcompete Special-Purpose Tuning? Case Study in Medicine*. https://doi.org/10.48550/arXiv.2311.16452.

OECD. (2023). *Artificial Intelligence in Science: Challenges, Opportunities and the Future of Research*. OECD Publishing. https://doi .org/10.1787/a8d820bd-en.

OpenAI Blog. (n.d.) Overview. https://openai.com/news.

OpenAI. (2023). GPT-4 system card. Retrieved from https://cdn .openai.com/papers/gpt-4-system-card.pdf.

Partnership on AI. (n.d.). Partnership on AI. Retrieved from https://partnershiponai.org.

Peng, Y., Liu, E., Peng, S., et al. (2022). Using artificial intelligence technology to fight COVID-19: A review. *Artificial Intelligence Review* 55: 4941–4977.

Popli, N. (2022, December 14). He used AI to publish a children's book in a weekend. Artists are not happy about it. *Time*. https://time.com/6240569/ai-childrens-book-alice-and-sparkle-artists-unhappy/.

Prendiville, A., Gwilt, I., & Mitchell, V. (2018). Making sense of data through service design. In *Designing for Service*, D. Sangiorgi & A. Prendiville (Eds.), 225–236. London: Bloomsbury.

Prieto, S., Mengiste, E. T., & de Soto, B. G. (2023). Investigating the use of ChatGPT for the scheduling of construction projects. *Buildings* 13 (4): 857.

PwC. (2024). PwC's global artificial intelligence study: Exploiting the AI revolution. https://www.pwc.com/gx/en/issues/data-and-analytics/publications/artificial-intelligence-study.html.

Qiu, Y.-H., Yang, X., Li, Z-Z., Zhang, C., & Chen, S.-X. (2021). Investigating the impacts of artificial intelligence technology on technological innovation from a patent perspective. *Applied Mathematics and Non-Linear Sciences* 6 (1).

Radu, A., & Duque, C. (2022). Neural network approaches for solving Schrödinger equation in arbitrary quantum wells. *Scientific Reports* 12 (2535).

Ray, P. (2023). ChatGPT: A comprehensive review on background, applications, key challenges, bias, ethics, limitations and future scope. *Internet of Things and Cyber-Physical Systems* 3: 121–154. https://doi.org/10.1016/j.iotcps.2023.04.003.

Safian, R. (2018, September 11). 5 lessons of the AI imperative, from Netflix to Spotify. Fast Company. Retrieved from https://www.fastcompany.com/90234726/5-lessons-of-the-ai-imperative-from-netflix-to-spotify.

Sallinen, A., Sakhaeirad, A., Swamy, V., Krawczuk, I., Bayazit, D., Marmet, A., Montariol, S., Hartley, M.-A., Jaggi, M., & Bosselut, A. (2023). *MEDITRON-70B: Scaling Medical Pretraining for Large Language Models*.

Savage, N. (2023). Synthetic data could be better than real data. *Nature Outlook: Robotics and Artificial Intelligence*.

School of Engineering. (2023, May 3). Researchers develop novel AI-based estimator for manufacturing medicine. MIT News. Retrieved from https://news.mit.edu/2023/ai-based-estimator-manufacturing-medicine-0503.

Schopf, C. M., Ramwala, O. A., Lowry, K. P., Hofvind, S., Marinovich, M. L., Houssami, N., Elmore, J. G., Dontchos, B. N., Lee, J. M., & Lee, C. I. (2024). Artificial intelligence-driven mammography-based future breast cancer risk prediction: A systematic review. *Journal of the American College of Radiology* 21 (2): 319–328. https://doi.org/10.1016/j.jacr.2023.10.018.

Shen, T., Munkberg, J., Hasselgren, J., Yin, K., Wang, Z., Chen, W., Gojcic, Z., Fidler, S., Sharp, N., & Gao, J. (2023). Flexible isosurface extraction for gradient-based mesh optimization. *ACM Transactions on Graphics* 42 (4): 1–16. https://doi.org/10.1145/3592430.

Slack, G. (2022, September 19). Finding patterns of success across 50 years of innovation. Stanford Medicine, Scope Blog. Retrieved from https://scopeblog.stanford.edu/2022/09/19/finding-patterns-of-success-across-50-years-of-innovation/.

Sotirov, S. (2023, October 3). The role of AI in digital transformation. LinkedIn. Retrieved from https://www.linkedin.com/pulse/role-ai-digital-transformation-stanimir-stan-sotirov/.

Sowa, K., Przegalinska, A., & Ciechanowki, L. (2021). Cobots in knowledge work: Human–AI collaboration in managerial professions. *Journal of Business Research* 125: 135–142. https://doi.org/10.1016/j.jbusres.2020.11.038.

Thadani, N. N., Gurev, S., Notin, P., Youssef, N., Rollins, N. J., Ritter, D., Sander, C., Gal, Y., & Marks, D. S. (2023). Learning from prepandemic data to forecast viral escape. *Nature* 622: 818–825. https://doi.org/10.1038/s41586-023-06617-0.

Thierry, A. (2023). Circulating DNA fragmentomics and cancer screening. *Cell Genomics*.

Touvron, H., Lavril, T., Izacard, G., Martinet, X., Lachaux., M.-A., Lacroix, T., Rozière, B., et al. (2023). *LLaMa: Open and Efficient Foundation Language Models*. https://doi.org/10.48550/arXiv.2302.13971.

Van den Broeck, L., Bohsale, D. K., Song, K., de Lima, C. F. F., Ashley, M., Zhu, T., Zhu, S., et al. (2023). Functional annotation of proteins for signaling network inference on non-model species. *Nature Communications* 14 (4654).

van der Aalst, W. (2014). Data scientist: The engineer of the future. *Enterprise Interoperability* 7: 13–26. Cham: Springer International Publishing.

Vincent, N., & Hecht, B. (2023). Sharing the winnings of AI with data dividends: Challenges with "meritocratic" data valuation. *EAAMO '23*.

Wang, D., Lu, C.-T., & Fu, Y. (2023). Towards Automated Urban Planning: When Generative and ChatGPT-like Ai Meets Urban Planning. https://doi.org/10.48550/arXiv.2304.03892.

Wang, H., Fu, T., Du, Y., Gao, W., Huang, K., Liu, Z., Chandak, P., et al. (2023). Scientific discovery in the age of artificial intelligence. *Nature* 620: 47–60.

Wettersten, J., & Malmgren, D. (2018, March 5). What happens when data scientists and designers work together. *Harvard Busines Review*.

Weyl, E. G. (2022). Sovereign nonsense: A review of *The Sovereign Individual* by James Dale Davidson and Lord William Rees-Mogg. RadicalxChange.

WIPO (World Intellectual Property Organization). (n.d.). Artificial intelligence and intellectual property. Retrieved from https://www.wipo.int/about-ip/en/frontier_technologies/ai_and_ip.html.

Wired. (2024). Artificial Intelligence. https://www.wired.com/tag/artificial-intelligence/.

Wong, F., Zheng, E., Valeri, J., Donghia, N., Anahtar, M., Omori, S., Li, A., et al. (2023). Discovery of a structural class of antibiotics with explainable deep learning. *Nature* 626: 177–185.

World Economic Forum. (2024). *AI Governance Alliance Briefing Paper Series.* https://www3.weforum.org/docs/WEF_AI_Governance_Alliance_Briefing_Paper_Series_2024.pdf.

Xu, Y., Liu, X., Cao, X., Huang, C., Liu, E., Qian, S., Liu, X., et al. (2021). Artificial intelligence: A powerful paradigm for scientific research. *The Innovation* 2 (4): https://doi.org/10.1016/j.xinn.2021.100179.

Zhao, W. X., Zhou, K., Li, J., Tang, T., Wang, X., Hou, Y., Min, Y., et al. (2023). *A Survey of Large Language Models.* https://doi.org/10.48550/arXiv.2303.18223.

Złotkowska, E., Alazlo, A., Kielkiewicz, M., Misztal, K., Dziosa, P., Soja, K., Barczak-Bryzek, A., & Filipecki, M. (2024). Automated imaging coupled with AI-powered analysis accelerates the assessment of plant resistance to Tetranychus urticae. *Scientific Reports* 14: 8020.

INDEX

WRAP-UP